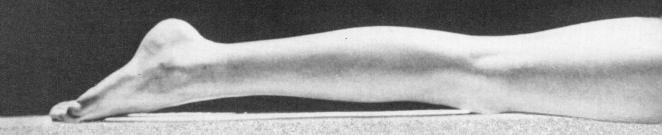

VOGUE BOOK OF

REINHARDT

BARBARA TIMS

DIETS AND EXERCISE

Allen Lane

ALLEN LANE
536 King's Road
London SW10 OUH

First published 1980
Copyright © Barbara Tims, 1980

Illustrations copyright © The Condé Nast
Publications Ltd

ISBN 0 7139 1244 8

Designed by Yvonne Dedman
Set in Monophoto Photina by
Filmtype Services Limited, Scarborough, Yorkshire
Colour Separations by
Culvergraphics, Lane End, Buckinghamshire
Printed in Great Britain by
Butler & Tanner Limited, Frome and London

From the many hundreds of diets that have appeared in *Vogue* over the years we have chosen for this book those that have proved most popular and most successful. We are grateful to the many experts and dieticians who originally compiled the diets and to the Editors and Beauty Editors who arranged for them to be published; also to the artists and photographers whose work give the book visual excitement as well as practicality. Special thanks go to Alex Kroll, editor of Condé Nast Books, who has masterminded the whole book and to Jacky Cole who has guided it from beginning to end. We would also like to thank Eleo Gordon and Esther Sidwell of Allen Lane/Penguin Books.

FOREWORD

In the 1980s a woman's appeal will lie in her image of super fitness, a look that expresses today's ideal of health and shape. The beginnings of it all lie in attitude towards diet, simply because it is the most determining factor when it comes to the way you feel and look. It affects not only weight and measurements, but general physical fitness, mental capacity and emotional well-being.

Over the years Vogue has been foremost in offering advice on nutrition and has presented many special diets and exercise programmes. Now they are gathered in one book, as Barbara Tims has sifted through sixty years of dietary features and adroitly selected the best, the most effective. She has formulated standard calorie charts, and has added a glossary of all dietary terms and related problems. The result is a compact encyclopaedia on diet giving all the facts and findings, the variations and values.

BRONWEN MEREDITH

VOGUE

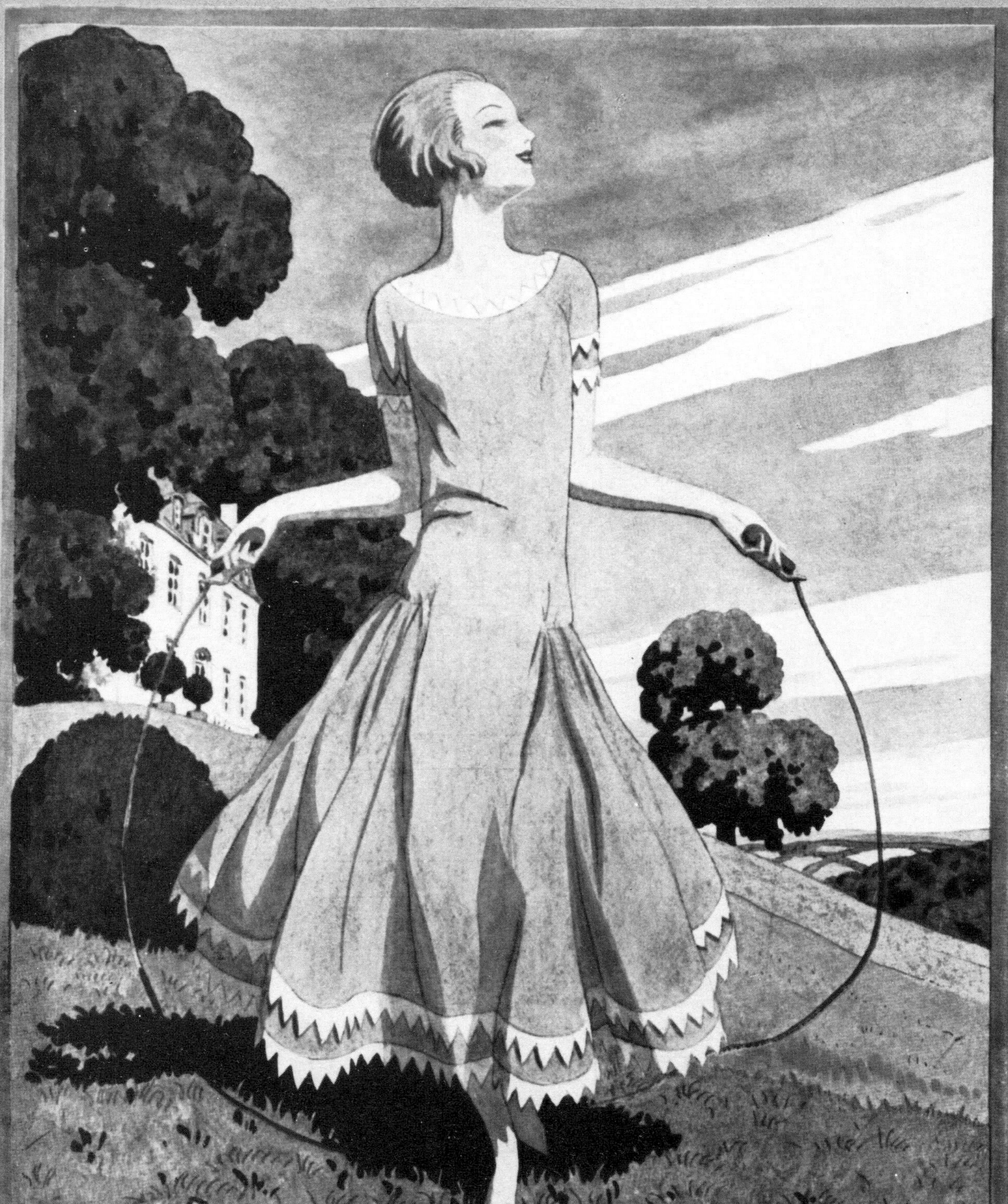

Late May 1925

Price One Shilling

INTRODUCTION

'Between the tango and the fashion for the tight, clinging gowns there has arisen a perfect rage for "being thin"... New "doctors" and new methods for melting the too solid flesh spring into existence over night, and while in the past this aesthetic side of the health question was left to the Institut de Beauté, women are now scurrying about to get real counsel from real physicians.' This was one of the first reports of slimming in *Vogue* – and it came from Paris in 1914. The 'real counsel from real physicians' consisted of amazing electrical treatments by Orcier 'the celebrated beauty doctor' including iodine baths with 'big plaques of electricity stuck into each end'. And Dr Bruno de Laborde's 'system of plaques whereby he guarantees to take the flesh off any given section of the body without in any way disturbing for instance the oval of the face or the rounded plumpness of the arms'. His patient sat in a brass-plated electric chair with plaques of lead bound over her hips, bust, and back, while the 'work of demolition was carried on by a current'. If by chance the electric chair didn't appeal to you, an alternative way to be 'most divinely thin' was to visit Dr Rivière's establishment where he had 'a veritable arsenal of fixtures and apparatus' and his patients were offered 'a colour bath without water or iodine, or with both; they were also invited to try any position on any kind of mechanical steed, with any kind of gait'. For his 'valuable contributions to science' Dr Rivière was awarded the Légion d'honneur and among his many distinguished patients 'one of the first to come to his establishment was the late King Edward of England'.

Meanwhile, in London, 'banting' became the fashion, so called after the obese William Banting who slimmed on a diet devised by his doctor which allowed him to eat as much meat, fish and poultry as he liked but cut out all sweet and starchy foods. Plenty of water and a fair quantity of claret were permitted, too. 'A most grateful draught,' the dieter wrote, 'as the water seems to carry away all the dregs left in the stomach after digestion.'

In July 1917 *Vogue* warned, 'When a Woman's Dearest Enemy Whispers, "But My Dear, Aren't You Getting a Little Stout", Then Black Godmother Fear Crouches in Her Heart and Then Banting Begins.' A complete cure was promised by Madame de Croquebiche, Director of the Institute of Beauty in Paris, on condition that her advice was followed

'Here Dr Rivière's patients sit as calmly as their temperaments will let them while the work of demolition goes on.'

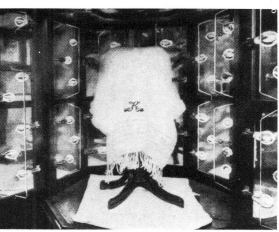

1914

ARLEN 1925

ARLEN 1925

(Above) 'Charles remarks with justice that Clementina's theories have gone to her head, when he comes upon her in this reverse position, which is guaranteed to make pounds vanish in thin air.'

(Below) 'Suzette, whose resemblance to a rag doll is somewhat marked here, goes through her matutinal battle with determination, but little resistance. These, perversely enough, it would seem, are called setting-up exercises.'

in every detail. These were her rules: first, never to have breakfast served in bed; second, after a bath, to lift each leg to waist level twelve times in succession; third, to remain standing or walking if possible for half an hour after each meal; fourth, never to take water with meals, but in the middle of the day to drink a large glass of warm water; fifth, to give up bread, sauces, sugar.

The corset makers were eager to help the figure conscious, offering 'a Reducing Corset on an entirely new principle. It does not compress the abdominal organs but reduces the figure two to five inches'... and it cost 18s 11d. At the beginning of the First World War *Vogue* reminded its readers that 'Figures Were Made Before Frocks' and reported: 'The shortage of fine corset material has become a serious consideration with the good corset manufacturers, just as the increasing cost of steel and cotton is forcing the makers of less expensive corsets either to raise prices or to substitute an inferior article ... the makers cannot, of course, control conditions; they can only do their best to meet them.'

After the war, women wanted to be thin, wanted to keep their figures ... But for this, what must one do?

'One woman utilizes her spare moments by standing on her head, and does it at any hour of the day or night! You enter her house, look about for her – where is Madame? "Here," she will cry to you from a corner of the room where a mass of cushions lies heaped upon the ground. "I will be with you in a moment; my exercise is practically over." Forthwith you perceive her, legs in the air, balanced on her head, as if this were the most natural of attitudes. This, according to her, prevents the acquisition of too much flesh. Another woman, who is miraculously young at fifty, plays with a medicine ball twice a week, after her fencing. Still another employs a Swedish instructor who gives her such violent and unmerciful exercise each morning that she is left like one dead, and these are only a few of the methods employed by various persons anxious to retain the slender and supple movements composing that captivating person, the modern woman.'

No need to be ashamed of your Ankles!

CLARK'S *Reducing* PASTE

5/6 *per pot*
At all Chemists and Stores.

THE woman who has thick ankles suffers a great disadvantage in these days. Fashion decrees that ankles are never hidden, and lucky is the person who has shapely ones. Everyone can have slim ankles. A daily massage with Clark's Thinning Paste will soon reduce the fattest of ankles to the slim, elegant shape which is so admired.

HEPPELLS, Ltd., 164 Piccadilly, W.1, and at Brighton

1925

Meanwhile advertisements offered 'Obesity Bath Sachets – when dissolved in your bath helps the evacuation of all superfluous fat through the intestines' and 'Obesity Soap – Will remove all fat on neck, hips, stomach etc.' If that didn't work you could resort to 'the mysterious rays of electricity ... the tried and tested friend of Beauty. These electrical treatments combined with a massage of nourishing skin-food are both logical and intelligent and are so efficacious that even the woman of sixty may attain the freshness of thirty-five.'

By 1925 'Daily Dozens for Débutantes' *(below)* suggested boxing, wrestling, high jumping, sprinting and high diving – 'in order properly to execute a dive the only necessity is a bridge, picturesque if possible, and spanning water of sufficient depth, say, twenty feet. The head and feet are then carefully reversed and the entire body plunged into the stream. Care should be taken to learn to swim before diving, or the sport may develop badly' – but of course they weren't really serious. Unlike

MARTIN 1925

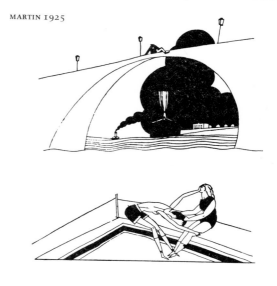

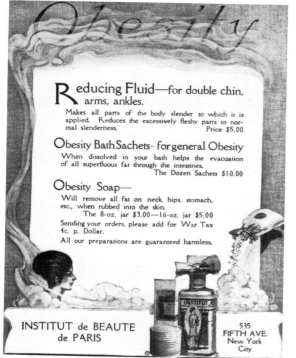

Obesity

Reducing Fluid—for double chin, arms, ankles.

Makes all parts of the body slender to which it is applied. Reduces the excessively fleshy parts to normal slenderness.   Price $5.00

Obesity Bath Sachets—for general Obesity

When dissolved in your bath helps the evacuation of all superfluous fat through the intestines.
The Dozen Sachets $10.00

Obesity Soap—

Will remove all fat on neck, hips, stomach, etc., when rubbed into the skin.
The 8-oz. jar $3.00—16-oz. jar $5.00
Sending your orders, please add for War Tax 4c. p. Dollar.

All our preparations are guaranteed harmless.

INSTITUT de BEAUTE de PARIS

535 FIFTH AVE. New York City

1920

(Above) 'There are so many ways in which wrestling can be appropriately cultivated that it is hard to choose between them. If you have a woman friend who has swiped the idea of your favourite gown there is nothing so satisfactory as a good old-fashioned head-lock. In the gruelling bout which we see here, Mrs Smith-Jones is just about to get a stranglehold on her cook, which she will only consent to release when respiration ceases.'

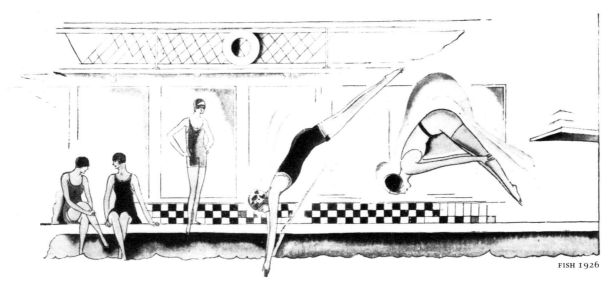

FISH 1926

'Diana', who was taking a course of ju-jitsu 'It's more exciting than an apache dance and I'm pining for a cat burglar to come into my house so that I can practise on him. Apart from that I've lost five pounds in weight' . . . or 'Hermione' in a 'white topped, black-knickered gym-suit' who discovered a school of acrobatic dancing and learnt to do cartwheels 'passably' and arabesques and pirouettes. It wasn't surprising that overweight was causing a problem when a 'light supper for a June evening' consisted of no less than ten dishes: 'artichauts d'Athènes, consommé aux pointes d'asperges, cotelettes de saumon Piedmontaise, épaule d'agneau à Langounoise, pommes de terre, petits pois, salade moraine, timbales de ris de veau à la chartreuse, flan de fraises, petites crèmes de fromage'. 'Taking the cure' became all the rage: the Baden Baden *Kur* where husky *mädchens* in waterproof boots sprayed staggering streams on excessive ounces . . . Karlsbad where the day began with two glasses of *Markbrunn* and ended with a glass of cold *Felsenquelle*, with hot peat packs spread on your liver and bubble baths in between.

Nevertheless people were beginning to be calorie-conscious even if they didn't call them calories – 'food values are no secret from the younger generation and rice pudding is refused, not because one does not like it – oh, no, but

FISH 1926

training for a tennis tournament lamentably re-
stricts the starch element of one's diet. Currants,
however, when not cooked and eaten in abun-
dance, are found most stimulating.'

And there were still corsets for every occasion
'for hunting, riding, dancing, day and evening
wear' and they imported to the 'woman of
generous proportions' the exact outline of the
more slender figure, while affording 'comfort to the
wearer: observe the triplex elastic at waist and
cutely cut gore at the side'. But inflation – or the
war – had taken the price up to 42s.

In the twenties 'Bodyline Building in *Vogue*' was
nothing to do with the human figure – it was a
Humber at Rootes, a Bentley at Owens or a Rolls

Royce at Jack Barclay. But with the thirties women
became more conscious of their bodies and the
great open-air cult from Germany had them
sunbathing, hiking and going to nudist camps. The
emphasis was on keeping fit and slim and the new
silhouette was an accepted fact. 'To some of us
making the best of it means resigning ourselves to
the fact that we do not look as well in the new
clothes as we did in the old (and this is a mistake).
To others, it means losing pounds (and this is
frequently wise). To a great many, it means
purchasing a new and firm corset (and this is
almost a necessity).' *Vogue* readers were ordered to
exercise their way to beauty and told 'the truth
about sport' – 'some charming people who like

(Opposite above) *'Diving and dipping
in the clear blue-green waters of the
Bath Club gives one a glorious feeling
of lively youth.'*

(Opposite below) *'The beginnings of
acrobatic dancing – the favourite form
of popular dancing today – induces
suppleness that renews both body
and mind.'*

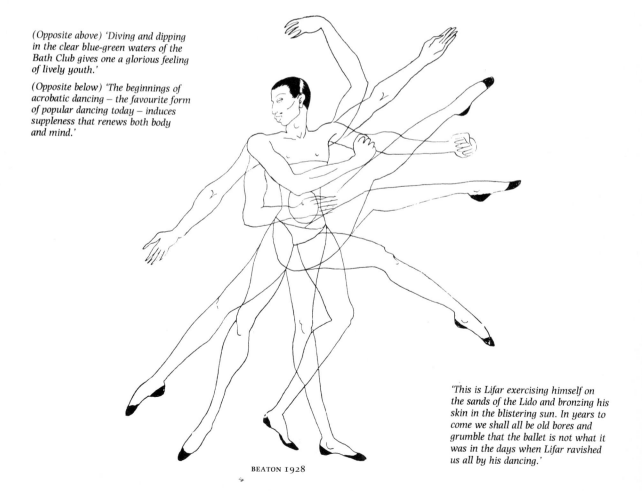

BEATON 1928

*'This is Lifar exercising himself on
the sands of the Lido and bronzing his
skin in the blistering sun. In years to
come we shall all be old bores and
grumble that the ballet is not what it
was in the days when Lifar ravished
us all by his dancing.'*

1928

Exercise for Beauty's Sake

jollity have been known to make up parties and go to Cricklewood Rink to perform on roller skates'. The placid and statuesque was definitely out of date – 'the modish woman will omit almost anything rather than her morning limbering up, which is, she finds, a really exhilarating beginning to her day'. Posture, too, was important 'so make a point of drawing your chest high and your chin up, several times a day'.

By 1932 the smart woman was determined 'to keep her pounds within bounds' but she attacked her problem with sense instead of desperation and gave her luncheon guests the following 'delicious lunch within dietary restrictions: vegetable hors d'oeuvre, bouillon or consommé borsch, lamb fillets en brochette, watercress, gluten crisps, moulded spinach ring, frozen and fresh fruit compote, café noir'. A mere eight dishes. The science of

dietetics was comparatively new – 'the result of increased knowledge of food values and of the action of food upon the digestive organs of the body ... beware Auto-intoxication. For every woman who suffers because her diet is wrong, either through deficiency or excess, ten are the victims of self-poisoning'. As few *Vogue* readers did their own cooking in the mid-thirties it was essential, if you wanted the *Vogue* Figure, to know 'what to tell your cook'.

'Cook, I have just returned from the doctor and he says I must go on a diet – but, as it is you who will have to prepare this food, can I try to explain to you what it was he told me to do – and still more important, what not to do?

'First of all I have to avoid fat in all forms. I am not to have in future any of your delicious salad dressing but must satisfy myself with a plain vinegar dressing. I must avoid milk, nuts and of course preparations which involve milk or its products such as some forms of cheese, Welsh rabbit – and, oh dear, all the things I like so much. He said, however, if you made a junket, the fat got separated by some chemical process – so that it was less rich. Therefore, I could have junket dishes, cook.

'He stressed how important proteins were and I was to rely on these for my food as far as possible. In addition, too, fresh uncooked food supplies the essential vitamins – so, cook, a small wine glass of orange juice before breakfast, please, or else some nice crisp salads. Clear soups can be taken if you free them from fat and meat particles – especially if made with one of the beef extracts – because these are stimulating, but contain no food value. I can have a small cup of Bovril and water in the middle of the morning.'

Cook's reaction to this was unrecorded – as are her views on 'a nice dressing of the mayonnaise type can be made by taking the yolk of an egg, 3 cups of paraffin (medicinal), juice of $\frac{1}{2}$ lemon, mustard and pepper to taste and 1–2 tablespoonfuls of vinegar'.

While doctors prescribed, hostesses decided how to apply diet to life ... 'abandon the idea that

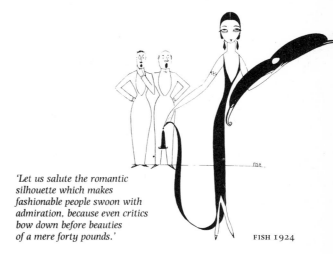

'Let us salute the romantic silhouette which makes fashionable people swoon with admiration, because even critics bow down before beauties of a mere forty pounds.'   FISH 1924

vegetable cookery need be tedious. It can and should be epicurean so aim for a cook who is good with vegetables and salads and remember it's not only healthy but also elegant to make your meals centre round vegetables and fruit'.

In 1936 one doctor suggested a short fast: 'If any reader cares to leave off eating altogether for forty-eight hours and at the same time take plenty of water, she will probably experience the following sensations: first, ravenous hunger, which will soon

'It was a man with no taste who declared that the Venus de Milo was the prototype of feminine elegance.
All that changed a long time ago; the slim woman is fashionable and the statues of the Louvre no longer figure in the reckoning.'

FISH 1924

Mrs Somerset Maugham   BEATON 1937

pass off; secondly, loss of thirst; thirdly, temporary headaches and listlessness; and, lastly, a feeling of well-being and complete absence of appetite. By a series of such short fasts with an intervening period of seven to ten days, many very serious conditions can be greatly benefited, and even cured.'

Another warned, 'Dieting can be definitely dangerous; women who use up a lot of energy should not put themselves on the extreme diet that would be safe for the plump woman of even, lazy temperament; and the diet prescribed for a too fat adolescent girl would obviously differ from one planned to slim a smart woman of thirty-five.'

Nevertheless Mrs Somerset Maugham described how 'I starved for six weeks. Yes, literally, for six weeks I ate nothing at all. Nothing. I drank water, of course – lots of it, and orange juice occasionally. Yet I never missed a day's work and after the first week I didn't even feel muzzy. I lost two stone and am not putting it on. I feel better than I can ever remember.'

For those who wanted to get their weight down but were neither strong enough nor strong-minded enough to starve *Vogue* recommended the milk and bread diet: 'the point is that you must take $1\frac{1}{2}$ to 2 pints of milk every day; and $\frac{1}{2}$ lb of bread every day, in any of the following forms: baked custard with one egg; bread and butter pudding; rice or tapioca pudding; or just bread and milk. Your lunch would consist of any of these dishes. At tea and breakfast you are allowed two cups of tea with milk and bread and butter to make up your quota of $\frac{1}{2}$ lb but no more. For dinner, eat what you like, so long as it includes fresh fruit and vegetables, and meat in moderation.'

In 1937 came the revolution. 'Down with Diets': 'Dieting in public is definitely out-of-date, and the woman who refuses good food because she's on a diet is now admitted to be a bore. Strawberries and cream at Lord's, hampers at Henley, lobsters at Ascot and bombes glacés at parties are all part of the fun of life and the London season, and should be enjoyed ... The slenderizing woman is never really beautiful. She is not natural and she cannot be fit because she is undernourished; she has to draw upon her nerves to supplement her short rations. *Vogue* has consulted a famous doctor who is of opinion that since many fat people neither overeat nor under-exercise, the answer to their problems lies elsewhere; their metabolism needs adjusting.'

'She had begun by eating too much; she corrected the error by resolving not to eat at all.'

1917

HOYNINGEN-HUENÉ 1931

DRTIKOL 1932

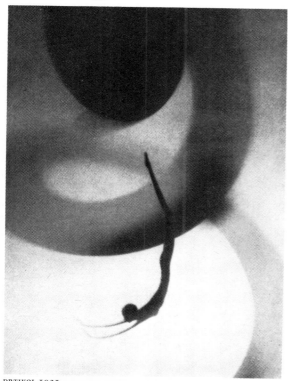

DRTIKOL 1931

'A rippling movement to give balance and poise.'

1936

HOYNINGEN-HUENÉ 1931

STEPS TO BEAUTY
*A Famous Dancer's Daily Dozen:
'Morning exercises, even as a prelude
to the most ordinary activities,
are often astonishingly strenuous.
Much more so are the exercises
of Miss Jean Barry, the exquisite
dancer who has charmed us so often
in Mr C.B. Cochran's revues.'*

Perhaps the Second World War came just in time. Rationing was introduced on 8 January 1940 with 12 oz sugar a week, 4 oz bacon, 4 oz butter. Before the end of the year tea was rationed to 2 oz a week, cooking fat 2 oz, meat worth 1s 10d. And worse was to come: 1 oz cheese a week, 2 oz bacon a fortnight, 1 oz cooking fat, 4 oz butter, 10d worth of meat. Nevertheless the average Briton's diet during the war was actually improved because the overall quantity of food was closely watched and more were in a position to eat out because 5s was the maximum price for a meal in a restaurant. And because people were asked to dig up their rose beds and plant vegetables in the 'Dig for Victory' campaign they were eating more and fresher vegetables. *Vogue* said, 'The time we spend in the garden and the space we usually devote to flowers can be better occupied by growing vegetables for food and in providing as many as possible with those elements of nutrition which may become scarce', and gave instructions for 'turning a lawn into a good vegetable-growing land'.

People were forced to eat a more healthy diet: honey and treacle and dried fruits such as dates, figs and prunes instead of sugar ... a little meat was made to go a long way by cultivating the use of such foods as eggs, cheese, beans, rice, macaroni and vegetables. Constance Spry wrote, 'You can't eat your cake and have it is a silly proverb; but that's just what you *can* do with a vegetable border.'

In 'Good Eating in Wartime' *Vogue* recommended soups of the peasant variety that make 'at least half a meal – pot-au-feu, onion soup with plenty of grated cheese and crusty bread, thick and savoury soups made from potatoes, peas, celery, artichokes, and eaten with fried croutons to give a pleasantly crunchy contrast to their smoothness. Soups can be made of almost anything that is eatable. Use plenty of vegetables and add pearl barley, rice, dried peas, bean flour or seed tapioca to give nourishment. Do not forget the excellence

(*Right*) EXERCISE FOR CHILDREN
Modern Ideas and Methods

ABBÉ 1931

Diet Without Tears   1935

of fish soups, particularly that variety which is somewhere between a soup and a stew ... Two courses can make a sturdy meal and are all that most people want in a time like the present.'

By 1941 the Ministry of Food was preaching that 'the right food is beauty's first aid'. *Vogue* warned 'lack of vitamins may show itself in different ways' and recommended carrots for vitamin A – 'not just an occasional sprinkling on salad, but a fair size one, preferably raw, every day' – herrings, kippers, sardines, salmon for vitamins A and D and milk for those who lacked calcium. For loss of appetite and nervousness, two teaspoons of Marmite in hot water were recommended for its vitamin B-1; *Vogue* warned 'go easy on alcohol, it uses up this vitamin'.

In some ways the post-1945 diet was more frugal than the wartime one. As *Vogue* said, 'Peace is here, but not yet plenty.' And Maurice Edelman, MP, writing about the new unorthodox Minister of Food – John Strachey – said that the Ministry was both a duty and a challenge. Doris Lytton Toye announced in 1947 that the 'key to true beauty is in a well-tempered body and most good figures are carved with knife and fork. Without embarking on a stringent diet (well nigh impossible these days) we can do a lot, and enjoy the doing, to tone up our interior workings. Fat or thin, we shall all be the better for a short cure at home.'

Her 'pointers' included hot water or a health drink first thing in the morning, muesli for breakfast, raw salads for lunch, a simple soup and grilled meat dinner and a tisane – camomile, vervain or peppermint – at bedtime to induce sound sleep. 'Shophound in the Kitchen' recommended 'the waterless method of cooking' to prevent shrinkage and to preserve the maximum amount of vitamins, mineral salts and roughage.

By 1950 *Vogue* was publishing serious calorie-counted diets: a ten-day skim-milk weight-reducing diet – probable loss 10 lb ... and a three-day diet with a liquid day, an alkaline-forming day and a protein day 'to be repeated in rotation until the weight is normal'. In 1953 'four out of every ten women are following some form of reducing diet. An even greater number are planning to reduce and many more are talking about it' ... Much the same as it is today.

Rationing finally ended in July 1954, and diets proliferated: The Liquid Diet, Diet X, The Man and His Middle, Diet for a Spring Suit Figure, Nothing to Lose but Weight, More Taste than Calories ... And then: 'Because the subject of diet and weight reduction is so much a matter of public interest and because one new diet theory frequently flies in the face of another, *Vogue* establishes *Vogue*'s Diet Authority – a board of scientists equipped to examine diet ideas *scientifically*.'

Exercise became increasingly important: in 'How to Give Your Figure a Sporting Chance' *Vogue* said, 'Active people experience less tension, have greater physical strength and rarer weight problems than the inactive who show the definite signs of age much earlier. Therapists, doctors, exercise experts, as well as the people who follow the simple directions, stress the very real, sometimes extraordinary, sense of well-being that blooms from exercise'. Readers were encouraged to hunt (for firmer thighs, leaner ankles) to play golf (firmer arms, smaller waist), swim underwater (sleeker hips, thighs, calves, ankles), dance (sleekness in general) and play tennis (midriff, hips).

Long cool diet drinks 'to help your own personal air-conditioning system work efficiently' included coolers, cobblers, and a no-calorie 'Horse's Neck'.

1947

The sixties saw the beginning of the back-to-nature trend: growing your own vegetables, buying free-range eggs and wheatgerm from the mushrooming health food shops. With the youth cult and the mini-skirt more and more of the body was bared and what showed had to be worth looking at.

In spite of this, in the early sixties, diets were rare – and imprecise – in *Vogue*. In 'How to Stay Slim and Like It', foods were divided into Friends, Foes and Acquaintances: meat, fish, vegetables, fruit and dairy produce were Friends. Flour, pasta, dried vegetables, tinned fruit, jam, ice-cream, chestnuts, soft drinks and beer were Foes. Root vegetables, broad beans, nuts, crispbread, vermouth, dry wine and an occasional whisky and soda were Acquaintances.

'The simplest do-it-yourself answer,' said *Vogue*, 'is – we're sorry to say – some kind of crash diet ... it's human nature to want quick results so, for quick returns, cut out starch and sugar, eat meat, fish, game, cheese, eggs, leafy vegetables and not much else, for a fortnight. Some people find it helps to use one of the meal-in-a-glass or biscuit aids to replace the meal occasionally.'

1959

= tauter midriff, tauter hips, firmer legs

(Above) 'You may have a strong healthy body, but it may not be a figure, and a figure is what you need for fashion.'

There were all kinds of 'meals-in-a-glass', usually a 225-Calorie mixture, and *Vogue* guinea-pigs reported that they did 'definitely satisfy hunger' – they also contained seventy grammes of protein, vitamins and minerals and cost 8s 6d for a half-pound tin.

'But', a medical obesity expert warned, 'don't expect wonders from any quick-quick weight-loss produced by pill or injection in which a diuretic is a factor; weight stays lost only until you eat and drink liquids again.' One doctor asked: 'Don't they realize they're losing the *same* four pounds over and over?'

The Giant Roller   *Weights and Measures*

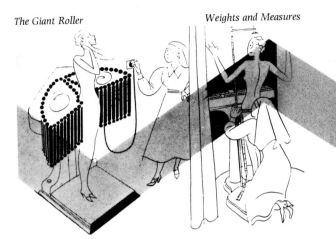

La Toilette

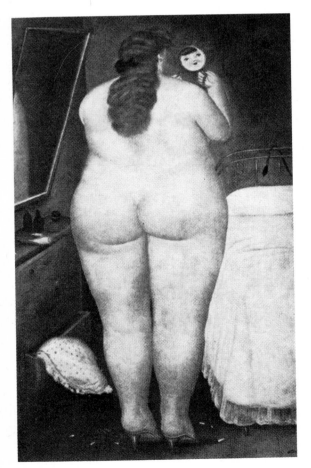

BOTERO 1971

To help them lose weight *Vogue* readers were encouraged to visit the excellent new 'resorts' – 'if you can really give up time to it (and sign the cheque at the end) you'd be silly not to retire gracefully to one' – where treatments included dry-heat baths, wet-heat baths, Swedish body massage, ultrasonic treatment, osteopathy and even hydrotherapy. Although *Vogue* admitted there were people 'sceptical by instinct who are convinced they are a racket ("What, pay thirty quid a week for a few glasses of fruit juice?")' the 'nature cure' establishments flourished. New ones opened up and others expanded; most had waiting-lists. There were plenty of people to defend them: Ian Fleming 'put himself in the hands of the sorcerers and lost pounds in a week' . . . Robert Carrier found it 'marvellous to rest, write – and lose weight – at the same time' and Jill Bennett went for 'short stays and just slept and slept'.

If you could not – or would not – go to a nature-cure establishment in 1965 you could shed pounds 'as easily as water from a duck's back' with Robert Carrier's Gourmet Diet, based on the premise that protein turns into energy, carbohydrates into fat. 'One of my first gourmet diet meals,' he wrote, 'was a fresh crab salad dressed with one tablespoon of mayonnaise and one tablespoon of lemon juice, followed by two braised quails served with green vegetables. My companion and I split a bottle of Corton Grancey, then we each had a brandy with our coffees. That weekend I lost 5 lb.'

The Paraffin Bath

The Shower

For spring 1966 *Vogue* proposed a 'Diet in a Nutshell' – 'easy, nutritionally sound, painless, inexpensive and devised by one of Britain's leading nutrition consultants.' Average weight loss in a week was 6½ lb (see p. 105).

If you didn't fancy nuts perhaps you could be tempted by the Caviar and Nectarine Diet – which you could follow indefinitely, substituting lobster and peaches should you wish.

But by the time the seventies arrived there was a thoroughly researched answer to every problem of health, diet and exercise. Gone were the days of trial and error: eating regimes were nutritionally sound and medically checked. The attitude to dieting was discussed in articles such as 'Think Yourself Slim' and 'Why Do We Eat So Much?' and exercises were planned for strength and energy, to relieve tension and encourage relaxation, as well as for figure perfection. Weight Watchers, started in 1964, introduced a New Programme of Eating, based on 'the most advanced medical and scientific research carried out by internationally known doctors and dieticians.'

The *Vogue* Super Diet, devised with the guidance of Dr Robert Atkins, was followed by people all over the world. There were diets for extra energy, high vitality, general good health; diets with a high-fibre content to avoid constipation, with

After the Bath

Massage

(Above and right) The Road to Beauty

Ultra-violet Rays

LIBIS 1934

extra calcium for bone strength and with large amounts of vitamin C for followers of Dr Linus Pauling who believed that the answer was a lemon (or an orange or grapefruit) three times a day.

Today people are more than just aware of being overweight, they are doing something about it. And with expert advice so readily available via magazines, books, television and radio phone-ins, they know exactly what to do. They are told precisely how many calories it will take to put on an extra pound and – more important – how many calories allied to how much exercise it will take to lose it again. Health farms – the former 'nature-cure establishments' – abound, exercise places and beauty salons become more luxurious, the reasons for eating are analysed and health warnings sounded: 'A person carrying ten extra pounds acquires the same health risk as someone smoking twenty cigarettes a day' ... 'People who are fat-prone must not only take steps to reduce their weight but must be prepared to sustain treatment, perhaps all their lives, in order to keep the body at the desired weight. Slimming is hard work and only 5–10 per cent of people who begin a slimming regime keep it up. But the returns should make the effort worthwhile, for not only do we look better for losing weight but we also stand a better chance of being healthier.'

Fitness is everything now. As we go into the eighties, to be obese is as much an offence against society as it is against yourself.

(Right) Vogue staff work it off

1971

REINHARDT

PART I

DIETS

Metric equivalents are approximate throughout. For instance 1 oz = 28.35 g, and this has been rounded off to 30 g.

An asterisk * indicates that you will find a recipe in the recipe section, pages 131–95.

FINDING THE DIET THAT WORKS FOR YOU

Not every diet works for everyone, even though it may be a sound, sensible diet. One reason is that we all have psychological preferences that make some diets appealing and others dreary. Many diets rely on having to count calories, others group foods into those allowed and those forbidden. It is not that one method is necessarily better than another: the best is the one that appeals to you and therefore works for you.

Some diets are strictly for one day only, others for a week or more, some can be continued indefinitely for they are a sensible way of eating. In any case do not exceed the stated time given. *Remember that diets are for healthy people, if in doubt check with your doctor.*

High-protein diets

These are diets on which you eat protein almost exclusively. Very lean meats, chicken and fish, cottage cheese, hard cheese and eggs make up the bulk of such a diet. The most well known is probably the Stillman diet developed by the late Dr Irwin Stillman. Some people refer to it as the water diet because you are required to drink at least eight glasses of water a day.

For: You often see spectacular results from this diet, usually during the first week or ten days. It can be effective for losing a few pounds quickly.

Against: Even Dr Stillman warned that a dieter must supplement this diet with vitamins because with any kind of limited eating you are in danger of depriving yourself of some essential nutrients.

Also, a protein-only diet sets up certain chemical reactions in your body that can be dangerous, especially for people with diseases such as diabetes. In addition, the diet is boring and difficult to stay on because the foods are so limited. In his later years Dr Stillman began to change his mind and to come round to a less exclusive point of view, saying that most people need some carbohydrates, especially on a long-term diet. Generally a high-protein diet that excludes almost all carbohydrate should not be tried without your doctor's consent.

Low-carbohydrate diet

Low- or minimal-carbohydrate diets encourage the dieter to eat protein and fats (as contrasted with high-protein diets that do not allow you to eat fat), but almost no carbohydrates. You are permitted fatty meats like steak, even bacon, fish, poultry, eggs and some dairy products. The Atkins Diet, (p. 30), originated by Dr Robert Atkins, is probably the best known. Putting yourself on one of these diets will automatically force you to eat fewer calories because carbohydrates are high-calorie foods. They are also the foods most readily turned into fatty tissue.

For: This kind of diet does reduce calorie intake and cause weight loss. It provides you with plenty of body-building protein, plus some fats for energy.

Against: Everyone needs some carbohydrates and it is difficult for the dieter who needs to lose a lot of weight to know just where to draw the line on eliminating them. Some people can get by with very few. Others experience a sharp drop in blood sugar with accompanying feelings of mental inefficiency and irritability and fatigue. A doctor's advice on how to regulate your carbohydrate intake on this kind of diet is essential. There is also a psychological drawback with a minimal-carbohydrate diet. Carbohydrates cause your body to hold water. When you cut down on them, especially when you cut down to practically nothing, your body dumps a lot of water quickly, resulting in a quick loss of weight. You can only lose so much water, however, and after a few weeks the water loss is not so dramatic and neither is your weight loss. It can be difficult to get by this plateau without being discouraged, but you will continue to lose weight – just more slowly.

Special food diets

These are diets that suggest you eat one or two foods exclusively, e.g. grapefruit, bananas. Without exception these diets are unbalanced and ineffective except for fast weight loss of a few pounds. Followed for any length of time – say over a week – they can cause health problems. When they work it is often because you get so bored with one sort of food you do not eat much of it.

Fasting

Fasting means not eating or eating almost nothing. A fast should never be attempted without medical supervision. It can be dangerous and result in problems more serious than overweight. Sometimes a modified kind of fast is used under strict medical supervision for really obese people.

Sensible eating plans

The most successful diet is a well-balanced one, low in carbohydrates (but not eliminating them), high in proteins and limited in fats. The resulting weight loss may not be fast or dramatic but it is steady. Dieting this way also has the advantage of changing your eating habits over a long period, causing you to eat more healthily and sensibly.

AVERY 1924

LOW-CARBOHYDRATE, HIGH-PROTEIN DIETS

THE TAKE-IT-OFF, KEEP-IT-OFF SUPER DIET

This diet was devised for *Vogue* with the guidance of Dr Robert Atkins and planned in a series of D-Days. In the first four you can eat steak and salad vinaigrette; grilled lobster with garlic butter; prawns or crabs; chicken rosemary; eggs as you like them. In the next four days add home-made cheesecake: specified amounts of vegetables, cream, cottage cheese. In D-Days 9–16 you gradually add more treats. By D-Day 16 you should not only have lost at least 10 lb (4.5 kg) but you should not have suffered one single hungry or bored moment – and you should have felt better every day. Your appetite and metabolic system should have normalized so that you will want to stay on this diet – and stay 10 lb thinner –for the rest of your life.
Possible weight loss: 10 lb (4.5 kg) in sixteen days.
Time: for the rest of your life.

D-DAYS 1–4
Anything on the following list and nothing that is not on the list.

Meat: steaks, lamb chops, hamburgers, any kind of meat in any quantity except meat with fillers such as bologna, sausage, hot dogs, meat-balls.

Poultry: duckling, turkey, chicken, anything with wings, no stuffings.

Fish: caviar, salmon, lobster, shrimps, any kind of seafood including oil-packed and smoked – except oysters, mussels and pickled fish.

Eggs: boiled, fried, scrambled, poached, omelette – any style.

Salads: two small green salads a day (less than one cupful) made of salad material listed on page 31. Dressings with oil, vinegar, salt, dry spices, herbs, grated cheese or anchovies.

Fats: butter, margarine, oils, shortening, pure mayonnaise in judicious quantities.

Cheese: 4 oz (115 g) a day of any hard cheese, no cream cheese or cheese spreads.

Puddings: jelly with artificial sweeteners.

Seasonings: salt, pepper, mustard, horse-radish, vinegar, vanilla and other extracts, artificial sweeteners, any dry powder spice without sugar.

Drinks: water, mineral water, soda water; Marmite or powdered beef or chicken broth, bouillon; sugar-free soft drinks; coffee, tea.

D-DAYS 5–8
Now you may add daily: home-made cheesecake;* a vegetable serving – one 4 oz (115 g) portion of any vegetable listed on p. 31; double cream – 1 oz (30 g) a day in coffee or cooking; cottage cheese – 3 oz (85 g) a day.

D-DAYS 9–12

Now you may add oysters and mussels to seafood menus and start to use wine in cooking – and have a glass of dry table wine with dinner. Or you can exchange the glass of wine for fruit – a small portion such as quarter of a canteloupe, half a grapefruit, half an apple. Walnuts, almonds, water chestnuts may be added to recipes. But no peanuts, cashews, chestnuts ... And you may now have unlimited cottage cheese.

D-DAYS 13–16

Now you can have fruit and a glass of wine or 2 fl oz (55 ml) vodka, gin or whisky. And you may add sour cream to recipes.

D-DAY 17

Survey your remarkable accomplishment. Make a decision about your future eating plans. Don't go back to old eating patterns if you want to stay 10 lb (4.5 kg) thinner.

Super dont's

Put these out of your life (and your recipes):

bread	potatoes
cereal	pulse vegetables
corn	rice
ice-cream	spaghetti
ketchup	sugar
macaroni	sweets/chewing gum
milk	water biscuits

Note: One piece of chewing gum can spoil the whole chemical balance.

The super vegetables

Eat as much as you like of these:

artichokes	cauliflower
asparagus	courgettes
aubergine	marrow
avocado	mushrooms
bamboo shoots	onions
beans, green	peppers
broccoli	pumpkin
Brussels sprouts	spinach
cabbage	spring greens

The super salad material

Eat as much as you like of these:

celery	onion
chicory	pickle (sour or dill)
Chinese cabbage	pimento
cucumber	radishes
endive	spring onions
lettuce	tomato
olives, green or black	watercress

The super rules

1. Eat all the allowed foods you need to avoid hunger.
2. Never eat when you are not hungry.
3. Don't finish everything on your plate.
4. Take as much or as little water or calorie-free drinks as thirst requires.
5. Frequent small meals are fine, but only to stave off hunger.
6. If weakness results from rapid weight loss, salt depletion may be the cause. Take plenty of salt and no purgatives.
7. Take a multi-vitamin pill daily.
8. Check labels on low-calorie drinks, syrups, desserts. Only those with no carbohydrate content are allowed.
9. If in doubt about any food, leave it out.

ARLEN 1925

SUPER SUMMER DIET[1]

This low-carbohydrate, low-fat diet was planned by Helen Corbitt, an expert dietician, for the famous beauty spa, The Greenhouse, midway between Dallas and Fort William in the United States. She believes that meals can be well-balanced and nutritious, attractive and delicious, even though they add up to only 850 Calories a day. They are planned with your family in mind. There is no reason for you to eat different food, just add more for them.

Do

1. Use artificial sweeteners instead of sugar.
2. Limit your use of salt (or try using salt substitutes).
3. Use skimmed milk in recipes calling for milk.
4. Use vegetable oils, like corn oil. Do not use mineral oil as this prevents absorption of vitamins.
5. Use soft margarines. On the whole you will use much less.
6. Eat raw carrots, tomatoes, celery or similar vegetables for snacks.
7. Drink tea or coffee black and have a glass of water between meals.
8. Exercise regularly.

Don't

1. Do not fry any food: use non-stick pans which do not need fat.
2. Do not eat breads, potatoes, pastas, dried beans, peas, corn, rice – you know only too well what things to avoid.
3. Do not use sauces, e.g. tomato ketchup – or only the merest trace if you must.
4. Do not eat fruits packed in syrup.
5. Do not drink spirits and limit soft drinks.
6. Do not drink water with your meals.

You probably will not follow these menus and recipes exactly: they are intended to be useful guidelines. Adopt the idea of eating smaller-than-average helpings – and no second helpings.

Sample menu

Breakfast
½ grapefruit
1 slice melba toast
2 cups black coffee or tea

Mid-morning
½ pint (2.8 dl) vegetable broth or bouillon

Lunch
½ cold boiled lobster
Shredded cucumbers and capers (all you wish)
Spinach salad mimosa: ½ hard-boiled egg white, chopped; 2 level teaspoons wine vinegar dressing*
Black coffee or tea

Tea
Hot tea with lemon

Dinner
Cold consommé served on the rocks in a small wine glass
2 or 3 shrimps
½ grilled double poussin
2 tablespoons green beans
1 braised celery heart
Green salad with ½ tomato and 1 teaspoon dressing
1 dessertspoon puréed strawberries and baked custard
Black coffee or tea

First week

If you are slimming, start with cutting down at breakfast. A half grapefruit, or a sliced orange, or your favourite fruit, fresh or freshly cooked without adding sugar. Black coffee or tea. A slice of melba toast, if you must, but make it yourself, and, if you think the world looks too dismal, have an egg poached or boiled as well (leave the yolk on the plate).

Hot tea or coffee between meals is permissible, and a cup of hot vegetable broth* mid-morning will make the world look brighter; it is filled with vitamins, especially potassium.

If you crave something in the middle of the afternoon, fresh fruit of any kind, put into a blender with crushed ice, makes a good pick-me-up; use it for a before-dinner cocktail too. Take a few pieces of fresh pineapple, a few strawberries, a small piece of melon, any fruit as long as it is fresh – about $\frac{1}{2}$ pint (2.8 dl) altogether – add a couple of ice cubes and a sprig of mint and purée them in the blender. This is low in calories, but very refreshing.

DAY 1

Lunch

Grapefruit grilled with cinnamon
$\frac{1}{4}$ grilled chicken, rubbed with lemon juice before grilling
Asparagus with grated orange peel

Dinner

Iced madrilène (Serve in shallow crystal bowls with crab meat and capers in the centre. It is a beautiful low-calorie sight to sit down to. A twist of lemon. Serve sour cream for those who are not dieting.)
Grilled fillet steak, lightly rubbed with brown mustard before cooking
Fresh green beans, sprinkled with dill
Lemon ice*

DAY 2

Lunch

A small cup of hot chicken broth
Half a fresh pineapple, scooped out and filled with orange and grapefruit sections, slivers of cold chicken on top; yogurt dressing*

Dinner

Chilled tinned celery-heart salad sprinkled with finely chopped hard-boiled egg white and parsley; wine vinegar dressing*
A thick grilled lamb chop, all the fat cut off
Fresh spinach soufflé*
A baked half tomato sprinkled with oregano and Parmesan cheese
Fresh pears in red wine*

DAY 3

Lunch

Cold boiled lobster with jellied cucumber salad* and yogurt remoulade*

Dinner

Gazpacho (a small glass before dinner)*
Thin slices of boiled lean beef with fresh little white onions cooked in the broth
Fresh cabbage quarters, cooked covered in boiling water, garnished with a few peas and chopped parsley
Marinated beetroot*
Stewed apples and mandarin oranges*

DAY 4

Lunch

Cheese custard*
Fresh spinach and mushroom salad*

Dinner

A tray of nibbles before dinner: raw carrot sticks, thin slices of raw white turnips, baby tomatoes and cucumber fingers all ice cold and crisp (and you can eat all you like)
Grilled whole baby poussin with pink apple sauce, flavoured with horse-radish (make it pink with vegetable colouring or beetroot juice)
Mushroom soufflé*
Broccoli with piquant sauce*
Pots de crème*

DAY 5

Lunch

Hot tomato bouillon*
Sliced egg and tinned artichoke salad with wine vinegar dressing*
Fingers of fresh pineapple

Dinner

Yogurt soup* (serve in crystal over a green leaf from the garden)
Oven-baked fresh salmon steak*
Swedish cucumbers*
A bouquet of vegetables: baby beetroots with capers, okra, courgettes
Grapefruit sections with puréed strawberries

DAY 6

Lunch

Grilled hamburger

Baked half tomato with spinach purée*
German coleslaw*

Dinner
Tinola* (boiled chicken with vegetables), served from the pot you cooked it in
Relish salad*
Three-fruit sorbet*

DAY 7 (SUNDAY)

Dinner
Jellied spring salad*

Turkey breast Singapore*
Fresh green beans, onion rings tossed and sprinkled with coconut
Carrot pudding*
Very cold tinned apricots with warm custard

Supper
Hot claret consommé
Slices of ripe cantaloupe, thin slices of Swiss cheese and cold meat (Buy lean, very thin slices of salt beef; this goes well with the melon and the cheese.)

THE HIGH-PROTEIN DIET

This diet is based on the recommendations of Dr Edgar S. Gordon, professor of medicine at the University of Wisconsin Medical Center in the USA.

Protein food has a high specific dynamic action – that is, it costs more calories to digest and use so that, in effect, a certain amount of food energy is wasted as heat and is, therefore, unavailable for filling energy needs or for storage as fat.

On the basis of research findings, Dr Gordon recommends a high-protein diet that provides 105 g protein, 65 g carbohydrate, and 50 g fat, for a total of about 1,100 Calories daily. It is nutritionally adequate and almost never attended by hunger, he says.

Possible weight loss: $2\frac{1}{2}$–3 lb (1.1–1.4 kg) per week.
Time: indefinitely.

The formula

Milk: skimmed or low-fat, $\frac{3}{4}$ pint (4.3 dl).

Eggs: one, prepared in any way as long as no fat is added. 1 oz (30 g) meat may be substituted.

Meat, poultry or fish: 9 oz (255 g) cooked weight (see note). Remove all fat, preferably before cooking. May be grilled, roasted or boiled. Lean cured meats are allowed, also pickled, smoked or kippered fish or fish packed in water (not oil).

Permissible substitutes: for 1 oz (30 g) meat: 2 oz (55 g) cottage cheese or 1 dessertspoon peanut butter (not more than twice a week); for 2 oz (55 g) meat: 1 egg (never eat more than two a day) or 1 oz (30 g) Swiss, Cheddar or American cheese (no other types and only one substitution a day).

Vegetables (1): 8–16 oz (225–455 g). Either raw, cooked or combined. Select from the following including at least 4 oz (115 g) of one of the starred vegetables at least every other day:

asparagus	mangetout peas
aubergine	marrow
bean sprouts	mushrooms
beans, green	peppers
*broccoli	radishes
cabbage	*spinach
cauliflower	*spring greens
celery	spring onions
chicory	tomato juice
courgettes	(not more than
cucumber	1 cup a day)
endive	tomatoes
*kale	*turnip tops
lettuce	watercress

Vegetables (2), or grain: one portion of the size indicated.

1 oz (30 g) potatoes; 2 oz (55 g) any of the following: beetroot, Brussels sprouts, white onions, peas, pumpkin.

Or ½ slice bread, 1 oz (30 g) cooked cereal, 1½ oz (45 g) cooked rice, 1 oz (30 g) cooked spaghetti, noodles or macaroni, 1 water biscuit.

Fruit: two portions of the size indicated. Choose from:

apple, 2 inch (5 cm)	grapefruit, ½ small
apricots: fresh, 2 medium; dried, 4 halves	honeydew melon, ⅛ medium
banana, ½ small	mango, ½ small
blackberries, 4 oz (115 g)	nectarine
blueberries, 4 oz (115 g)	orange, 1 small
	peach, ⅓ medium
cantaloupe, ¼	pear, 1 small
cherries, 10 large	pineapple, small slice
dates, 2	prunes, 2 medium
figs: fresh, 2 large; dried, 1 small	raspberries, 4 oz (115 g)
grapefruit juice, small glass	strawberries, 4 oz (115 g)
	tangerine, 1 large

Fat: four portions of size indicated. Should be mainly vegetable fat. Total allowance may be in form of oil, but none should be used for frying. Each of the following is equal to one portion: 1 teaspoon oil; 1 teaspoon mayonnaise made with corn oil (no more than 2 teaspoons a day); 1 teaspoon margarine (no more than 3 teaspoons a day); 4–5 walnut halves or 1 dessertspoon chopped (no more than 10 halves or 2 dessertspoons a day).

Note: According to Dr Gordon the size of portions is of vital importance to the effectiveness of the high-protein diet, so that in many cases we have indicated the proper amounts on the menus. When not indicated there you will find them in the lists of vegetables and fruits. Meat portions refer to cooked weight. If you have no kitchen scales, you can judge as follows: a 3 oz (85 g) portion of meat is approximately equal to a quarter of a 2–3 lb (0.9–1.4 kg) cooked chicken; two 4 × 2 × ¼ inch (10 × 5 × 0.6 cm) slices of any roast meat; 1 medium loin chop, ¾ inch (2 cm) thick; a 4 × 2 × ½ inch (10 × 5 × 1.2 cm) piece of steak or fish. When meat is given for a between-meal snack, it might consist of some left over from a previous meal. If there are any items on the menus that you particularly dislike or have difficulty obtaining, substitute something else that will meet Dr Gordon's specifications.

Menus

DAY I

Breakfast
1 tangerine
1 oz (30 g) grilled ham
1 poached egg
Coffee or tea

Mid-morning
1 oz (30 g) cold meat
1 cup low-fat milk

Lunch
2 oz (55 g) grilled fish with lemon wedge
Courgette and tomato baked in casserole with a little tomato juice and seasonings

Mid-afternoon
1 oz (30 g) Swiss cheese
½ cup low-fat milk

Dinner
Melon
Herb-grilled calf's liver: cover ¼ inch (6 mm) thick piece of liver with lemon juice, parsley, shallots, mushrooms, salt and pepper; grill 1½ minutes each side
Endive and beetroot salad
Vinaigrette dressing made with 1 teaspoon oil
Broccoli with lemon
1 teaspoon margarine

Evening
1 oz (30 g) meat
½ cup low-fat milk

DAY 2

Breakfast
Small orange
1 oz (30 g) grilled bacon
½ slice wholewheat toast, 1 teaspoon margarine
Coffee or tea

Mid-morning
1 oz (30 g) Swiss cheese
1 cup low-fat milk

Lunch
Hot beef consommé
Prawns baked in foil*
Raw vegetable salad (lettuce, bean sprouts, mush-
   rooms, cauliflower, green beans, celery and
   tomatoes) with low-calorie dressing*

Mid-afternoon
2 oz (55 g) meat or 1 oz (30 g) cheese
½ cup low-fat milk

Dinner
Honeydew melon and powdered ginger
3 oz (85 g) marinated grilled lamb chop: trim fat,
   marinate in minced garlic, lemon zest and juice
Quick ratatouille*

Evening
1 oz (30 g) meat
½ cup low-fat milk

DAY 3

Breakfast
¼ small canteloupe melon
1 scrambled egg (with low-fat milk)
1 grilled chicken liver
Coffee or tea

Mid-morning
1 oz (30 g) meat
1 cup low-fat milk

Lunch
Cottage cheese salad: mix together cottage cheese,
   tomato, cucumber, spring onions, radishes; season; arrange on lettuce; half a slice of toast with
   1 teaspoon margarine
Spiced iced tea

Mid-afternoon
2 oz (55 g) meat
½ cup low-fat milk

Dinner
2 raw stuffed mushrooms (stuffing: cottage cheese
   creamed with a dessertspoon milk, parsley,
   chives, marjoram, dash of Worcestershire sauce)
Orange roasted chicken*
Asparagus with lemon and 1 teaspoon margarine
1 apple
3 walnuts

Evening
1 oz (30 g) meat
½ cup low-fat milk

DAY 4

Breakfast
Small glass grapefruit juice
Sausage
½ slice rye toast with ½ teaspoon margarine
Coffee or tea

Mid-morning
1 oz (30 g) meat
1 cup low-fat milk

Lunch
Artichoke stuffed with shrimps*
Low-calorie mayonnaise*

Mid-afternoon
2 oz (55 g) cheese
½ cup low-fat milk

Dinner
Grilled veal cutlet
Grilled mushrooms
Braised spinach (braise in chicken stock with
   grated onion, nutmeg, rosemary, salt and pepper; drain and squeeze out liquid)
Orange ice (1 part frozen unsweetened orange
   concentrate mixed with 2 parts water, frozen
   and shaved into slivers)

Evening
1 oz (30 g) meat
½ cup low-fat milk

DAY 5

Breakfast
1 large tangerine
1 oz (30 g) grilled ham
½ slice rye toast
1 teaspoon margarine
Coffee or tea

Mid-morning
1 oz (30 g) meat
1 cup low-fat milk

Lunch
Hot tomato bouillon
Salade niçoise*
Low-calorie salad dressing*

Mid-afternoon
2 oz (55 g) meat
½ cup low-fat milk

Dinner
Herbed pork chop (trim off fat; score surface and press in minced parsley and shallots; season and grill)
2 oz (55 g) cauliflower with parsley, chives and 1 teaspoon margarine
Mushroom, watercress and chicory salad
Garlic dressing made with 1 teaspoon oil
4 oz (115 g) strawberries

Evening
1 oz (30 g) meat
½ cup low-fat milk

DAY 6

Breakfast
½ small banana
1½ oz (45 g) cereal
1 poached egg
1 teaspoon margarine
Coffee or tea

Mid-morning
1 oz (30 g) meat
1 cup low-fat milk

Lunch
Hot chicken broth
Garlic hamburger*

Spinach, mushroom and walnut salad
2 teaspoons oil and vinegar dressing

Mid-afternoon
2 oz (55 g) meat
½ cup low-fat milk

Dinner
Chicken roasted with soya sauce
Mangetout peas with 1 teaspoon butter
Tomato grilled with oregano and seasonings
Orange

Evening
1 oz (30 g) meat
½ cup low-fat milk

DAY 7

Breakfast
Small pear
1 oz (30 g) chopped chicken scrambled with 1 egg flavoured with tarragon
½ slice toast with 1 teaspoon margarine
Coffee or tea

Mid-morning
1 oz (30 g) meat
½ cup low-fat milk

Lunch
Beef bouillon
Fillet of sole en papillote*
Braised celery

Mid-afternoon
2 oz (55 g) meat
½ cup low-fat milk

Dinner
Roast veal stuffed with mushrooms, garlic, pepper, salt
Green beans
Watercress and orange salad
2 teaspoons curry-flavoured French dressing
4 walnut halves
4 halved apricots poached with cloves and cinnamon

Evening
1 oz (30 g) meat
½ cup low-fat milk

FAVOURITE FOOD DIET

This diet was originally created for the late Aga Khan and incorporates many of his favourite foods. It has since been followed the world over. It permits as much tea and coffee as you like and allows milk in both; artificial sweetener only; salt and pepper for seasoning; vinegar for salad dressing; it *excludes* all fat, cream, sugar either on their own or in the preparation of a dish; all frying and, above all, no alcohol. You may substitute one meal for another provided you eat the liver prescribed and you may eat the three meals for each day in whatever order you like. It is *forbidden* to eat less than the diet prescribes. A daily multi-vitamin tablet is recommended.

DAY 1

Breakfast
6 half apricots stewed or preserved without sugar

Lunch
Large grilled steak
Large salad: lettuce, tomato and cucumber
½ glass of skimmed milk

Dinner
Glass grapefruit juice
Small grilled steak
Small portion green beans

DAY 2

Breakfast
1 poached or boiled egg
1 slice brown bread or toast

Lunch
1 boiled or poached egg
8–10 asparagus tips
½ glass skimmed milk

Dinner
1 cup clear soup
Large portion grilled calf's liver
Small portion cauliflower
1 sliced tomato

DAY 3

Breakfast
Tomato juice

Lunch
Large grilled steak
Small portion green beans
Boiled or raw cabbage with oil-free dressing
½ glass skimmed milk

Dinner
1 cup clear soup
2 lean pork cutlets
Small portion boiled celery
Mixed salad

DAY 4

Breakfast
1 boiled or poached egg
1 slice brown bread or toast

Lunch
1 boiled or poached egg
Small portion spinach
4 sticks raw celery
½ glass skimmed milk

Dinner
1 cup of clear soup
Large portion grilled chicken
Mixed salad
Sliced orange

DAY 5

Breakfast
1 poached or boiled egg
1 slice brown bread or toast

Lunch
1 poached egg on boiled spinach
Small portion boiled cauliflower
½ glass skimmed milk

Dinner
1 cup clear soup
Large portion grilled white fish with lemon (not greasy fish like salmon, mackerel, herring)
Salad of chopped cabbage and grated carrots

DAY 6

Breakfast
Grapefruit juice
1 boiled or poached egg

Lunch
Large grilled steak
Boiled cabbage and small portion green beans
½ glass skimmed milk

Dinner
Tomato juice
2 grilled lamb or pork chops, lean meat only
8–10 asparagus tips

DAY 7

Breakfast
Grapefruit juice
1 boiled or poached egg

Lunch
1 cup clear soup
Large portion roast beef, no fat, or half a chicken
Small portion spinach
Sliced tomato and lettuce salad

Dinner
2 slices cold roast beef or portion cold chicken
Small portion green beans
½ glass skimmed milk
Fresh peach

DAY 8

Breakfast
1 boiled or poached egg
1 slice brown bread or toast

Lunch
1 boiled or poached egg
Small portion grilled tomatoes
Finely chopped raw cabbage with sliced peppers
    and chopped parsley
½ glass skimmed milk

Dinner
Orange juice
2 grilled veal cutlets
½ grapefruit

DAY 9

Breakfast
Tomato and lettuce salad

Lunch
Small grilled steak
Large portion cabbage or raw cabbage salad with
    oil-free dressing
½ glass skimmed milk

Dinner
Tomato juice
Large portion calf's or lamb's liver
Small portion spinach
4 sticks raw celery

DAY 10

Breakfast
½ grapefruit

Lunch
2 boiled or poached eggs
Small portion grilled tomatoes
Boiled cabbage or cabbage salad
½ glass skimmed milk

Dinner
1 cup clear soup
2 slices roast veal or lamb, no fat
Salad

SUPER PROTEIN DIET

This seven-day slimming plan can be followed indefinitely and is high in protein, vitamins and minerals. Keep to the rules and, if you are overweight and normally eat too much, you should lose weight quite easily, with an added beauty bonus. Allow only ½ pint (2.8 dl) milk a day, including milk in tea and coffee. Restrict your butter to ½ oz (15 g) a day. Never fry foods, always grill, poach, bake or boil. Drink as much water, tea, coffee and meat extracts as you like. Replace sugar with artificial sweetener. Allow approximately 4 oz (115 g) meat or 6 oz (170 g) fish unless otherwise stated, and as many vegetables as you like chosen from the following: artichokes, asparagus, aubergines, French beans, runner beans, broccoli, Brussels sprouts, cabbage, carrots, cauliflower, celery, courgettes, marrow, mushrooms, onions, green or red peppers, spinach, swede, tomatoes and turnips.

DAY 1

Breakfast
Wineglass tomato juice
1 boiled egg
2 slices bread or toast

Lunch
Ham slices wound into rolls and stuffed with cottage cheese
Coleslaw (finely sliced cabbage and carrot blended with a little plain yogurt, lemon juice and tomato purée)
2 slices bread
5 oz (140 g) plain yogurt

Dinner
Slice melon
Fricassée of veal
Sliced carrots
Orange and grapefruit compote

DAY 2

Breakfast
Sliced orange

2 oz (55 g) cheese grilled on a slice of toast with grilled mushrooms

Lunch
Open sandwiches of liver pâté, sliced cucumber and small bacon twists on 3 slices bread
1 pear

Dinner
½ grilled grapefruit
Braised beef
Courgettes
Fresh fruit salad moistened with fresh lemon and orange juice

DAY 3

Breakfast
Tumbler unsweetened or fresh orange juice
1 rasher grilled bacon and grilled tomatoes
2 slices bread or toast

Lunch
Flaked, cooked, smoked cod stirred into a lightly scrambled egg on 1 slice toast
Spinach
1 apple

Dinner
½ avocado dressed with lemon juice
Roast chicken with bacon rolls
Broccoli
Rhubarb fool (i)*

DAY 4

Breakfast
½ grapefruit
Poached finnan haddock
2 slices bread or toast

Lunch
Spanish omelette (2 eggs)
Green salad
2 slices bread
1 apple

Dinner
Consommé
Baked ham with 2–3 drained apricot halves
Melon and grape salad

DAY 5

Breakfast
Wineglass tomato juice
1 poached egg on a slice of toast

Lunch
Open sandwiches of sliced chicken garnished with
  watercress on 3 slices bread
5 oz (140 g) plain yogurt

Dinner
Cold leeks in wine vinegar
Grilled Dover sole
French beans
1 oz (30 g) cheese with celery

DAY 6

Breakfast
½ grapefruit
Grilled lamb's kidneys with grilled tomatoes
2 slices bread or toast

Lunch
Grilled halibut flavoured with orange juice

Spinach
1 apple

Dinner
Smoked trout
Lamb, green pepper, tomato, mushroom and
  onion kebab
Mixed salad
½ peach topped with cottage cheese

DAY 7

Breakfast
1 poached egg and 1 rasher grilled bacon with
  grilled mushrooms
2 slices bread or toast

Lunch
Prawn salad with 2 slices bread
1 oz (30 g) cheese with celery

Dinner
Turtle soup
Grilled rump steak
Green salad
2 slices fresh pineapple

1926

BLANCH

EXERCISE BASICS

These exercises are based on an interview with Dr J. M. Marshall, Clinical Associate Professor of Surgery at the New York Hospital Cornell Medical Center.

To be effective an exercise programme has to be done regularly. The basic rule is that you must do it at least three times a week (five times a week is better). However, a lot depends on how much you are putting into it. If you are exercising every day but it is not stressing you effectively, you may be better off doing it less frequently and more intensely.

Here is an exercise plan that has it all: stretching, strengthening, endurance – with a warm-up at the outset, jogging between exercises and a cool-down at the end. You have everything you need for total fitness. Begin slowly and gradually work up to more repetitions of each exercise – and jog longer in between at a brisker speed. Finish by walking around the room for a couple of minutes, doing some light stretches and shaking loose. Total time, 20–30 minutes.

Flexibility plus warm-up: Exercises 1–4 stretch the ligaments and tendons and increase the range of motion. Do them slowly. Jog loosely for 15 seconds between the exercises. Go non-stop.

1. Sit and reach – Sit on exercise mat, legs straight, feet together, 1a. Keeping the back and legs straight slowly reach forward along the legs, 1b. Hold at a slight stretch for 10 seconds, 1c. Recover. Repeat 3 times. This stretches the hamstrings (muscles behind your thighs) and the lower back ... Jog.

EXERCISE BASICS

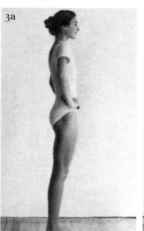

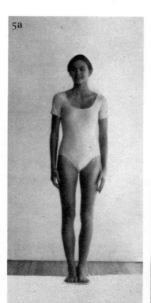

2. Touch toes *(above left)* – Stand with arms and legs outstretched, 2a. Keep the legs straight. Bend forward and touch the left foot with the right hand, 2b. Recover. Then touch the right foot with the left hand. Do 5–10 each side. This is another good hamstring and back stretcher and a light warm-up for waist and abdomen muscles . . . Jog.

3. Leg stretch *(above right)* – Stand with hands on hips, 3a. Move the left leg forward, knee bent slightly. Stretch the right leg back. Slowly move the pelvis forward and down, 3b. Hold 5 seconds. Recover. Do 2 with each leg. Work up gradually to 10-second holds. This stretches the hip and groin muscles, hamstrings and Achilles tendons, and strengthens the front thigh muscles as a bonus . . . Jog.

4. Achilles stretch *(left)* – Stand, body straight, hands against wall, feet flat on floor 2 or 3 ft (66 or 99 cm) back. Lean into wall, 4a. Hold 10–15 seconds. Push back. Repeat three times. Or move left foot back, right knee towards wall, 4b. Slowly stretch back heel down, and slightly bend back knee. Hold at a slight stretch for 10–15 seconds. Reverse the legs. Do two with each leg. This exercise stretches the Achilles tendon and calf and helps maintain ankle flexibility . . . Jog.

Strengthening plus endurance:
Exercises 5–6 use major muscle groups. Do the exercises briskly in order to keep your heart rate up to training level. And jog on the spot or round the room a minute or more between each exercise.

5. Jumping Jacks *(left)* – Stand erect, arms at sides, feet together, 5a. Jump, spread the legs while raising the arms, and clap your hands over your head, 5b. Recover by jumping back to the starting position. Land on toes. Repeat 10–20 times. This raises your heart rate, loosens the joints and is a good exercise for the ankles, calves, and arms . . . Jog.

Log hop *(large illustration on previous page)* – Put three thick books on the floor, a couple of feet apart. Hop over them without stopping, keeping the legs together. Do this once or twice. It is a rigorous workout for the legs and will put spring in your stride . . . Jog.

6. Hop kick – Stand erect, 6a. Spring off the left leg. At same time, kick the right leg out and extend the right hand to touch the right toe, 6b. Recover. Repeat, alternating sides. Do 5–10 times with each leg. An ankle, calf and front thigh conditioner . . . Jog.

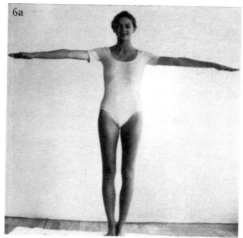

Flexibility plus strengthening plus cool-down:
Jog loosely for 15 seconds between exercises.

7. Sit-up – Lie on your back, legs well bent, 7a (this protects your back). Curl up slowly, keeping hands clasped behind head, 7b until elbows touch knees, 7c. Then go slowly down. If you cannot do it with your hands behind your head, keep them at your sides until you get better. Do this 5–10 times. This is an essential abdominal strengthener . . . Jog.

8. Back-over – Lie on the floor on your back. Bring your legs over your head and try to touch the floor with your toes while breathing out hard. Do this 1–5 times. This exercise stretches the hamstrings and lower back . . . Jog.

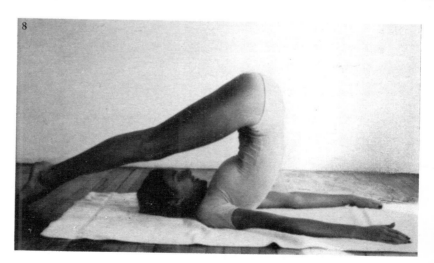

CALORIE CONTROLLED DIETS

Even though it takes only about 15 Calories a day to maintain each pound (455 g) of you it takes not eating 3,500 Calories to lose one pound. Which is why losing weight takes time.

To work out just how much and how fast you will lose weight on, for instance a 1,200 Calorie a day diet, multiply your weight by 15 (daily per-pound Calorie maintenance); subtract 1,200 (daily Calorie intake) from the result; multiply that number by 7 (days in a week) and divide that number by 3,500 (Calorie deficit necessary to lose one pound). The result is the number of pounds you should lose in a week. For example, if you weigh 150 lb (68 kg) you should lose about 2.1 lb (1 kg) a week on 1,200 Calories a day ($150 \times 15 = 2,250$; $2,250 - 1,200 = 1,050$; $1,050 \times 7 = 7,350$; $7,350 \div 3,500 = 2.1$). This would be a good dependable safe weight loss. If you want to boost the speed a little cut back to closer to 1,000 Calories a day by cutting out the evening snack. And you can increase the pounds shed by increasing your exercise (a 150 lb, 68 kg, person uses 19.4 Calories a minute running, 5.2 walking).

You usually lose extra the first week because of body fluid shifts and subsequent water loss; but this extra is not fat loss and it will not stay lost.

NO-DIET DIET

How is it possible to lose weight without going on a diet? By changing a few of your eating habits, says Marina Andrews. Here is a typical mid-week menu:

Daily menu

Breakfast
½ grapefruit with sugar
1 slice toast with butter, marmalade
1 cup coffee with 1 teaspoon sugar, milk

Mid-morning
1 cup coffee

Lunch
Plain omelette (2 eggs) made with milk and cooked in butter

2 crackers with Cheddar cheese (*add 55 if with butter*)
1 small glass wine
Coffee

Afternoon tea
1 cup tea with milk and sugar (*add 60 or more Calories if you have a biscuit*)

Dinner
Pre-dinner drink, gin and tonic
Small bowl clear soup
Chicken casserole with flour and wine
Average helping frozen peas
2 potato croquettes
Average slice fruit pie with cream

2 small glasses wine
1 cup coffee (*add 22 Calories if with cream*)

Total number of Calories: 2,050

I have been most liberal in the quantity of foods. However if, for example, you like more than one slice of toast for breakfast, rolls with your soup at dinner and the extra drink beforehand, or additional sugar in your coffee, you will see that the amount of Calories each day could be nearer 2,500. This is an excessive amount for most inactive people. How, therefore, to save calories and lose weight while keeping to the same diet? Below is one possible answer, with a saving of 950 Calories a day, 6,650 a week.

Breakfast
½ grapefruit
1 black coffee

Lunch
Omelette (2 eggs) with milk, in a non-stick pan
2 crackers, no butter
Edam or Gouda cheese
1 small glass wine
1 black coffee

Afternoon tea
1 cup tea with lemon

Dinner
Gin and tonic (Slimline tonic can save calories)
Chicken casserole – enrich with yogurt, not flour
Frozen peas
1 potato croquette
Fruit, no cream or pastry
1 small glass wine
1 black coffee

Total number of Calories: 1,100

If you like coffee or tea with a little milk, add about 20 Calories more a cup. Artificial sweeteners have no calories and can replace sugar. The liquid kind can replace sugar on fruit.
Possible weight loss: 2½ lb (1.1 kg) a week.
Time: indefinitely.

THE NEVER ON SUNDAYS, TUESDAYS, THURSDAYS DIET

This is a diet that alternates between austere and luxury days. There is always the feeling that there is jam tomorrow – and there really is. You start and end the week with luxury days. On luxury days the Calorie count is around 1,400; on austere days it is 1,000. Every day you can drink lemon tea or black coffee without sugar (but an artificial sweetener if you wish), and a little milk for breakfast. A glass of dry white wine at lunch on luxury days; and a glass of red or dry white wine every day for dinner. Eat fresh fruit only – no tinned varieties; starch-reduced bread, toast or crispbread with a scraping of butter; low-calorie soft drinks. Here is a week's chart with three alternatives for each meal each day – the approximate numbers of Calories of each is indicated in brackets.
Possible weight loss: up to 2 lb (0.9 kg) in seven days.
Time: you could continue this diet indefinitely, or as long as you take to get down to your right weight.

SUNDAY

Breakfast
6 oz (170 g) grilled trout with a slice of toast
(*225*)

4 oz (115 g) stewed figs with a little yogurt, 1 crispbread with a little marmalade
(*260*)

2 oz (55 g) grilled bacon with mushrooms and tomato, 1 slice of toast
(*300*)

Lunch
4 oz (115 g) grilled salmon steak with tomato, crisp roll
1 peach
(*574*)

6 fl oz (1.7 dl) consommé
4 oz (115 g) roast chicken with green beans and 2 small new potatoes
5 oz (140 g) fresh fruit salad with a little cream
(515)

4½ oz (125 g) fillet steak with mushrooms, tomato and ½ jacket potato
2 oz (55 g) ice-cream
(510)

Dinner
Small helping caviar with lemon
3 oz (85 g) roast duckling with apricots, asparagus with little melted butter and green salad
3 oz (85 g) fresh raspberries
(570)

Melon and Parma ham
6 oz (170 g) poached fillet of sole with grapes and salad
Orange salad
(570)

Avocado pear
½ lobster with green salad
3 oz (85 g) fresh pineapple with kirsch
(510)

MONDAY

Breakfast
4 oz (115 g) kedgeree
1 slice toast
(300)

2 oz (55 g) grilled liver, 1 oz (30 g) bacon, tomato
1 slice toast
(315)

½ grapefruit
1 poached egg with 2 rashers grilled bacon
1 crispbread
(290)

Lunch
4 fl oz (1.1 dl) clear soup
2 cheese biscuits
1 orange
(210)

3 oz (85 g) salmon with green salad
1 crispbread
(210)

4 fl oz (1.1 dl) fruit juice
1 oz (30 g) cheese with 1 crispbread
1 apple
(230)

Dinner
5 oz (140 g) tomato juice
4 oz (115 g) Scotch eggs with green salad
Fruit yogurt
(535)

5 oz (140 g) mushroom soup
2½ oz (70 g) grilled steak, French beans
Apple purée
(380)

½ grapefruit
4 oz (115 g) smoked mackerel with green salad, 2 small new potatoes
1 pear
(525)

TUESDAY

Breakfast
4 oz (115 g) finnan haddock poached in milk
2 crispbreads with a little marmalade
(210)

4 oz (115 g) stewed gooseberries
1 boiled egg with 1 slice toast
(165)

4 oz (115 g) grilled kipper with 1 slice toast
(225)

Lunch
½ avocado pear
2 grilled lamb chops with mushrooms and tomato
1 apple
(660)

1 slice melon
8 oz (225 g) grilled trout with green beans, 2 small new potatoes
3 oz (85 g) raspberries and cream
(585)

Opposite and overleaf: Penn, 1977, 1978, 1974

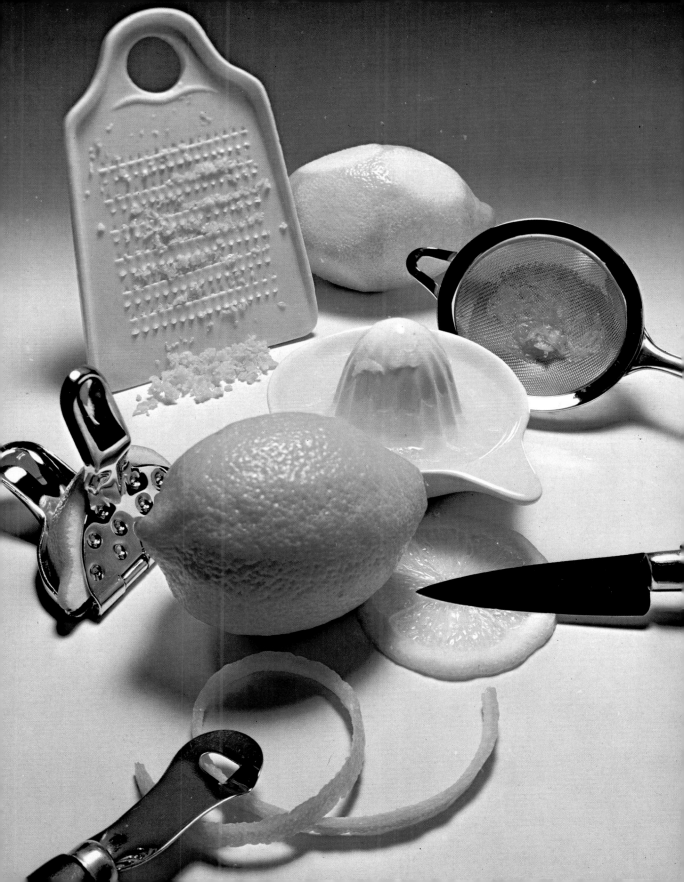

Small portion of smoked salmon
3 oz (85 g) cold duck with mixed salad
3 oz (85 g) pineapple
(545)

Dinner
Small portion smoked salmon
4 oz (115 g) roast capon with fresh asparagus, grilled tomatoes
1 oz (30 g) cheese with 2 water biscuits
(570)

Melon and orange cocktail
3 oz (85 g) roast lamb, peas, young carrots
Crème caramel*
(580)

Oeuf en cocotte*
3 oz (85 g) crab with green salad
4 oz (115 g) lychees flambé (cooked in kirsch and lighted)
(500)

WEDNESDAY

Breakfast
2–3 oz (55–85 g) cereal with ¼ pint milk
1 poached egg on 1 slice toast
(300)

4 oz (115 g) fresh fruit juice
1¾ oz (50 g) lean ham, tomato
1 crispbread
(220)

5 oz (140 g) apple purée
2 oz (55 g) sausage
2 tomatoes
1 slice toast
(255)

Lunch
2 oz (55 g) Brie
½ oz (15 g) walnuts
1 crispbread
(275)

4 oz (115 g) Scotch egg with green salad
1 peach
(370)

3 oz (85 g) cold beef with green salad
1 slice melon
(240)

Dinner
5 fl oz (1.5 dl) clear soup
3 oz (85 g) grilled chop, carrots, green beans
2 oz (55 g) ice-cream
(445)

½ grapefruit
4 oz (115 g) curried chicken
2 oz (55 g) boiled rice
5 oz (140 g) yogurt
(420)

4 fl oz (1.1 dl) tomato juice
3 oz (85 g) salmon with green salad
1 oz (30 g) cheese and 1 cream cracker
(425)

THURSDAY

Breakfast
2 oz (55 g) grilled cod's roe with tomato
1 slice toast
(120)

½ grapefruit
Scrambled egg on toast
(165)

1 oz (30 g) grilled bacon with tomato
1 crispbread
(160)

Lunch
Small prawn cocktail*
3 oz (85 g) roast duck with orange salad, 2 small roast potatoes
3 oz (85 g) fresh pineapple
(670)

Melon
4 oz (115 g) salmon with green salad, small helping of potato salad
1 peach
(545)

6 oz (170 g) grilled sole with spinach or asparagus
4 oz (115 g) bilberry pie and cream
(660)

Opposite: Penn, 1977

Dinner
½ avocado pear
4 oz (115 g) fillet steak, grilled, with French beans, grilled tomato
Small portion Camembert with 2 water biscuits
(570)

Small prawn cocktail*
3 oz (85 g) roast lamb with broccoli, braised celery
Fresh fruit salad
(580)

5 fl oz (1.4 dl) consommé
4 oz (115 g) roast beef with courgettes, French beans
Crème caramel*
(535)

FRIDAY

Breakfast
1 oz (30 g) cereal with ¼ pint milk
1 boiled egg
1 crispbread
(320)

5 oz (140 g) prunes
1 boiled egg
1 slice toast
(225)

4 fl oz (1.1 dl) orange juice
2 grilled kidneys, mushrooms
1 crispbread
(175)

Lunch
2 oz (55 g) cold chicken with lettuce and tomato
1 orange
(160)

3 oz (85 g) gammon, tomato
1 apple
(260)

2 oz (55 g) Edam cheese
2 crispbreads
(230)

Dinner
5 fl oz (1.4 dl) tomato juice
3 oz (85 g) grilled haddock, 2 small potatoes, cress
1 oz (30 g) cheese with 1 water biscuit
(410)

3 oz (85 g) tomato salad
4 oz (115 g) roast beef, roast potato, spinach
5 oz (140 g) yogurt
(615)

5 fl oz (1.4 dl) consommé
3 oz (85 g) veal cutlet, 2 oz (55 g) onions, French beans, 1 new potato
Fresh fruit salad
(465)

SATURDAY

Breakfast
Omelette (1 egg) with tomato
1 slice toast with little cherry jam
(220)

2 oz (55 g) cold gammon
1 slice toast with little marmalade
(205)

Melon
Boiled egg
1 slice toast with marmalade
(170)

Lunch
Shrimp cocktail
3 oz (85 g) grilled lamb chop with spinach and small Lyonnaise potatoes
Peach
(535)

Melon
Lobster with little mayonnaise, green salad
4 oz (115 g) strawberries and cream
(470)

½ grapefruit
4 oz (115 g) sauté kidneys with 2 oz (55 g) boiled rice and broccoli
5 oz (140 g) yogurt
(490)

Dinner
Melon with Parma ham
3 oz (85 g) lobster with green salad
2 oz (55 g) mushrooms on toast
(600)

½ avocado pear with shrimps
3 oz (85 g) veal escalope with green beans
Fresh fruit salad
(630)

Scampi meunière
4 oz (115 g) smoked breast of chicken with asparagus tips and grilled tomatoes, French beans
4 oz (115 g) strawberries and cream
(670)

THE GOURMET DIET

This diet includes one gourmet meal each day and a pudding for people who like something sweet. The diet should be followed for four weeks and anyone who is overweight should lose at least 8 lb (3.6 kg). Everyone should look and feel better after it. There is a light lunch and a more substantial dinner – except for Sundays when they are reversed. But all meals can be interchanged as long as there is one of each type each day. This diet is anti-potatoes but includes liberal amounts of one or two fresh vegetables (cooked quickly in lightly salted boiling water) and a small green salad with each main course. The quantities given for vegetables are the maximum – you can eat less, but not more. Apart from the slice of toast and butter for breakfast, no bread, biscuits or butter are allowed. Each day there are a few Calories in hand – sometimes over 200 – and you can use these for drinks. If you feel hungry during the day eat a radish, small tomato, carrot or slice of cucumber. If you want to eat something not listed below make sure you balance the Calories. Do not exceed 1,100 but do not go below 850 and do not omit any fish or meat. No sugar – artificial sweetener if you wish in tea or coffee and in puddings. If you have a little milk with your tea or coffee alter the Calorie count from 0 to 20. Have half a tumbler of orange juice instead of grapefruit for breakfast if you would rather but increase the Calorie count from 30 to 50. The number of Calories for each day is given in brackets.

Possible weight loss: average 8 lb (3.6 kg) over four weeks.
Time: four weeks or indefinitely.

Breakfast every day
½ grapefruit
1 egg – boiled, poached or dry-fried
1 slice toast
Scraping of butter
Black coffee or tea

SUNDAY *(975 Calories)*

Lunch
Herbed chicken*
4 oz (115 g) mushrooms
4 oz (115 g) spinach
Apple cream*
Black coffee or tea

Dinner
Onion soup*
Poached eggs mornay*
Pineapple and lettuce salad*
Black coffee or tea

MONDAY *(860 Calories)*

Lunch
Tumbler tomato juice
4 oz (115 g) lean beef

6 asparagus spears
4 small lettuce leaves
1 orange
Black coffee or tea

Dinner
Scallops mornay*
Gooseberry jelly*
Black coffee or tea

TUESDAY *(1,000 Calories)*

Lunch
Cucumber soup*
Rice salad*
1 apple
Black coffee or tea

Dinner
Corn on the cob
Duckling and turkey salad*
Hot coffee soufflé*
Black coffee or tea

WEDNESDAY *(900 Calories)*

Lunch
3 oz (85 g) cold lamb
1 hard-boiled egg
2 tomatoes
4 oz (115 g) carrot
4 small lettuce leaves
8 oz (225 g) strawberries

Dinner
Tumbler tomato juice
Sole aux crevettes*
4 oz (115 g) cauliflower
4 oz (115 g) peas
Blackcurrant fool*
Black coffee or tea

THURSDAY *(950 Calories)*

Lunch
2 oz (55 g) smoked salmon
2 tomatoes
¼ cucumber

4 small lettuce leaves
1 apple
Black coffee or tea

Dinner
Asparagus vinaigrette*
2 grilled tomatoes
2 grilled lamb cutlets
4 oz (115 g) broccoli
Oranges juliennes*
Black coffee or tea

FRIDAY *(960 Calories)*

Lunch
Teacup consommé
4 oz (115 g) chicken meat
4 small lettuce leaves
1 tomato
3 apricots
Black coffee or tea

Dinner
1 slice melon, with either artificial sweetener or a
    squeeze of lemon
Ham horns*
4 oz (115 g) cauliflower
Gooseberry jelly*
Black coffee or tea

SATURDAY *(1,000 Calories)*

Lunch
Plaice bonne femme*
4 oz (115 g) peas
4 oz (115 g) spinach
1 apple
Black coffee or tea

Dinner
Salad Clementine*
Marinated steak*
2 grilled tomatoes
2 oz (55 g) mushrooms
4 oz (115 g) runner beans
Banana soufflé*
Black coffee or tea

SUNDAY (*1,080 Calories*)

Lunch
Artichoke with lemon dressing*
Chicken and clam pancakes*
4 oz (1 1 5 g) runner beans
4 oz (1 1 5 g) broccoli
Apple cream*
Black coffee or tea

Dinner
1 stuffed tomato (ii)*
Grilled lamb chops with herbs*
4 oz (1 1 5 g) French beans
4 oz (1 1 5 g) carrots
1 slice melon
Black coffee or tea

MONDAY (*1,000 Calories*)

Lunch
Aubergine parmigiana*
2 tomatoes
8 oz (2 2 5 g) cherries
Black coffee or tea

Dinner
Asparagus vinaigrette
Omelette lorraine*
2 grilled tomatoes
4 oz (1 1 5 g) runner beans
Mint and grape mould*
Black coffee or tea

TUESDAY (*980 Calories*)

Lunch
8 oz (2 2 5 g) smoked trout
2 tomatoes
¼ cucumber
1 orange
Black coffee or tea

Dinner
Steak tartare*
Mushroom and tomato salad*
Pineapple ice-cream*
Black coffee or tea

WEDNESDAY (*850 Calories*)

Lunch
Chicken en gelée*
2 tomatoes
1 oz (3 0 g) cottage cheese
3 apricots
Black coffee or tea

Dinner
Grilled liver with mushrooms
4 oz (1 1 5 g) runner beans
4 oz (1 1 5 g) spinach
Raspberry and blackcurrant mould*
Black coffee or tea

THURSDAY (*900 Calories*)

Lunch
2 oz (5 5 g) prawns and shredded lettuce
2 tomatoes and ¼ sliced cucumber
2 oz (5 5 g) cottage cheese
8 oz (2 2 5 g) cherries
Black coffee or tea

Dinner
Orange and tomato soup*
Carré d'agneau conti*
4 oz (1 1 5 g) broccoli
4 oz (1 1 5 g) carrots
Instant chocolate and orange mousse*
Black coffee or tea

FRIDAY (*935 Calories*)

Lunch
Teacup consommé
Beef and lettuce salad*
2 peaches
Black coffee or tea

Dinner
Salmon mousse*
Sauté of veal créole*
4 oz (1 1 5 g) courgettes
4 oz (1 1 5 g) carrots
Zabaglione*
Black coffee or tea

SATURDAY (*1,030 Calories*)

Lunch
Tomato juice cocktail*
Chicken and mushroom salad*
4 oz (115 g) strawberries
Black coffee or tea

Dinner
1 slice melon
8 oz (225 g) grilled hake garnished with a little
  parsley
Rice salad*
4 oz (115 g) peas
Pineapple ice-cream*
Black coffee or tea

SUNDAY (*970 Calories*)

Lunch
Tomato and vegetable aspic*
4 oz (115 g) grilled fillet steak
Tossed green salad*
Raspberry cream*
Black coffee or tea

Dinner
Parisian salad*
3 apricots
Black coffee or tea

MONDAY (*890 Calories*)

Lunch
2 stuffed tomatoes (ii)*
4 oz (115 g) cottage cheese
¼ sliced cucumber
4 oz (115 g) gooseberries
Black coffee or tea

Dinner
Oeuf en cocotte aux champignons*
Seafood casserole*
4 oz (115 g) cauliflower
4 oz (115 g) runner beans
Chocolate bavaroise*
Black coffee or tea

TUESDAY (*855 Calories*)

Lunch
4 oz (115 g) chicken meat
2 tomatoes and ¼ sliced cucumber
3 oz (85 g) cottage cheese
1 slice melon
Black coffee or tea

Dinner
Watercress soup*
Stuffed green peppers (ii)*
2 grilled tomatoes
4 oz (115 g) runner beans
Crêpes aux pêches*
Black coffee or tea

WEDNESDAY (*1,000 Calories*)

Lunch
2 stuffed tomatoes (ii)*
4 oz (115 g) grated young carrots
4 small lettuce leaves
1 orange
Black coffee or tea

Dinner
Cucumber salad (ii)*
Baked chicken and pineapple*
4 oz (115 g) each peas and broccoli
Apple cream
Black coffee or tea

THURSDAY (*1,025 Calories*)

Lunch
2 oz (55 g) tongue
Roast pepper salad*
1 apple
Black coffee or tea

Dinner
Asparagus vinaigrette*
Baked lamb chops with tomatoes and cheese*
4 oz (115 g) each cauliflower and French beans
Oranges juliennes*
Black coffee or tea

FRIDAY *(890 Calories)*

Lunch
Teacup consommé
Chicken and mushroom salad*
8 oz (225 g) fresh cherries
Black coffee or tea

Dinner
Tomato juice frappé*
Sole casserole*
4 oz (115 g) cauliflower
2 oz (55 g) sweet-corn
Hot coffee soufflé*
Black coffee or tea

SATURDAY *(875 Calories)*

Lunch
Waldorf salad*
2 oz (55 g) cottage cheese
2 tomatoes
Black coffee or tea

Dinner
Cucumber soup*
Ham mousse*
4 oz (115 g) cauliflower
4 oz (115 g) peas
Apple and pear snow*
Black coffee or tea

SUNDAY *(1,055 Calories)*

Lunch
Teacup consommé with watercress garnish
4 oz (115 g) roast beef
4 oz (115 g) French beans
4 oz (115 g) broccoli
Raspberry cream*
Black coffee or tea

Dinner
4 oz (115 g) corn on the cob
3 oz (85 g) lean beef
Orange salad*
Black coffee or tea

MONDAY *(925 Calories)*

Lunch
Baked crab meat*
2 tomatoes
¼ cucumber
8 oz (225 g) strawberries
Black coffee or tea

Dinner
Artichoke with lemon dressing*
4 oz (115 g) grilled steak
4 oz (115 g) peas
4 oz (115 g) runner beans
Chocolate bavaroise*
Black coffee or tea

TUESDAY *(850 Calories)*

Lunch
Teacup consommé
Savoury banana salad*
4 oz (115 g) cottage cheese
Black coffee or tea

Dinner
Fish with garlic*
4 oz (115 g) broccoli
4 oz (115 g) runner beans
Pineapple japonaise*
Black coffee or tea

WEDNESDAY *(950 Calories)*

Lunch
Watercress soup*
2 stuffed tomatoes (ii)*
2 peaches
Black coffee or tea

Dinner
Prawn cocktail*
Koulibiaca*
Baked stuffed aubergine*
4 oz (115 g) spinach
Apple scallops*
Black coffee or tea

THURSDAY *(920 Calories)*

Lunch
5 oz (140 g) chicken drumstick
2 tomatoes
¼ sliced cucumber
8 oz (225 g) grapes
Black coffee or tea

Dinner
Sole voisin*
4 oz (115 g) cauliflower
4 oz (115 g) peas
Oranges juliennes*
Black coffee or tea

FRIDAY *(935 Calories)*

Lunch
Tumbler tomato juice
Caesar salad*
2 oz (55 g) cottage cheese
2 peaches
Black coffee or tea

Dinner
Egg broth*
French roast chicken*
4 oz (115 g) spinach
4 oz (115 g) carrots
Gooseberry jelly*
Black coffee or tea

SATURDAY *(1,000 Calories)*

Lunch
Spinach soup*
Duckling and turkey salad*
4 oz (115 g) strawberries
Black coffee or tea

Dinner
Liver shaslik*
4 oz (115 g) carrots
4 oz (115 g) peas
Blackcurrant crêpes*
Black coffee or tea

THE MINI-MIDI-MAXI PLAN

How much you eat depends greatly on where you are, who you are and who you are with. Some people have an eating pattern which is constant from day to day, others have no two days alike.

This diet plan, devised by Dr Margaret Allan, will help you to lose weight whatever your way of life. The flexibility comes about because you can decide which meals you eat and when you eat them. It is called the mini-midi-maxi plan because each day you can have:
- a mini-meal – about 200 Calories
- a midi-meal – about 500 Calories
- a maxi-meal – about 800 Calories

In the charts you will see mini-, midi- and maxi-meals (but only mini- and midi-breakfasts since it would be unusual and unwise to have your maxi-meal at breakfast time). The charts indicate the approximate calorie values of the different planned meals. There are nine choices for lunches and dinners; the first three (i) are the sort of meals you have at home; the second group (ii) is suitable for eating in the office or while travelling; the last three (iii) are planned to be chosen from restaurant menus. By choosing one mini-meal, one midi-meal and one maxi-meal you can be certain of keeping to a 1,500 daily Calorie allowance and you should stay fit and healthy while you lose weight.

Programming the diet to your life style

Mini-breakfast, midi-lunch, maxi-dinner
No time in the morning so you have a mini-breakfast, spend most of your lunch hour shopping so you take lunch to the office or buy something in a sandwich bar and, most days, have the maxi-meal in the evening. Or you go out to lunch and reverse the procedure, having your midi-meal in the evening.

Midi-breakfast, mini-lunch, maxi-dinner
Your job takes you out of the office much of the time. A typical day starts with a 9.30 appointment

followed by another an hour later and then another fifty miles away. Lunchtime is unreliable so you have a midi-breakfast, often in the hotel where you have stayed overnight followed by a mini-lunch, then a maxi-dinner. Or you have a maxi-lunch – business – and then a mini-dinner.

Midi-breakfast, maxi-lunch, mini-dinner
Your children are grown up and married, both you and your husband have full-time jobs and often the only meal you have time to enjoy together is breakfast. Most days both of you have business lunches which you make your maxi-meal and are content to have only a mini-dinner.

Mini-breakfast, maxi-lunch, midi-supper
Your children come home from school for lunch and some days your husband does too – and always at weekends – so your life works best with a mini-breakfast, maxi-lunch and midi-supper at 6 p.m. when homework is finished and television will be allowed afterwards.

Possible weight loss: $1\frac{1}{2}$ lb (0.7 kg) in one week; 10 lb (4.5 kg) at the end of ten weeks.
Time: indefinitely.

Mini-meals

Breakfasts
1 oz (30 g) cereal
$\frac{1}{4}$ pt (1.5 dl) milk
(210)

2 slices very lightly buttered toast
$\frac{1}{2}$ oz (15 g) marmalade
(205)

1 grapefruit
2 oz (55 g) lean ham
2 tomatoes
(200)

2 small lean rashers bacon, well grilled
1 tomato, grilled
(185)

1 egg, boiled
1 slice lightly buttered toast
(160)

1 small glass unsweetened fruit juice
1 egg, poached
1 slice lightly buttered toast
(210)

Lunches or dinners (i)
1 poached egg
1 slice lightly buttered toast
(160)

3 fish fingers or 4 oz (115 g) smoked salmon and 2 crispbreads (no butter)
(240)

2 oz (55 g) corned beef
2 oz (55 g) potatoes
2 small tomatoes
(205)

Lunches or dinners (ii)
2 oz (55 g) cheese
1 apple
(220)

Fruit-flavoured yogurt (5 oz, 140 g, carton)
1 orange
(200)

1 round of sandwiches
(250)

Lunches or dinners (iii)
$\frac{1}{4}$ pint (1.4 dl) thick soup
1 bread roll
(210)

$\frac{1}{2}$ pint (2.8 dl) beer or a glass of dry wine
Small packet crisps (1 oz, 30 g)
(245)

Plain omelette (2 eggs)
(200)

Midi-meals

Breakfasts
1 small glass unsweetened fruit juice
3 slices lightly buttered toast
2 oz (55 g) marmalade
(470)

1 oz (30 g) cereal
¼ pint (1.4 dl) milk
1 poached egg
2 oz (55 g) lean bacon, grilled
(520)

½ grapefruit
7 oz (200 g) poached kippers
2 slices lightly buttered bread
(505)

1 oz (30 g) cereal
¼ pint (1.4 dl) milk
7 oz (200 g) smoked haddock
1 slice lightly buttered bread
(500)

6 oz (170 g) porridge
¼ pint (1.4 dl) milk
2 oz (55 g) sausage, grilled
1 oz (30 g) lean bacon, grilled
(470)

1 oz (30 g) muesli or similar cereal
¼ pint (1.4 dl) milk
1 slice lightly buttered toast
Scrambled eggs (2 eggs)
(520)

Lunches or dinners (i)
½ pint (2.8 dl) thick soup
2 oz (55 g) grated cheese
2 slices lightly buttered toast
(480)

4 oz (115 g) grilled gammon
4 oz (115 g) group A vegetables
2 bananas
(440)

4 oz (115 g) fish in breadcrumbs
4 oz (115 g) group C vegetables
4 oz (115 g) potatoes
(450)

Lunches or dinners (ii)
Ham sandwiches: 4 slices lightly buttered bread
  and 2 oz (55 g) lean ham
(470)

1 bread roll
¼ oz (7 g) butter
2 oz (55 g) Cheddar cheese
½ pint (2.8 dl) beer, or glass dry wine
(520)

1 slice game or pork pie
1 apple
1 fruit-flavoured yogurt
1 banana
(465)

Lunches or dinners (iii)
½ pint (2.8 dl) thin soup
4 oz (115 g) roast beef
2 oz (55 g) potatoes
1 oz (30 g) Yorkshire pudding
(435)

5 oz (140 g) grilled steak
4 oz (115 g) group A vegetables
3 oz (85 g) potatoes
4 oz (115 g) group A or B fresh fruit
(425)

6 oz (170 g) grilled chicken
2 oz (55 g) group A vegetables
2 oz (55 g) potatoes
3 savoury biscuits, lightly buttered
4 oz (115 g) cottage or curd cheese
(525)

Maxi-meals

Lunches or dinners (i)
4 oz (115 g) minced beef or steak
4 oz (115 g) tomatoes
4 oz (115 g) mushrooms
2 oz (55 g) spaghetti
4 oz (115 g) apple pie
2 tablespoons single cream
(755)

7 oz (200 g) cod on the bone
4 oz (115 g) chips
3 oz (85 g) group C vegetables
4 oz (115 g) ice-cream
(810)

½ pint (2.8 dl) thick soup
4 oz (115 g) grilled liver
1 oz (30 g) bacon, grilled
2 oz (55 g) potatoes
4 oz (115 g) group B vegetables
1 banana
¼ pint (1.4 dl) custard (use artificial sweetener)
1 tablespoon double cream
(800)

Lunches or dinners (ii)
Salmon or tuna fish sandwiches: 4 slices lightly
   buttered bread and 2 oz (55 g) smoked salmon
1 banana
4 oz (115 g) grapes
2 oz (55 g) cheese and 1 crispbread
(785)

Scotch egg
Tomato, lettuce
Slice of cheesecake
4 oz (115 g) group A or B fruit
Glass of wine
(820)

½ pint (2.8 dl) thin soup
4 oz (115 g) veal and ham pie
2 tomatoes
Fruit-flavoured yogurt
1 oz (30 g) cheese and crispbread
Apple
(740)

Lunches or dinners (iii)
½ pint (2.8 dl) consommé
1 bread roll
5 oz (140 g) lean lamb chop
4 oz (115 g) group B vegetables
2 oz (55 g) potatoes
4 oz (115 g) crème caramel
(800)

8 oz (225 g) melon
8 oz (225 g) grilled sole
4 oz (115 g) group B vegetables
4 oz (115 g) potatoes
3 oz (85 g) fruit flan
2 oz (55 g) ice-cream
(755)

2 oz (55 g) smoked salmon
1 slice brown bread, lightly buttered
5 oz (140 g) roast chicken (or other poultry)
4 oz (115 g) group B vegetables
3 oz (85 g) boiled rice
6 oz (170 g) group A or B fruit
2 tablespoons single cream
(710)

Notes
1. You can drink as much water, black tea, coffee
or low-calorie drinks as you like. If you have a little
milk add about 20 Calories a cup.
2. With home-cooked dishes use the minimum of
fat and low-fat spread. Good non-stick pans, foil
and roasting bags all help to cut down on fat.
3. Make up alternatives by changing dishes
around or introducing others providing you know
their Calorie value and do not exceed the
allowance.
4. Vegetables and fruit are classified into three
groups, A, B and C. Potatoes can be replaced by
any boiled, baked or poached vegetable.

Group A

Fruit

apricots	raspberries
grapefruit	redcurrants
lemon	rhubarb
loganberries	strawberries
melon	tangerines

Vegetables

artichokes	lettuce
asparagus	marrow
aubergine	mushrooms
beans, runner	mustard and cress
broccoli	onions
Brussels sprouts	parsley
cabbage	radishes
carrots	spinach
cauliflower	spring greens
celery	swedes
chicory	tomatoes
courgettes	turnips
cucumber	watercress

Group B

Fruit

apples	greengages
blackberries	oranges
blackcurrants	peaches
cherries	pears
damsons	pineapples
gooseberries	plums
grapes	

Vegetables

bean sprouts	leeks
beans, broad	parsnips
beetroot	peppers

Group C

Fruit

bananas	prunes

Vegetables

avocado pear	peas
beans, baked	potatoes
beans, butter	sweet-corn

THE TWO-DIET PLAN TO REAL WEIGHT LOSS

First a two-week diet to lose 8 lb (3.6 kg), then a long-term diet to lose a further 2 lb (0.9 kg) a week.

Diet for two weeks only
No substitutes. No alcohol. Do not eat anything not mentioned in the diet and do not change lunch for dinner or vice versa. No eating between meals. All vegetables without butter, salads without oil or dressing, lean meat only and nothing fried. Eggs may be boiled or poached. Black coffee. Tea with lemon, no milk. No sugar. As much water as you like. Your weight should be reduced by about 8 lb (3.6 kg) in two weeks. The basis of the diet is chemical and normal energy is maintained while reducing. Quantities are of little importance except where indicated.
Possible weight loss: up to 8 lb (3.6 kg).
Time: exactly two weeks.

Breakfast: the same each morning – $\frac{1}{2}$ grapefruit, 1 or 2 eggs

MONDAY
Lunch: fresh fruit salad – put anything in it and eat as much as you like

Dinner: $\frac{1}{2}$ grapefruit, 2 eggs, mixed green salad, 1 piece dry toast

TUESDAY
Lunch: cold chicken, tomatoes
Dinner: steak, tomatoes, lettuce, celery, cucumber, olives

WEDNESDAY
Lunch: 2 eggs, tomatoes
Dinner: 2 lamb chops, celery, cucumber, tomatoes

THURSDAY
Lunch: as Monday
Dinner: 2 eggs, cottage cheese, shredded cabbage, 1 piece dry toast

FRIDAY
Lunch: 2 poached eggs, spinach
Dinner: $\frac{1}{2}$ grapefruit, fish, mixed green salad, 1 piece dry toast

SATURDAY
Lunch: as Friday
Dinner: plenty of steak, celery, cucumber, tomatoes

SUNDAY
Lunch: as Monday
Dinner: $\frac{1}{2}$ grapefruit, chicken, tomatoes, carrots, cooked cabbage

Long-term diet
This diet allows up to 1,400 Calories a day and is good for long-term weight watchers.
Possible weight loss: $1\frac{1}{2}$ lb (0.7 kg) a week.
Time: indefinitely.

FOOD
Breakfast: 150–250 Calories (approx.)
Snack (midday or evening): 150–250 Calories (approx.)
Main meal (midday or evening): 550–750 Calories (approx.)

DRINKS *(165 Calories)*
Alcoholic drink before, after or with snack. Any one of the following – whisky, gin, rum, vodka, brandy ($\frac{5}{6}$ fl oz, 25 ml), sherry, port, vermouth ($1\frac{2}{3}$ fl oz, 50 ml) plus any low-calorie drink – bitter lemon, tonic, ginger ale; 1 glass dry white wine.

Note: The diet contains a variety of different foods but you may repeat the meals up to four times. If you wish you can have two alcoholic drinks and miss out the wine or vice versa. You can also go without alcohol one day and have twice the amount the next day. Drink as much water as you like during the day. Use sugar substitutes if necessary in tea or coffee and not more than $\frac{1}{3}$ pint (2 dl) milk a day.

DAY 1

Breakfast
1 large boiled egg
2 pieces crispbread
$\frac{1}{4}$ oz (7 g) butter
(200)

Snack
Small glass grapefruit juice
$3\frac{1}{2}$ oz (100 g) crab meat
2 oz (55 g) green pepper
(100)

Meal
Slimmers' goulash*
2 oz (55 g) pasta or rice
3 oz (85 g) peas
(550)

DAY 2

Breakfast
Small glass orange juice
6 oz (170 g) smoked haddock, poached
(230)

Snack
2 pieces crispbread with $\frac{1}{4}$ oz (7 g) butter
1 oz (30 g) lean ham
(190)

Meal
4 oz (115 g) asparagus with $\frac{1}{4}$ oz (7 g) butter
Mixed grill (small chop, kidney, sausage, bacon)
Mixed salad (no dressing)
2 oz (55 g) sorbet
(660)

DAY 3

Breakfast
1 glass tomato juice
1 oz (30 g) grilled lean bacon
Mushrooms poached in lemon juice
(155)

Snack
1 cup consommé
2 pieces crispbread
2 apples
(185)

Meal
Coq au vin (i)*
Mixed salad
2 oz (55 g) ice-cream
(640)

DAY 4

Breakfast
2 pieces crispbread with $\frac{1}{4}$ oz (7 g) butter
$\frac{1}{2}$ oz (15 g) marmalade
(160)

Snack
Small glass orange juice
1 large hard-boiled egg
4 medium tomatoes
(175)

Meal
6 oz (170 g) melon
6 oz (170 g) smoked trout, 1 oz (30 g) horse-radish
 sauce
4 oz (115 g) cold roast beef
6 oz (170 g) mixed salad
2 oz (55 g) boiled potatoes
(535)

DAY 5

Breakfast
Small glass grapefruit juice
2 oz (55 g) cold lean ham
2 medium tomatoes
(205)

Snack
2 oz (55 g) salmon
2 pieces crispbread with ¼ oz butter
(205)

Meal
1 portion slimmers' macaroni cheese*
2 medium tomatoes
4 oz (115 g) apple pie
1 oz (30 g, 2 tablespoons) single cream
(585)

DAY 6

Breakfast
4 oz (115 g) kipper, poached
2 pieces crispbread
(240)

Snack
Small glass orange juice
4 oz (115 g) grilled chicken
(230)

Meal
4 oz (115 g) corn on the cob
¼ oz (7 g) butter
2 oz (55 g) roast pork, lean and fat

3 oz (85 g) Brussels sprouts
2 oz (55 g) boiled potatoes
Small crème caramel*
(650)

DAY 7

Breakfast
Small glass pineapple juice
6 oz (170 g) stewed prunes
(195)

Snack
1 oz (30 g) cold lean pork
2 pieces crispbread
¼ oz (7 g) butter
(215)

Meal
¼ pint (1.4 dl) thick soup (e.g. cream of chicken,
 tomato, onion)
1 portion fish casserole*
4 oz (115 g) boiled or mashed potatoes
4 oz (115 g) peas
6 oz (170 g) baked apple
¼ pint (1.4 dl) slimmers' custard*
(665)

DAY 8

Breakfast
Small glass tomato juice
1 poached egg
2 pieces crispbread
¼ oz (7 g) butter
(220)

Snack
1 orange
1 banana
½ oz (15 g) peanuts
(195)

Meal
Prawn cocktail*
8 oz (225 g) plaice or sole, grilled
4 oz (115 g) peas
4 oz (115 g) sweet-corn
1 slice (1 oz, 30 g) brown bread
¼ oz (7 g) butter

DAY 9

Breakfast
Small glass pineapple juice
6 oz (170 g) porridge made with water
2 fl oz (55 ml, 4 tablespoons) milk
(*190*)

Snack
2 pieces crispbread with ¼ oz (7 g) butter
1 oz (30 g) Edam cheese
(*200*)

Meal
1 portion slimmers' cottage pie*
4 oz (115 g) runner beans
1 portion hot sweet soufflé omelette*
(*545*)

DAY 10

Breakfast
Small glass grapefruit juice
5 oz (140 g) fruit-flavoured yogurt
(*185*)

Snack
2 pieces crispbread
3 oz (85 g) smoked haddock, poached
1 poached egg
(*230*)

Meal
2 oz (55 g) smoked salmon
1 slice (1 oz, 30 g) brown bread
¼ oz (7 g) butter
6 oz (170 g) grilled steak with mixed salad
(*570*)

DAY 11

Breakfast
1 oz (30 g) cereal with ¼ pint (1.4 dl) milk
(*210*)

Snack
Small glass tomato juice
2 pieces crispbread
2 oz (55 g) cottage cheese
1 apple
(*175*)

Meal
4 oz (115 g) grapefruit
1 portion liver parcel*
3 oz (85 g) carrots
3 oz (85 g) boiled potatoes
2 (4 oz, 115 g) bananas
¼ pint (1.4 dl) slimmers' custard*
(*720*)

DAY 12

Breakfast
Small omelette (2 eggs, minimal fat)
(*180*)

Snack
Small glass tomato juice
2 pieces crispbread with ¼ oz (7 g) butter
2 oz (55 g) smoked salmon
(*230*)

Meal
½ pint (2.8 dl) consommé
3 oz (85 g) gammon rasher, grilled
1 oz (30 g) pineapple
3 oz (85 g) broad beans
5 oz (140 g) trifle
(*550*)

DAY 13

Breakfast
Small glass orange juice
2 pieces crispbread
¼ oz (7 g) butter
(*165*)

Snack
1 oz (30 g) Cheddar cheese, grated
1 hard-boiled egg
(*190*)

Meal
4 oz (115 g) roast beef, all lean
3 oz (85 g) roast potatoes
1 oz (30 g) Yorkshire pudding
4 oz (115 g) Brussels sprouts
4 oz (115 g) carrots
1 oz (30 g) roast parsnips
(*585*)

DAY 14

Breakfast
Small glass tomato juice
2 fishcakes
¼ oz (7 g) butter (for shallow frying)
(205)

Snack
2 pieces crispbread
¼ oz (7 g) butter

½ pint (2.8 dl) thin soup (e.g. chicken noodle)
(165)

Meal
4 oz (115 g) pork chop
2 oz (55 g) rice, boiled
4 tomatoes
6 oz (170 g) fresh fruit salad
1 oz (30 g) single cream
(660)

THE MULTIPLE-CHOICE DIET

You know your own body best ... so lose weight *your* way. It is all a question of a little dieting and a lot of exercising, which could be anything from disco dancing to jogging. Here are three different plans which work at three different speeds.

Two-week plan
If you would rather work harder but for a shorter time go for losing 6 lb (2.7 kg) in two weeks. It is also a good way to get a long-range diet off to a fast start. In fact, this plan is the basis of the other two.
The 1,000 Calorie diet should help you lose 6 lb (2.7 kg) of fat in two weeks. The key to the plan is exercise: a daily workout increases your metabolism and tends to curb your appetite as well. Half an hour's jogging burns about 300 Calories so twelve days' jogging means another pound lost. Choose whatever exercise you enjoy – walking, dancing, skipping – the point is to get moving. This diet has been computer-tested in the USA to make sure that it is nutritionally sound. It contains everything you need except iron: an iron supplement is recommended. Have at least one glass of milk or one carton of unsweetened, natural yogurt each day for calcium, and include 2 teaspoons of vegetable oil.
Possible weight loss: 5 – 6 lb (2.3 kg – 2.7 kg).
Time: two weeks.

Approximately 1,000 Calories a day

Breakfast, under 200 Calories
Plain yogurt, or 2 small eggs boiled or poached, with 1 crispbread; ½ grapefruit; coffee or tea without sugar or milk.

Lunch, under 300 Calories
A thin slice wholemeal bread with a scraping of butter; egg, tuna fish or ham salad, no mayonnaise; 1 glass of skimmed milk.

Dinner, under 450 Calories
1 cup consommé with a sprinkling of chives; ¼ chicken without skin or 6 oz (170 g) grilled white fish with lemon and parsley or 2 thin slices veal or low-calorie stuffed pepper or low-calorie chicken in the pot given in the recipe section, plus a large portion of steamed courgettes, carrots or spinach with lemon and herbs and a big salad.

Snack, under 100 Calories
Once a day, at teatime or before going to bed, choose from: 1 bunch grapes, ½ cantaloupe melon, 1 apple, 1 orange, 1 small banana, 10 oz (285 g) skimmed milk.

Three-week plan
Try this system if you want to lose less than 6 lb (2.7 kg), or if you have already lost 6 lb (2.7 kg)

after the two-week plan and you are ready for a follow-up.

First rule: do not stop exercising. If you have already lost some weight it is especially important. Follow the 1,000 Calorie diet plan but increase the Calories to 1,500 by adding the following:

- a piece of wholemeal toast with pat of butter to your breakfast
- dressing on your salad
- a baked potato for dinner (but with cottage cheese instead of butter)
- lean red meat twice a week for lunch (not more than 4 oz, 115 g)
- extra chicken or fish at dinner
- glass of dry white wine with dinner.

Four-week plan

On this time-scale you can lose weight just by sticking to a nutritionally sound eating pattern. If you exercise as well three times a week – the minimum for maintaining your level of fitness – you should easily lose 6 lb (2.7 kg) in four weeks. Cut out all desserts, between-meal snacks, sugar, cheese, nuts, alcohol (with the exception of a glass of wine at dinner) and excess fat. Most women tend to put on weight in this order: hips and thighs, stomach, arms, face. You can expect to lose it in reverse order. That means to get weight off your hips you have to be persistent. One last note: do not confuse stretching and bending routines with exercise like running, tennis, dancing and swimming. While leg lifts and sit-ups will tone muscles and give shape to your body, it is the vigorous calorie-burning exercise that really works off fat.

THE HIS-AND-HERS DIET

This is a diet based on the recommendations of Frederick J. Stare, MD, Chairman of the Department of Nutrition at Harvard University School of Public Health, and Jelia Witschi, MS, Harvard University School of Public Health.

'Cutting up and cutting down instead of cutting out is the way to control weight,' says Dr Stare. By 'cutting up' he means using your muscles with frequency and moderation. He sums up his advice in four words, 'Exercise more not less', calling attention to the fact that he puts exercise first. It is '... essential for those who want to lose excess pounds. Exercise facilitates the use of the stored calorie sources (that is, fat) by creating greater caloric demands. At the same time that the body is demanding a larger amount of calories, the overweight person should eat less in order to cause his body to draw on more of the stored fat and hence bring about a loss of weight. Primarily, eating less means cutting down on portion sizes and second helpings. But this advice applies only to those who are eating a sufficient variety of food to ensure good nutrition – that is, an adequate supply of proteins, vitamins, minerals, carbohydrates and fats. We eat and need far more than calories alone.'

As you might expect 'eating less', according to Dr Stare, implies eating less of the most concentrated calorie sources – pastries, puddings, snack foods, sweetened and alcoholic drinks. But he does not object to a dieter substituting an occasional pudding for part of the daily allocation of bread (or other starch) and fat. The guidelines he gives are designed to supply adequate nutrition at Calorie levels of 1,000–1,200 Calories for women and 1,400–1,600 Calories for men. This should lead to a weekly weight loss of $2-2\frac{1}{2}$ lb (0.9–1.1 kg). But the rate could be stepped up by taking more exercise.

Possible weight loss: $2-2\frac{1}{2}$ lb (0.9–1.1 kg) a week.
Time: indefinitely.

The formula – foods to be eaten daily

Type	Amount for women	Amount for men
meat	2 portions of 3–3½oz (85–100g) each	2 portions of 3½oz (100g) each
low-fat milks	¾ pint (4.3dl)	¾ pint (4.3dl)
vegetables	1 raw salad 2oz (55g) cooked vegetables	1 raw salad 2oz (55g) cooked vegetables
fruits	1 portion citrus fruit 2–3 portions other fruit	1 portion citrus fruit 2–3 portions other fruit
bread	3–4 portions	5–6 portions
fat	1 portion	3–5 portions

Meat: fish; poultry; lean trimmed cuts of beef, veal, lamb or pork; cheese; eggs. No fat to be added in cooking.

Vegetables: dark green or dark yellow varieties should be included daily.

Fruits: vary widely in carbohydrate content and portions should vary accordingly. Fresh fruit should be used whenever possible. (The syrup added in tinned fruits approximately doubles the calorie content.)

Bread (including cereal, biscuits, potatoes and other starchy vegetables): each of the following is equivalent to one portion – 2 oz (55 g) dried beans or peas; 1 oz (30 g) baked beans; 2 water biscuits; 5 saltines.

Fat: butter or margarine – 1 teaspoon a portion; 1 dessertspoon salad dressing or oil; 1 slice bacon; 1 dessertspoon cream.

Daily menus

DAY 1 (*1,150 Calories*)

Breakfast
½ grapefruit grilled with allspice
1 slice rye toast
½ teaspoon butter
Coffee or tea with low-fat milk

Lunch
1 cup beef consommé
Chef's salad: 1 oz (30 g) creamed cottage cheese, 1 oz (30 g) chicken, 1 oz (30 g) ham, green pepper, lemon juice, salt, freshly ground pepper and lettuce
5 saltines
1 apple

Any time
1 cup low-fat milk
2 water biscuits

Dinner
2 grilled lamb chops
2 oz (55 g) broccoli
½ teaspoon butter
4 oz (115 g) strawberries with juice of ½ orange

DAY 2 (*1,025 Calories*)

Breakfast
½ cantaloupe
1 slice wholewheat toast
½ teaspoon butter
1 cup low-fat milk
Coffee or tea (with low-fat milk)

Lunch
Oeuf en gelée on lettuce*
2 slices melba toast
1 pear

Any time
1 cup low-fat milk
1 oatmeal biscuit*

Dinner
Jellied consommé madrilène with capers and 2 tablespoons crab meat
3½ oz (100 g) chicken diable (grilled with coating of hot mustard, lemon juice, tarragon, black pepper)
2 oz (55 g) string beans with mushrooms
½ teaspoon butter
Watercress and radish salad
Egg-yolk dressing*
1 large orange

DAY 3 *(1,080 Calories)*

Breakfast
Small portion cornflakes with 1 sliced banana
1 cup low-fat milk
Coffee or tea with low-fat milk

Lunch
1 cup chicken consommé with raw sliced mushrooms
Raw spinach and hard-boiled egg salad with 1 slice crumbled bacon
2 slices crispbread
1 teaspoon butter
Egg-yolk dressing*
1 large orange
1 cup low-fat milk

Any time
1 cup low-fat milk
1 oatmeal biscuit*

Dinner
3½ oz (100 g) peppered steak
2 oz (55 g) endive or celery braised in chicken stock with salt, pepper, lemon juice
2 dried figs

DAY 4 *(1,150 Calories)*

Breakfast
½ grapefruit
1 poached egg
1 slice wholewheat toast
1 cup low-fat milk
Coffee or tea with low-fat milk

Lunch
Vegetable salad: tomato, mushrooms, cucumber, raw cauliflower and 2 oz (55 g) potato (cooked and diced) on lettuce
1 dessertspoon oil and vinegar dressing
1 slice crispbread
3 oz (85 g) pineapple
1 cup low-fat milk

Any time
1 cup low-fat milk
1 oatmeal biscuit*

Dinner
1 cup tomato bouillon (1 beef cube dissolved in 1 cup hot tomato juice, with chopped parsley)
Scallops (5 oz, 140 g) and water chestnuts en brochette
3 artichoke hearts with lemon juice and oregano
1 baked apple with cloves and orange juice
Tea or coffee

DAY 5 *(1,070 Calories)*

Breakfast
1 large orange
1 slice wholewheat toast with ½ teaspoon butter
1 cup low-fat milk
Coffee or tea with low-fat milk

Lunch
Jellied watercress soup*
1 tomato, ¼ cucumber and hard-boiled egg-white salad
Egg-yolk dressing*
1 slice white toast with ½ teaspoon butter
1 pear
1 cup low-fat milk

Anytime
1 cup low-fat milk

Dinner
5 oz (140 g) herb-poached chicken
2 halves grilled tomato flavoured with basil, garlic, pepper
5 oz (140 g) corn on the cob
2 inch (5 cm) wedge honeydew melon with chopped mint
Coffee or tea with low-fat milk

DAY 6 *(1,200 Calories)*

Breakfast
1 cup fresh orange juice
1 slice wholewheat toast
1 cup low-fat milk
Coffee or tea with low-fat milk

Lunch
Mushroom, green bean and chive salad
1 dessertspoon caper dressing

1 slice Cheddar cheese on 1 slice rye bread, toasted
1 apple
1 cup low-fat milk

Anytime
1 cup low-fat milk

Dinner
3½ oz (100 g) ginger marinated roast beef (marinade: beef bouillon, soya sauce, grated ginger root brought to a boil and poured over meat to marinate 3 hours; drain meat and roast, basting with marinade during cooking)
2 oz (55 g) cauliflower with 1 dessertspoon freshly grated Parmesan cheese melted under grill
6 grapes
4 oz (115 g) fruit tart
Coffee with low-fat milk

DAY 7 (*1,030 Calories*)

Breakfast
2 oz (55 g) unsweetened cooked prunes
1 slice wholewheat toast
Coffee or tea with low-fat milk

Lunch
Cold roast beef salad*
3 saltines
1 cup low-fat milk

Any time
1 cup low-fat milk

Dinner
5 oz (140 g) veal cutlet en papillote (put lightly sautéed veal cutlet on a large piece of foil; spoon over cooked tomato and courgette and season; fold foil to seal and bake at 375°F, 190°C for 10–15 minutes)
1 tangerine
1 oatmeal biscuit*
Coffee with low-fat milk

1926

THE SPA DIET

An 850-Calorie-a-day diet from the Vail Club Spa, Colorado, USA. It incorporates a balanced variety of foods and fresh ingredients; it begins with Sunday dinner and ends the following Sunday morning but can be followed on any seven consecutive days.
Possible weight loss: up to 3 lb (1.4 kg) a week.
Time: seven days.

EVERY DAY

Breakfast
This is the same each day, except for Tuesday and Friday, when 1 poached, boiled or scrambled egg is allowed
½ grapefruit or ¼ melon
1 tablespoon cottage cheese
1 slice melba toast
Tea or coffee

Health cocktails
Served every evening before dinner: 8 fl oz (2.3 dl) blended vegetable drink, made with tomato, parsley, celery, watercress and other crudités with dip of whipped cottage cheese and chives

SUNDAY (*330 Calories*)

Dinner
¼ grilled chicken, seasoned with fresh herbs and lemon, and garnished with fresh mandarin orange slices
Small portion brown rice
½ grapefruit, grilled, with sherry and cinnamon

MONDAY (*790 Calories*)

Lunch
Cheese and mushroom omelette (use a non-stick pan and the minimum of oil)
Mixed salad with yogurt and lemon dressing
3 slices of apple

Dinner
Celery-heart salad, garnished with ½ chopped hard-boiled egg white and parsley, with wine vinegar dressing*

4 oz (115 g) lamb chop, trimmed of all fat
4 oz (115 g) baked tomatoes sprinkled with herbs and Parmesan cheese
Fresh peach or apricot with 2 tablespoons low-fat yogurt

TUESDAY (*835 Calories*)

Lunch
1 cup hot chicken broth
1 slice chicken with fresh pineapple, orange and grapefruit salad

Dinner
4 oz (115 g) lean beef hamburger, grilled
2 tablespoons coleslaw with wine vinegar and oil dressing
Fresh fruit in season

WEDNESDAY (*810 Calories*)

Lunch
4 oz (115 g) tomatoes stuffed with 3 oz (85 g) chicken, on lettuce or watercress
2 slices fresh pineapple

Dinner
1 cup hot spinach soup
4 oz (115 g) baked fresh salmon with dill and cucumber
3 oz (85 g) lightly cooked French beans
$\frac{1}{4}$ fresh pear

THURSDAY (*780 Calories*)

Lunch
1 cup jellied consommé, with 1 oz (30 g) each of baby shrimps and chopped raw vegetables
8 oz (225 g) spinach salad with grilled bacon pieces and $\frac{1}{2}$ chopped hard-boiled egg
$\frac{1}{4}$ apple

Dinner
2 artichoke hearts with yogurt and lemon juice dressing
2 oz (55 g) slice veal with lemon and caper sauce
1 baked potato skin
4 oz (115 g) tomato and spring onion salad with wine vinegar dressing*
$\frac{1}{4}$ cantaloupe melon

FRIDAY (*760 Calories*)

Lunch
1 cup crab and tomato bisque
4 oz (115 g) steamed broccoli
1 pomegranate or fruit in season

Dinner
6 oz (170 g) poached fillet of sole
4 oz (115 g) steamed ratatouille
Small wedge Cheddar cheese

SATURDAY (*850 Calories*)

Lunch
4 oz (115 g) tomato jelly with sliced hard-boiled egg
2 tablespoons red caviar on bed of chopped lettuce
$\frac{1}{2}$ medium orange

Dinner
$\frac{1}{2}$ roast poussin
Grilled tomato
2 oz (55 g) grilled mushrooms with herbs and lemon juice
Orange sorbet in orange skin

SUNDAY (*335 Calories*)

Lunch
1 slice cold lean roast beef
Mixed salad with wine vinegar dressing*
Fresh fruit in season

1926

THE COMPUTER-APPROVED DIET

These menus are more than a well-balanced diet: they have been computer-approved. This means that each day's meals have been checked against a computer programme incorporating statistics like calorie counts, nutritional content and the USA recommended dietary allowances for vitamins and nutrients. In the not-too-distant future you may be able to punch your menu plans into a simple home computer terminal and the print-out will instantly show if you are lacking in calcium or overloading yourself with protein. The diet is based on approximately 1,200–1,500 Calories a day and you should lose a steady 1½–2 lb (0.7–0.9 kg) a week – and have extra energy. Drink as much mineral water as you like; use skimmed milk in tea and coffee, but no sugar. Use a minimum of margarine or butter on your bread.

The menus are nutritionally balanced by the day so whole days are interchangeable.

Possible weight loss: 1½–2 lb (0.7–0.9 kg) a week.
Time: indefinitely.

DAY 1 (*1,230 Calories*)

Breakfast
½ grapefruit
Small bowl bran cereal with 4 fl oz (1.1 dl) skimmed milk
Tea or coffee

Lunch
3 oz (85 g) lean hamburger with lettuce
Small tomato
1 small wholemeal roll
1 apple
1 glass skimmed milk

Dinner
3 oz (85 g) steak, grilled (trim off the fat)
1 baked potato with 1 tablespoon cottage cheese and chives
Small portion peas

Small raw spinach and mushroom salad* with 1 tablespoon safflower oil and vinegar dressing
1 slice fresh pineapple
Coffee or tea

Snack
1 peach
1 glass skimmed milk

DAY 2 (*1,280 Calories*)

Breakfast
7 fl oz (2 dl) orange juice
1 poached egg on 1 slice wholemeal toast
Coffee or tea

Lunch
Toasted ham and cheese sandwich
1 apple
1 glass skimmed milk

Dinner
3 oz (85 g) grilled halibut or any white fish
Small portion French beans
1 new potato with mint
1 peach and cottage cheese salad
Coffee or tea

Snack
1 low-fat fruit yogurt

DAY 3 (*1,250 Calories*)

Breakfast
6 fl oz (1.7 dl) fruit juice
Boiled egg
1 slice wholemeal toast
Coffee or tea

Lunch
Tuna fish and salad sandwich in granary bread
1 orange
1 glass skimmed milk

Dinner
Crudités (raw celery, carrot, radish, etc)
4 oz (115 g) roast beef or ham
1 small baked yam or potato
2 or 3 branches broccoli
Coffee or tea

DAY 4 *(1,370 Calories)*

Breakfast
1 orange
Small bowl bran cereal with 4 fl oz (1.1 dl) skim-
    med milk
Coffee or tea

Lunch
Salad of raw spinach, watercress, green pepper and
    hard-boiled egg with lemon juice
1 apple and 1 small roll
1 glass skimmed milk

Dinner
4 oz (115 g) chicken livers sautéed in 1 tablespoon
    vegetable oil
Grilled tomato, halved
Small portion green beans or 4 asparagus tips
Orange and banana slices

Snack
Raw cauliflower flowerettes with dip made from 2
    tablespoons low-fat cottage cheese, 1 teaspoon
    mayonnaise and 1 carrot, liquidized
1 glass dry white wine

DAY 5 *(1,500 Calories)*

Breakfast
Fresh orange and grapefruit salad
1 poached egg with a rasher grilled lean bacon and
    1 slice wholemeal toast
Coffee or tea

Lunch
Salad of lettuce, pieces of turkey, ham, cheese and
    carrots with lemon wedge with 1 brown roll
1 glass skimmed milk

Dinner
1 grilled chicken breast (with skin removed)
Small portion peas
Mixed salad with chopped parsley and onion,
    lemon juice, soaked wheatgerm and 1 table-
    spoon safflower oil
Small bunch grapes with 1 wafer biscuit
1 glass skimmed milk

Snack
1 low-fat plain yogurt and 1 tablespoon raisins

DAY 6 *(1,300 Calories)*

Breakfast
6 fl oz (1.7 dl) orange juice
1 slice wholemeal toast with marmalade
Coffee or tea

Lunch
Toasted cheese and tomato on 1 slice wholemeal
    bread
Salad of lettuce, raw carrots with lemon juice
1 apple
1 glass skimmed milk

Dinner
1 lean pork chop
1 small boiled potato in skin with parsley
4 oz (115 g) spinach
Salad of lettuce, raw courgettes and spring onions
2 plums
Coffee or tea

Snack
1 banana
1 glass skimmed milk

DAY 7 *(1,210 Calories)*

Breakfast
$\frac{1}{2}$ grapefruit
Small bowl porridge with skimmed milk
1 slice wholemeal bread
Coffee or tea

Lunch
Crudités (raw celery, carrot, cucumber)
Creamed asparagus and sliced hard-boiled egg on
    wholemeal toast
1 orange
1 glass skimmed milk

Dinner
6 oz (170 g) grilled sole
1 small baked potato
2 or 3 branches broccoli
Fresh fruit salad

Snack
4 fl oz (1.1 dl) skimmed milk
1 wafer
1 fruit yogurt

THE SECRET DIET

By slightly adjusting your eating habits it is quite simple to halve the number of calories you consume in a week. The two menus given here show how it can be done. You will see that the original diet reaches a staggering 3,030 Calories in a day – far too many for people with a normal sedentary daily routine. The calorie-controlled menu comes to approximately 1,200 Calories. By rethinking your diet in this way you could lose 2 lb (0.9 kg) a week.

Possible weight loss: 2 lb (0.9 kg) in the first week.
Time: until you are down to your ideal weight.

Original diet (*3,030 Calories*)

Breakfast
½ grapefruit, 1 teaspoon sugar
1 cup cornflakes with 1 teaspoon sugar and ¼ pint (1.4 dl) milk
1 slice toast, butter and marmalade
2 cups coffee, milk and sugar

Mid-morning
1 cup coffee, milk and sugar

Lunch
Omelette (2 eggs) with milk, ham filling, cooked in butter
Mixed salad, with 1 tablespoon French dressing (tomato, lettuce, cucumber, watercress)
Cheddar cheese
2 digestive biscuits, butter

Tea
2 cups of tea with milk, sugar
2 chocolate wholemeal biscuits

Dinner
Large whisky and ginger ale
Avocado pear with shrimps and mayonnaise
2 grilled lamb chops
Fried potatoes
2 grilled tomatoes
Brussels sprouts
Orange salad and cream
2 glasses red wine
2 cups coffee with cream

Secret diet (*1,215 Calories*)

Breakfast
½ grapefruit, no sugar
1 cup cornflakes
¼ pint (1.4 dl) milk
1 crispbread, scraping low-fat margarine
1 cup coffee, black

Mid-morning
Lemon tea

Lunch
Omelette (2 eggs) with milk, cooked in non-stick pan, no butter, mushroom filling
Green salad, lemon juice
1 oz (30 g) Edam cheese
2 water biscuits

Tea
Lemon tea

Dinner
Dry vermouth
½ avocado pear with lemon juice
1 grilled lamb chop
Boiled potato
1 grilled tomato
Brussels sprouts
Orange salad
1 glass red wine
Black coffee

LOW-COST LOW-CALORIE DIET

This special one-week budget diet was planned by Weight Watchers and is based on their successful programme which changes, or re-educates, the dieter's eating habits so that she chooses nutritious, slimming foods instead of fattening unnutritious foods.

Eating lunch out

Appetizers: tomato or mixed vegetable juice, beef, chicken or onion bouillon.

Entrées: choice of open sandwiches (1 slice enriched white or wholemeal bread with grilled steak; grilled cheese and tomato; sliced chicken, turkey, ham or roast beef); tinned tuna or salmon; shrimps with 1 tablespoon mayonnaise; cottage cheese with fruit or vegetables; 2 eggs (poached, soft- or hard-boiled or scrambled without fat; all-beef frankfurter; all-beef hamburger; smoked salmon.

With any of these (except sandwiches) have 1 slice enriched white or wholemeal bread.

Vegetables: green pepper rings, sliced cucumber, dill pickle, green salad with oil and vinegar or 1 tablespoon mayonnaise, sliced tomato *plus* baked potato, enriched rice or noodles instead of bread *plus* cooked vegetables without butter.

Drink: hot or iced tea or coffee, diet soft drink or skimmed milk.

Fruit: choice of melon, grapefruit or orange, $\frac{1}{4}$ fresh pineapple.

Menu notes

- Drinks: make your choice from tea, coffee or low-calorie drinks.
- The fruit allowed at lunch may also be taken as a snack or added to your milk shake.
- Wherever the menu calls for skimmed milk, you may substitute instant non-fat dried milk, reconstituted – it is less expensive.

- You might like to turn the $\frac{1}{2}$ cup of skimmed milk allowed at each meal into a between-meals snacks or before-bed snack – see recipe for Weight Watchers' bonus milk shake.*

Menus

MONDAY

Breakfast
$\frac{1}{2}$ grapefruit
1 oz (30 g) cereal with liquid skimmed milk
Tea or coffee with skimmed milk

Lunch
Spinach omelette (1 egg)
1 tomato
Lettuce
1 slice bread
2 level teaspoons margarine
Floating islands*
Any low-calorie drink

Dinner
Coq au vin (ii)*
4 oz (115 g) butter beans
Broccoli
1 level teaspoon margarine
1 orange
Tea or coffee with skimmed milk

TUESDAY

Breakfast
4 fl oz (1.1 dl) orange juice
1 oz (30 g) cereal with liquid skimmed milk
Tea or coffee with skimmed milk

Lunch
4 oz (115 g) baked white fish
Broccoli
1 slice bread
1 peach
Any low-calorie drink

Dinner
Curried chicken with rice*
Green beans
Green salad
1 tablespoon mayonnaise
3 apricot halves with 1 teaspoon juice (unsweetened)
Tea or coffee with skimmed milk

WEDNESDAY

Breakfast
4 fl oz (1.1 dl) grapefruit juice
1 oz (30 g) hard cheese
1 slice toast
1 level teaspoon margarine
Tea or coffee with skimmed milk

Lunch
Veal with pimento dressing*
Salad (cucumber, celery, radishes)
1 medium apple
Any low-calorie drink

Dinner
Soya-bean loaf* with mushroom sauce*
Courgettes
Wedge of lettuce
2 teaspoons mayonnaise
¼ medium pineapple
Tea or coffee with skimmed milk

THURSDAY

Breakfast
2 small tangerines
1 oz (30 g) cereal with liquid skimmed milk
Tea or coffee with skimmed milk

Lunch
Beef patties*
1 tomato, sliced
1 pickled cucumber, lettuce
4 oz (115 g) peas
1 slice bread
2 teaspoons mayonnaise
5 oz (140 g) grapefruit sections with 2 tablespoons juice
Any low-calorie drink

Dinner
4 fl oz (1.1 dl) tomato juice
Fish pie*
Courgettes
Spinach with nutmeg
1 level teaspoon margarine
Pear mousse*
Tea or coffee with skimmed milk

FRIDAY

Breakfast
1 small orange
1 poached egg
1 slice toast
1 level teaspoon margarine
Tea or coffee with skimmed milk

Lunch
4 fl oz (1.1 dl) mixed vegetable juice
4 oz (115 g) tuna fish
Mixed salad
1 slice bread
2 teaspoons mayonnaise
3 oz (85 g) raspberries
Any low-calorie drink

Dinner
Lentil soup with ham*
Green salad with 1 tomato, 4 oz beetroot
2 teaspoons mayonnaise
1 slice bread
Fresh peach
Tea or coffee with skimmed milk

SATURDAY

Breakfast
½ medium grapefruit
1 oz (30 g) hard cheese
1 slice toast
1 level teaspoon margarine
Tea or coffee with skimmed milk

Lunch
Liver and onions with fennel*
Kale
1 medium pear
Any low-calorie drink

Dinner
Fish with bonus sauce*
Cauliflower with pimento strips
1 fresh peach
Tea or coffee with skimmed milk

SUNDAY

Breakfast
4 fl oz. (1.1 dl) orange juice
1 scrambled egg on 1 slice toast
1 level teaspoon margarine
Tea or coffee with skimmed milk

Lunch
Chop suey*
Mixed green salad
2 oz (55 g) sliced beetroot
4 oz (115 g) pineapple chunks with juice
Any low-calorie drink

Dinner
6 oz (170 g) grilled lemon sole
6 oz (170 g) courgettes
Wedge of lettuce with 2 teaspoons mayonnaise
½ medium grapefruit
Tea or coffee with skimmed milk

THE VEGETARIAN DIET

This diet has been devised by Dr Judith Stern. On a vegetarian diet you can eat more – as it is bulk for bulk much 'cheaper' in calories than meat – a filling fooling for dieting stomachs. A body needs only about 44 g of protein daily, an amount easily obtainable without meat. The egg, in fact, comes closest to being the perfect protein. (And certain non-meat proteins are more valuable in combinations than alone; skimmed milk and potatoes, for example, give you more usable protein if eaten together than the same amount eaten at different times.)

The Vegetarian Diet is lacto-ovo as opposed to 'pure' vegetarian – that is, eggs and milk products are included. If you drop these animal-derived products from your diet, you run a risk of running short of vitamin B-12, but this diet requires no vitamin supplements or elaborate protein counts.

The Vegetarian Diet is based on a nutritionally balanced 1,100–1,200 Calories a day, including each of the four general food groups: bread–cereal, milk products, high protein (like eggs, beans), vegetable–fruit. If it is not possible to cook your own lunch, here are some suggestions that add up to the same number of calories as the menu's lunches: a cup of plain yogurt and fresh fruit; a big salad dressed with lemon or tomato juice. (But do

not use oil in the dressing; 1 fl oz, 30 ml, of oil is 270 Calories.)

Possible weight loss: 2 – 3 lb (0.9 – 1.4 kg) in the first week.

Time: until correct weight is achieved.

DAY 1 (*1,160 Calories*)

Breakfast
6 fl oz (1.7 dl) tomato juice
4 oz (115 g) cooked porridge with 4 fl oz (1.1 dl) skimmed milk and 1 teaspoon wheatgerm
Coffee or tea

Lunch
½ grapefruit
Soya-bean salad*
1 slice wholemeal toast with 1 teaspoon margarine
Iced tea

Dinner
Spicy egg curry*
Rice pulao*
Spicy salad*
Lemon tea

Evening snack
1 glass skimmed milk
1 medium-size fresh fruit

DAY 2 *(1,150 Calories)*

Breakfast
6 fl oz (1.7 dl) unsweetened grapefruit juice
2 oz (55 g) high-protein dry cereal with ½ sliced
    banana and 4 fl oz (1.1 dl) skimmed milk
Coffee or tea

Lunch
Sliced fruit and cottage cheese*
1 slice wholemeal toast with 1 teaspoon margarine
Tea

Dinner
6 fl oz (1.7 dl) tomato juice with a slice of lime
Vegetables with bean curd sauce*
2½ oz (70 g) boiled white rice
Cucumber salad (i)*
Jasmine tea

Evening snack
Same as Day 1

DAY 3 *(1,200 Calories)*

Breakfast
½ grapefruit
2 slices raisin bread with 1½ teaspoons margarine
Coffee or tea

Lunch
Cold vegetable soup*
1 oz (30 g) cheese and tomato on toast
1 medium apple

Dinner
6 fl oz (1.7 dl) tomato juice with a slice of lime
Low-calorie macaroni and cheese*
Green salad, 2 tablespoons low-calorie dressing*
Orange Pekoe tea

Evening snack
Same as Day 1

DAY 4 *(1,160 Calories)*

Breakfast
1 orange, sliced
1 oz (30 g) muesli with 4 or 5 strawberries, sliced,
    and 4 fl oz (1.1 dl) skimmed milk
Coffee or tea

Lunch
½ grapefruit
Lentil salad*
1 slice wholemeal bread with 1 teaspoon margarine
Tea

Dinner
¼ small cantaloupe
Ratatouille (i)*
Baked potato with 2 tablespoons yogurt and chives
1 slice wholemeal bread with 1 teaspoon margarine
Coffee or tea

Evening snack
Same as Day 1

DAY 5 *(1,200 Calories)*

Breakfast
6 fl oz (1.7 dl) unsweetened grapefruit juice
1 oz (30 g) muesli with 4 fl oz (1.1 dl) skimmed milk
Coffee or tea

Lunch
Fresh mango with yogurt*
1 slice wholemeal bread with 1 teaspoon margarine
Tea

Dinner
Cheese buttermilk soufflé*
6 oz (170 g) broccoli
Mixed green salad
2 tablespoons low-calorie dressing*
Coffee or tea

Evening snack
1 glass skimmed milk
1 slice wholemeal toast with ½ teaspoon margarine

DAY 6 *(1,110 Calories)*

Breakfast
½ grapefruit
Muffin with 1 oz (30 g) cheese, grilled
Coffee or tea

Lunch
Spinach salad*
1 slice wholemeal bread with ½ teaspoon margarine
Tea

Dinner
Stuffed green peppers (ii)*
Pan-fried carrots*
Cucumber salad (i)*
Coffee or tea

Evening snack
1 glass skimmed milk

DAY 7 *(1,120 Calories)*

Breakfast
¼ small cantaloupe
2 oz (55 g) high-protein cereal with 4 or 5 straw-
    berries and 4 fl oz (1.1 dl) skimmed milk
1 slice wholemeal toast with ½ teaspoon margarine
Coffee or tea

Lunch
Quick onion soup*
2 pineapple rings, water-packed, with 4 oz (115 g)
    low-fat cottage cheese
Tea

Dinner
Egg foo yung*
4 oz (115 g) mangetout peas or green beans with
    water chestnuts
2½ oz (60 g) boiled rice
4 oz (115 g) fresh grapes
Jasmine tea

Evening snack
Same as Day 1

THE SUMMER HOLIDAY NO-COOKING DIET

Nobody wants to spend sunny days cooking in the kitchen so turn your summer holiday into a diet holiday, keeping food preparation to the minimum and making the most of summer fruits and salads. On this one-week diet you can drink as much tea or coffee as you like provided you do not use more than ½ pint (2.8 dl) of milk a day for everything. You can also have low-calorie soft drinks but no alcohol. (These must be added to the total daily calorie intake.)
Possible weight loss: 3 lb (1.4 kg).
Time: one week.

DAY 1 *(800 Calories)*

Breakfast
Slice of melon with lemon
1 crispbread with plum jam
Coffee or tea

Lunch
Cold consommé
1½ oz (45 g) Brie
1 crispbread
Iced lemon tea

Dinner
4 oz (115 g) cold beef
Cucumber and spring onions with yogurt dressing
Orange sorbet

DAY 2 *(890 Calories)*

Breakfast
Tomato juice with lemon slice
1 oz (30 g) cream cheese with fresh apricots
1 crispbread
Coffee

Lunch
5 oz (140 g) yogurt with fresh blackberries
1 crispbread with 1 oz (30 g) Cheddar cheese
Celery

Dinner
Chef's salad (hard-boiled egg, ham, lettuce, tomato
    with low-down dressing*)
Fresh peach

DAY 3 *(900 Calories)*

Breakfast
½ grapefruit
1 crispbread with a little Marmite and tomato
Coffee

Lunch
4 oz (115 g) tuna fish with lettuce and a little
    mayonnaise
1 crispbread with a little butter
1 apple

Dinner
4 oz (115 g) steak tartare* with lettuce, watercress
    and radish salad and low-down salad dressing*
4 oz (115 g) fresh pineapple with Cointreau

DAY 4 *(930 Calories)*

Breakfast
1 orange
1 crispbread with a little butter and marmalade
Coffee

Lunch
3 oz (85 g) cold beef with pickles and watercress
1 crispbread
5 oz (140 g) flavoured yogurt

Dinner
4 oz (115 g) poached salmon
4 oz (115 g) asparagus with lemon juice
Sliced mushroom and carrot salad with low-down
    dressing*
Fresh plums or apricots

DAY 5 *(870 Calories)*

Breakfast
Cornflakes with skimmed milk and raspberries
Coffee

Lunch
Gazpacho*
1 crispbread with sardines, endive and tomatoes

Dinner
Tomato juice
4 oz (115 g) peeled prawns with low-down
    dressing*
Green salad
2 crispbreads with scraping of butter
Lemon sorbet

DAY 6 *(940 Calories)*

Breakfast
Hard-boiled egg with sliced tomato
1 crispbread
Coffee

Lunch
4 oz (115 g) cold ham with tomato and watercress
    salad
1 oz Cheddar cheese
1 crispbread

Dinner
4 oz (115 g) cold chicken breast with crudités:
    carrots, green pepper, radishes, spring onions
2 crispbreads with scraping of butter
4 oz (115 g) strawberries

DAY 7 *(990 Calories)*

Breakfast
5 oz (140 g) yogurt with banana and cinnamon
Coffee

Lunch
3 oz (85 g) cold roast beef
Green salad
1 crispbread

Dinner
Vichyssoise
2 slices ham with 2 oz (55 g) cottage cheese and
    chives
Cucumber and tomato salad with low-down
    dressing*
2 crispbreads with a scraping of butter
Orange salad with dash of Grand Marnier

THE SPARKLING WINE DIET

How to lose weight and enjoy all the good things of summer ... fresh fish, lean meat, salads, strawberries, even cream and champagne. The daily allowance is two glasses of champagne or sparkling wine, to be drunk whenever you like. The natural sugar content helps to cut out any cravings for sweet things that often attack dieters. Use artificial sweeteners in tea and coffee, but a fruit salad can be sweetened with sparkling wine which is far better for you than sugar. Doctors say that champagne is a good reviver and tranquillizer, it also acts as a diuretic which can help weight loss. Before a meal it can tone and help the circulatory system by dilating blood vessels and, in turn, stepping up metabolism. The types of fish available through the summer vary from week to week so that the diet has little chance to grow repetitive. Try mixing shellfish with firm white fish, both an excellent source of vitamin B complex, vitamin D and certain minerals. Include as much fresh raw fruit and vegetables as possible – keep to low-calorie varieties like lettuce, endive, batavia and cress, raspberries, strawberries, oranges, grapefruit, gooseberries and apples. The diet does not include mid-morning or teatime extras but you are allowed lemon tea, black coffee, Marmite or Bovril, or subtract the fruit course from a main meal and eat it mid-morning or mid-afternoon. The daily allowance is 1,200 Calories – if you keep to the diet for one week you could lose 2 lb (0.9 kg). Providing you are healthy, this diet can be followed indefinitely – the weight loss will not be so large as it is when you follow most other diets, but it will be steady.

Possible weight loss: 2 lb (0.9 kg) in the first week.
Time: indefinitely.

MONDAY (*1,170 Calories*)

Breakfast
Fruit salad with a little All Bran
Thin slice toast, a little margarine
Lemon tea or black coffee, no sugar

Lunch
4 fl oz (1.1 dl) champagne
2 oz (55 g) smoked salmon
1 slice wholemeal bread
4½ oz (125 g) grilled lamb chop
Small portion green beans
1 orange

Dinner
4 fl oz (1.1 dl) sparkling wine
1 oz (30 g) crab with lemon slice
6 spears asparagus
3 oz (85 g) cold turkey
Small mixed salad
1 dessertspoon French dressing*

TUESDAY (*1,180 Calories*)

Breakfast
4 fl oz (1.1 dl) fresh orange juice
Poached egg
Thin slice wholemeal toast
Tea, coffee, no milk, no sugar

Lunch
4 fl oz (1.1 dl) sparkling wine
2 oz (55 g) smoked cod's roe with 2 oz (55 g) cottage cheese
1 dessertspoon French dressing*
Salad (celery, tomato, cucumber)
1 piece crispbread
1 apple

Dinner
4 large Mediterranean prawns
1 tablespoon home-made mayonnaise
3 oz (85 g) roast veal
Small portion mangetout peas
2 oz (55 g) zabaglione*

WEDNESDAY (*1,190 Calories*)

Breakfast
½ large grapefruit
1 oz (30 g) muesli
1 cup coffee with milk
5 oz (140 g) low-fat yogurt

Lunch
4 fl oz (1.1 dl) sparkling wine

1 oz (30 g) lobster chopped with raw mushrooms and spring onion
1 dessertspoon French dressing*
1 oz (30 g) lean ham and 1 oz (30 g) chicken on a bed of watercress
1 oz (30 g) wholemeal toast with a little margarine
Fresh pineapple

Dinner
4 fl oz (1.1 dl) champagne
Seafood kebab: skewer 1 oz (30 g) pieces halibut, prawns, bacon, tomato, green pepper, leek, brush with margarine and grill
1 oz (30 g) boiled rice
Fresh fruit salad with 2 fl oz (55 ml) white wine

THURSDAY (*1,240 Calories*)

Breakfast
4 fl oz (1.1 dl) tomato juice
2 slices crispbread
2 rashers well-grilled bacon
Tea or coffee, no milk, no sugar

Lunch
4 fl oz (1.1 dl) champagne
Prawn salad: 2 oz (55 g) prawns, avocado, celery, cucumber
4 oz (115 g) veal escalope
4 oz (115 g) green beans
1 sweetmeal biscuit

Dinner
4 fl oz (1.1 dl) sparkling wine
1½ oz (40 g) dressed crab
5 oz (140 g) grilled red mullet
4 oz (115 g) broccoli
Mixed salad
1 dessertspoon French dressing*
Water biscuit
½ oz (15 g) Edam cheese
1 small apple

FRIDAY (*1,190 Calories*)

Breakfast
4 oz (115 g) honeydew melon
1½ oz (40 g) All Bran
3 fl oz (85 ml) skimmed milk

10 raisins
Lemon tea or black coffee

Lunch
4 fl oz (1.1 dl) sparkling wine
1 crispbread
Eggs florentine*
Small banana
1 tablespoon single cream

Dinner
4 fl oz (1.1 dl) champagne
6 spears asparagus with 1 dessertspoon French dressing*
4 oz (115 g) grilled lobster
6 oz (170 g) ratatouille (ii)*
5 oz (140 g) low-fat yogurt
6 strawberries

SATURDAY (*1,240 Calories*)

Breakfast
Thin slice melon
1 oz (30 g) All Bran with a few sultanas
4 fl oz (1.1 dl) fresh orange juice
1 poached egg
Thin slice wholemeal toast
Lemon tea or black coffee, no sugar

Lunch
4 fl oz (1.1 dl) sparkling wine
Crudités (raw carrot, cauliflower, spring onion, radishes)
2 scrambled eggs with 2 tablespoons crab meat
1 small apple sliced with ½ oz (15 g) Edam cheese

Dinner
4 fl oz (1.1 dl) champagne
5 oz (140 g) smoked trout with little horse-radish sauce
2 oz (55 g) roast duck
2 oz (55 g) new peas

Opposite: Newton, 1977
Overleaf left: Reinhardt, 1979
Overleaf right: Scavullo, 1975

THE COUNTRY GARDEN DIET

A good diet for people who have access to really fresh fruits, vegetables and herbs in the summer. It allows a drink before dinner and a little wine with it, and includes several orange and cheese picnic lunches. When it is difficult to have a diet meal, eat moderately and replace your next meal with an orange and cheese picnic – the next two, if you have had a fair amount to drink as well. Your total calorie consumption over a two-day period should remain the same, and should be about 2,800 Calories.

This diet is based on approximately 1,300 Calories a day and on it you should lose about 2 lb (0.9 kg) a week. If all wine and spirits are omitted the weight loss could be 3 lb (1.4 kg). No sugar is allowed – artificial sweeteners only. Low-calorie soft drinks only. Half a pint (2.8 dl) milk or one pint (5.7 dl) skimmed milk allowed daily. The orange and cheese picnic consists of 3 oz (85 g) Edam cheese with a large orange.

Possible weight loss: up to 2 lb (0.9 kg) a week.
Time: indefinitely.

EVERY DAY

Breakfast
1 small glass freshly squeezed unsweetened orange juice *or* ½ grapefruit
1 thin slice granary bread, plain or toasted with ¼ oz (7 g) butter
1 oz (30 g) Edam cheese *or* 1 boiled or poached egg *or* 1 rasher lean bacon with 4 medium mushrooms or 2 medium tomatoes

MONDAY (*1,270 Calories*)

Lunch
2 oz (55 g) smoked salmon rolled and stuffed with 2 oz (55 g) prawns with lemon slice
1 thin slice brown bread and butter
Lettuce heart with lemon dressing
Fresh apple
Coffee with milk from allowance

Dinner
¼ pint (1.4 dl) cold consommé garnished with fresh chopped chives and lemon slices
2 oz (55 g) cold lean roast lamb
3 oz (85 g) cold runner beans
1 tablespoon vinaigrette
Blackberry and apple compote: 3 oz (85 g) apples plus 1 oz (30 g) blackberries
Coffee with milk from allowance

Drinks
1 single gin with tonic
1 glass red wine

TUESDAY (*1,330 Calories*)

Lunch
Orange and cheese picnic with mustard and cress
4 oz (115 g) fresh cherries *or* 2 apricots
Coffee with milk from allowance

Dinner
Watercress soup: 2 oz (55 g) watercress made to ¼ pint (1.4 dl) with milk and stock
4 oz (115 g) grilled chicken and tarragon
2 oz (55 g) new boiled potatoes
5 oz (140 g) Swiss chard *or* spinach flavoured with basil
Fresh fruit salad (½ apple, ½ banana, ½ orange)
Coffee with milk from allowance

Drinks
1 glass dry sherry
1 glass rosé wine

WEDNESDAY (*1,315 Calories*)

Lunch
Spiced avocado salad: ¼ avocado, sliced with medium tomato and 1 oz (30 g) Edam cheese, mixed with lemon dressing
1 slice lean ham
3 oz (85 g) fresh black grapes *or* 2 apricots
Coffee with milk from allowance

Dinner
4 oz (115 g) melon
3 oz (85 g) grilled lamb kebabs
2 oz (55 g) raw onion and mint salad marinated in lemon juice

Opposite: Chatelain. 1979

4 oz (115 g) stewed plums flavoured with orange
  zest and cardamom seeds
1 tablespoon single cream
Coffee with milk from allowance

Drinks
1 single whisky and water
1 glass red wine

THURSDAY (*1,360 Calories*)

Lunch
Orange and cheese picnic
4 oz (115 g) celery
Coffee or tea with milk from allowance

Dinner
2 oz (55 g) Dublin Bay prawns on ice served with
  lemon
8 oz (225 g) roast guinea fowl on the bone
3 oz (85 g) runner beans
3 oz (85 g) spinach
4 oz (115 g) loganberry and orange salad
Coffee with milk from allowance

Drinks
1 dry sherry
1 glass red wine

FRIDAY (*1,260 Calories*)

Lunch
Orange and cheese picnic
Coffee or tea with milk from allowance

Dinner
Globe artichoke with 1 tablespoon vinaigrette
  dressing
½ lobster, cold
3 oz (85 g) cucumber tang: shredded cucumber
  with lemon dressing flavoured with fresh tarragon and chervil
1 oz (30 g) lettuce heart and 1 oz (30 g) watercress
  salad with lemon dressing
2 oz (55 g) fresh figs
Coffee with milk from allowance

Drinks
1 single gin and tonic
1 glass dry white wine *or* 1 glass champagne

SATURDAY (*1,450 Calories*)

Lunch
Egg florentine (1 egg)*
1 fresh apple
Coffee or tea with milk from allowance

Dinner
¼ pint (1.4 dl) gazpacho*
3 oz (85 g) calf's liver with fresh sage and shallots
3 oz (85 g) spinach
3 oz (85 g) boiled courgettes
4 oz (115 g) pear with cinnamon and cloves baked
  in red wine
Coffee with milk from allowance

Drinks
1 single whisky and water
1 glass red wine
1 brandy

SUNDAY (*1,330 Calories*)

Lunch
3 oz (85 g) cold boiled courgettes with lemon
  dressing
3 oz (85 g) fresh poached salmon
2 oz (55 g) fresh peas cooked with ½ oz (15 g)
  chopped spring onions
3 oz (85 g) small boiled new potatoes with ¼ oz
  (7 g) butter
Sliced fresh peach
Coffee or tea with milk from allowance

Dinner
4 oz (115 g) melon
Herb omelette (2 eggs)
4 oz (115 g) tomato salad with 2 oz (55 g) lemon
  dressing*
1 oz (30 g) fresh Edam cheese
Fresh pear
Coffee with milk from allowance

Drinks
1 single gin and tonic
1 glass dry white wine

THE WINTERPROOF DIET

In winter you use up energy to keep warm and need more protective foods; there is a psychological need for hot satisfying meals. This eating plan supplies all these needs with a Calorie value of between 1,200 and 1,300 a day. It contains all the nutrients and protective foods the body requires and can be followed indefinitely to keep weight under control. Because it contains adequate supplies of protein and small but vital amounts of animal and vegetable fats, the diet causes no hardship and no risk to health. Obviously it is more enjoyable with intelligent variation, for example, any roast or grilled meat or grilled fish as a main course, cheese instead of a pudding, any fruit or vegetable in season – except bananas and root vegetables.

The foods that protect against cold and fatigue are the proteins, mainly meat, fish and eggs. The protectors against dry, parched skins are small quantities of animal and vegetable fats. They should be controlled but not entirely limited in the winter. The protectors against colds, coughs and flu are the vitamins and minerals contained in fresh, raw fruit and juice and green vegetables, as well as in the protein foods. Mild deficiencies in vitamins can easily occur in winter when fresh raw fruit and vegetables are scarce.

Possible weight loss: up to 2 lb (0.9 kg) a week.
Time: indefinitely.

How to use the Winterproof Diet

1. Divide 8 oz (225 g) butter in eight equal portions. Each portion is a day's allowance.
2. Eat one of the breakfasts every day. This meal is an important part of a winter diet for, expecially in cold weather, blood sugar levels drop swiftly after a breakfast of tea and toast and you will feel cold and tired by mid-morning. It is the essence of the diet to maintain blood sugar levels evenly through the day as well as to provide essential and protective foods.

3. Use artificial sweeteners for tea, coffee and cooking.
4. Allow four crispbreads each day (not the starch-reduced variety).
5. Allow $\frac{1}{2}$ pint (2.8 dl) milk a day. If you like hot milk at bedtime you must save enough for this from your daily allowance.
6. If you wish have a glass of wine before or with the main meal of the day.
7. Follow this eating pattern: choose a breakfast menu each morning; have a hot drink and crispbread mid-morning; choose one A meal and one B meal each day; have tea or coffee with 1 crispbread each day at 4–4.30 p.m.

Breakfast menus

You may have all the tea or coffee you like, using milk from your daily allowance and artificial sweetener instead of sugar. Each day have a glass of orange or grapefruit juice, fresh or frozen, before or with your breakfast; have a crispbread and butter from your daily allowance, and one of the following:

1. A large egg, coddled or boiled
2. 3 oz (85 g) portion boned smoked haddock or 5 oz (140 g) portion on the bone
3. Large poached egg on 1 slice brown toast – when having toast omit crispbread
4. 3 oz (85 g) lamb's kidney grilled with 1 large tomato
5. 5 oz (140 g) kipper on the bone or 3 oz (85 g) kipper fillet, grilled

A meals

1. A breakfastcup of clear soup with julienne of vegetables; omelette or soufflé with spinach or tomato filling – two standard eggs and about 3 oz (85 g) cooked weight of filling
2. 6 oz (170 g) chicken portion or 3 oz (85 g) chicken off the bone grilled or roasted with a large grilled tomato; large pear or bunch of grapes
3. 4 oz (115 g) grilled or sautéed kidneys with 3–4 oz (85–115 g) Brussels sprouts
4. Half a $2\frac{1}{2}$ lb (1.1 kg) lobster boiled or grilled with 4 oz (115 g) tomato and cucumber salad with 1 teaspoon vinaigrette; 3 oz (85 g) fresh pineapple

5. 3 oz (85 g) lean roast lamb with 2 oz (55 g) runner beans; 3 oz (85 g) fresh fruit salad with 1 dessertspoon plain yogurt

6. Hot or cold globe artichoke with 1 dessertspoon vinaigrette; 3 oz (85 g) thinly sliced boiled ham or gammon, 4 oz (115 g) braised celery or chicory

7. Half a large grapefruit (dissolve liquid sweetener with a drop of vanilla in a little orange or grapefruit juice and pour over the fruit); 6–7 oz (170–200 g) grilled trout with horse-radish sauce or lemon; 3 oz (85 g) any green vegetable

B meals

1. 4 oz (115 g) lean roast beef with 2–3 oz (55–85 g) green vegetable

2. Slice of melon (about 5 oz, 140 g) with ginger and/or lemon juice. Shrimp or prawn omelette made with 2 standard eggs and 2 oz (55 g) fish

3. Scrambled eggs (2 standard) on 3–4 oz (85–115 g) asparagus tips seasoned with black pepper; a peach or nectarine or a small bunch of grapes

4. Crab or chicken soufflé (one quarter of a soufflé made in a two-pint, one-litre dish); mandarin or satsuma

5. 8 oz (225 g) grouse or guinea fowl (weighed on the bone) with clear gravy and 4 oz (115 g) any one or two green vegetables; 3 oz (85 g) pear meringue – slice pears thinly, cook in very little vanilla-flavoured water, sweeten if necessary with artificial sweetener and top with stiffly beaten egg white; brown in a hot oven for 3–4 minutes

6. 6 oz (170 g) fillet of sole poached in a little white wine with 2 oz (55 g) white grapes and 2–3 oz (55–85 g) mushrooms; 3–4 oz (85–115 g) green figs

TEENAGE DIET

If you have been brought up to eat sensibly you should have no difficulty in maintaining your ideal weight throughout your teens. The trouble is that many things that young people like – chocolate, biscuits, colas – are high in calories.

To keep to a well-balanced diet means eating one food from each of the following groups each day:

Group 1: lean meat, poultry, offal, fish, eggs
Group 2: milk, cheese, yogurt
Group 3: bread, flour, cereal, pulses (beans, peas, lentils), nuts
Group 4: butter, margarine, low-fat spread, cooking oil or fat
Group 5: fruit and vegetables.

Learn to recognize the high-energy foods that should be eaten only in small amounts or cut out entirely while you are seriously slimming. *High energy foods* have a high fat and starch content and may also have a high sugar content: butter, oil, cheese, cream, fat meat, cakes, bread, biscuits, pastries, puddings, sweets, honey, jam, chocolate, all fried foods. Choose instead *low energy equivalents*: low-fat spread, crispbread or slimmers' bread; low-fat powdered or skimmed milk; artificial sweeteners instead of sugar; low-calorie soft drinks.

This diet has been planned especially for teenagers.

The daily allowance is about 1,500 Calories.
Possible weight loss: 1½ lb (0.68 kg) per week.

Daily allowances

- ½ pint (2.8 dl) milk
- 3 small slices wholewheat bread or up to 6 slices slimmers' bread
- 1 oz (30 g) low-fat spread
- as much tea and coffee as you wish, using milk from your daily allowance
- artificial sweetener if you wish
- low-calorie soft drinks

You should also have one meal from each list: breakfast, lunch, dinner, snack.

Breakfast menus
Choose from:
1. 2 boiled or poached eggs
2. 2 rashers grilled back bacon with tomato
3. 1 carton fruit yogurt
4. Cereal with $\frac{1}{4}$ pint (1.4 dl) milk (no sugar)
5. 2 oz (55 g) thinly sliced cheese, toasted
6. 1 slice cheese toasted on 1 slice bread with low fat spread from allowance

Lunch menus
Choose from:
1. Omelette (2 eggs) with 1 oz (30 g) grated cheese and green salad
2. 4 grilled fish fingers with peas and 1 grilled tomato
3. 4 oz (115 g) steak with 2 oz (55 g) boiled onions and 2 oz (55 g) spinach
4. 1 Scotch egg with celery and tomato
5. 3 oz (85g) lean ham or corned beef in a sandwich with bread and low-fat spread from day's allowance; lettuce and tomato
6. 1 grilled pork sausage (hot or cold) with hard-boiled egg; 1 piece of fresh fruit, e.g. apple, orange, few grapes, pear

Dinner menus
Choose from:
1. 4 oz (115 g) lean roast meat, 1 medium potato, green vegetable, little gravy
2. 8 oz (225 g) beef or lamb casserole with green vegetable, small potato
3. 2 grilled sausages with 2 tablespoons mashed potato, green vegetable or salad
4. 6 oz (170 g) macaroni cheese with green salad
5. Well-grilled pork chop with a little apple sauce, green beans, carrots
6. 4 oz (115 g) veal with green beans and grilled tomato; 1 piece fresh fruit

Snack to have during the day
Choose from:
1. 1 banana
2. 2 small apples
3. 4 Ritz biscuits
4. 1 carton natural yogurt
5. Glass of milk
6. 1 oz (30 g) Edam cheese
7. 1 oz (30 g) peanuts
8. $\frac{1}{2}$ pint (2.8 dl) dry cider
9. $\frac{1}{2}$ pint (2.8 dl) apple juice

FISH 1924

CARD TRICKS

Each of these exercises is designed to work on one or more of your most annoying figure problems, but doing them all will give the most beauty benefits. They were designed by Larry Lorence of Gala Fitness and all you need is a pack of cards.

VIDOL

1. Waist, buttocks and thighs (*above*) – Throw a pack of cards in front of you. Stand, feet slightly apart. Slowly go into a deep knee bend, 1a, and continue bending until you pick up a card, keeping the back straight, 1b. Now slowly straighten up, 1c. and drop the card to one side. Keeping legs straight, bend over, 1d. pick up another card. Stand and drop card. Repeat 5 times, alternating between deep knee bend and straight leg bend.

2. Thighs and buttocks (*right*) – Stand with the cards on the floor in front of you, feet slightly apart. Keeping the knees straight bend over and pick up a card, 2a. Straighten up, 2b, and bend knees and turn at waist. Keep bending, 2c, and turning until you are almost but not quite sitting on your heels. Drop the card behind you, 2d. Stand and repeat 10 times. Repeat on other side.

3a

3b

3c

3d

3e

3f

3. Thighs and waist (*left*) – Drop the cards on the floor and stand above them, feet apart, hands on hips, 3a. Bend to right, putting weight on right foot, 3b. Continue to bend, 3c, until you can pick up card at your right foot with left hand, 3d. Now make an arc on the floor with your hand, swinging hand from right to left foot, 3e, dropping card at left foot, 3f. Repeat, bending left knee, until you have picked up half the pack.

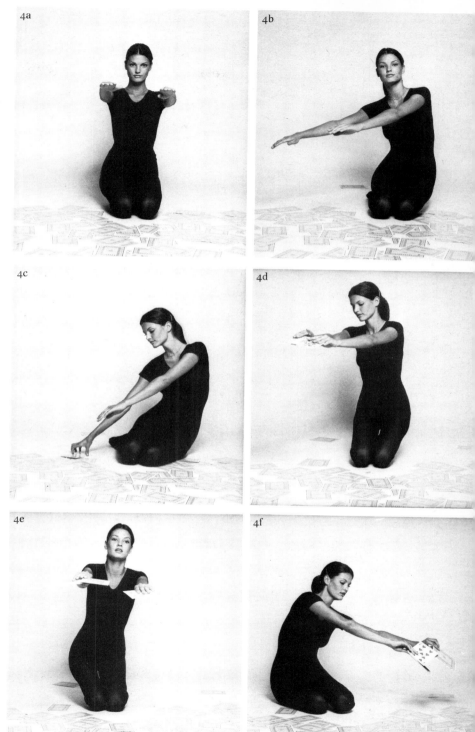

4. Hips and outer thighs (*right*) – Drop a pack of cards on the floor. Sit as in 4a, feet under you. Extend arms in front. Now reach to right, sitting to left side as you do so, 4b. Reach and pick up two cards, 4c. Now swing your body in the other direction, 4d, until you are sitting on right side, 4e and 4f. Put cards down. Repeat 6 times.

CARD TRICKS

5a

5b

5c

5d

5e

5f

5. Stomach *(left)* – Throw a pack of cards on the floor. Lie flat on floor, arms above you, 5a. Pick up a card or two from behind you. Pull forward, 5b and 5c, and put cards down at left toes, 5d. Lie down again and repeat, this time placing cards at right toes, 5e and 5f. Repeat 6 times.

6a

6b

6c

6d

6. Bosom and upper back *(right)* – With the cards at your feet, bend over, arms hanging loose, legs wide apart, 6a. Cross arms in front of you as much as possible, 6b. With arms still crossed, pick up a card in each hand, 6c and 6d, and begin straightening up, 6e, uncrossing arms to position 6f. Repeat 10 times.

6e

6f

SPECIAL FOOD DIETS

SEVEN-DAY FRUIT AND VEGETABLE DIET

The seven-day fruit and vegetable diet devised by Marina Andrews is a wonderful way of losing weight and ridding the body of the toxins so often associated with meat diets. During the seven days alternate one vegetable day and one fruit day. The ingredients are packed full of the vitamins that are essential for good health. It is a very simple diet that will not involve much shopping or special preparation.

Possible weight loss: up to 8 lb (3.6 kg).
Time: one week.

Vegetable day

Breakfast
1 glass vegetable juice (tomato and carrot mixed)
3 large tomatoes, grilled with pepper and lemon juice
1 crispbread thinly spread with butter
1 small black coffee

Lunch
Vegetable health salad (small beetroot, green pepper, red pepper, grated carrot, ½ cucumber, 1 celery stick, dessertspoon raisins, small bunch watercress) with natural yogurt and paprika
Lemon tea

Teatime
Lemon tea

Dinner
1 glass vegetable juice (tomato and carrot mixed)
6 large grilled mushrooms with a little sherry, sea-salt, black pepper and a lemon wedge on a bed of watercress
1 small black coffee

Fruit day

Breakfast
1 glass fresh fruit juice
1 large orange or grapefruit with a small carton of natural yogurt
1 small black coffee

Lunch
Fruit health salad (1 apple, 1 pear, 1 banana, 1 peach)
1 dessertspoon raisins, natural yogurt, pinch of fresh ginger
Lemon tea

Teatime
Lemon tea

Dinner
3 large slices fresh pineapple, spread thinly with honey, sprinkled with ginger and grilled for 3 minutes, served on bed of mustard and cress with a few peeled grapes
1 small black coffee

THE APPLE DIET

This diet is planned on two levels: a basic 1,200 Calorie a day diet on which you should lose around 2½ lb (1.1 kg) a week, and a 1,400 Calorie a day plan which allows you three extras each day. On the 1,400 Calorie diet you may substitute a glass of wine for the additional fruit if you wish – as long as it is dry or white wine. No sugar; use synthetic sweeteners if you wish. If you don't like drinking skimmed milk use it to make coffee or chocolate and have it hot or iced. Use salt and pepper, lemon juice or Worcestershire sauce for extra flavouring.

Apples provide an extra bonus by helping to clean your teeth and massaging the gums; the iron content helps maintain healthy blood and apples also have a natural antiseptic called malic acid which keeps breath fresh and the intestines clean. **Possible weight loss:** 2½ lb (1.1 kg) a week on the 1,200 Calorie plan; 2 lb (0.9 kg) a week on the 1,400 Calorie plan.
Time: as long as you wish.

1,200 Calorie diet

Breakfast
1 apple or orange
Egg with toast and margarine or butter
1 oz (30 g) cereal with skimmed milk
Tea or coffee with skimmed milk, no sugar

Lunch
2 oz (55 g) meat, fish, poultry or cheese
Green vegetables or crunchy apple salad* with
    low-calorie dressing*
1 slice wholemeal bread with margarine or butter
Lemon tea

Dinner
3 oz (85 g) meat, fish or poultry
1 medium potato with margarine or butter
Green vegetable
Salad or apple coleslaw*
Apple stewed with lemon juice and synthetic
    sweetener
Coffee

Evening
1 apple, 2 water biscuits
A glass of skimmed milk

1,400 Calorie diet
This is the same as the 1,200 Calorie diet but with a few additions, as follows.

Mid-afternoon
1 apple, pear or peach

Dinner
1 oz (30 g) more meat, fish or poultry

Evening
1 piece of extra fruit or biscuit, e.g. apple cakes*

THE AVOCADO DIET

Avocados are versatile and nutritious and a wonderful health and beauty aid. They contain 2.1 per cent protein; 25 per cent vegetable oil; fourteen vitamins and eleven minerals; no starch, practically no sugar and only 100 Calories a half.

They are such a complete food that in some countries babies are weaned on them and elderly people with digestive problems survive on them. Marina Andrews has created this four-day diet and suggests that you give yourself a beauty treatment while you lose weight: when you have eaten the avocado, turn the skin inside out and massage your face and neck and the backs of your hands and legs; after fifteen minutes wash off with warm water. The natural oils of the avocado will leave your skin soft and nourished.
Possible weight loss: up to 7 lb (3.2 kg).
Time: four days.

Breakfast
½ avocado with wedge of lemon squeezed over
Thin slice toast
1 cup herbal or mint tea

Mid-morning
Yogurt cocktail: 1 small carton natural yogurt, 1
  teaspoon tomato pureé, 1 teaspoon Worcestershire sauce, 4–5 ice cubes and 2 thin slices
  cucumber for garnish

Lunch
1 whole avocado, cut in half, stone removed and
  the centre filled with finely chopped dried apricots and walnuts – serve with wedge of lemon
  on a bed of crisp lettuce and celery tops
1 cup herbal or mint tea

Mid-afternoon
Yogurt cocktail

Dinner
½ avocado, mashed with squeeze of lemon and
  served on a slice of toast
1 cup herbal or mint tea

Bedtime
1 cup hot water with ½ teaspoon honey

After your four-day diet, continue to eat avocados
for your health.

THE CITRUS-FRUIT DIET

Followers of Dr Linus Pauling, who believes that
large amounts of vitamin C can 'provide protection
against the common cold and influenza' will find in
the Citrus-Fruit Diet the best sources of this vitamin.
As well as keeping you healthy it will help you
to shed about 2½ lb (1.1 kg) a week according to
how overweight you are to begin with and how
strictly you adhere to the plan. The diet is low on
fat and carbohydrate foods and has good vitamin
and mineral foods to help improve your skin and
the condition of your hair. Menus for six days are
given. The seventh day – which can be any day
you choose – is an all-fruit day when you choose
from the special fruit menus given. If you want to
speed up your weight loss you could have two fruit
days in your week.
Possible weight loss: 2½ lb (1.1 kg).
Time: one week.

Daily treats
Choose a treat every day from the following:
1. 1 glass dry sherry
2. 1 glass dry white wine
3. 1 low-fat yogurt
4. ½ pint (2.8 dl) dry cider
5. 1 measure spirits with low-calorie drink
6. 1 apple, pear, peach
7. Small portion potatoes
8. 1 oz (30 g) boiled sweets
9. 1 glass Buck's Fizz made from two parts cold
   champagne to one part orange juice
10. Andalucia – two parts iced orange juice with
   one part dry sherry

Non-alcoholic drinks
You are allowed ½ pint (2.8 dl) milk a day. You may
have coffee or tea as often as you like provided
you use artificial sweetener. Drink low-calorie
squashes, lemon juice and water as you wish.

Notes: Use artificial sweetening only. If you like
early morning tea, drink it with a slice of lemon or
orange, or milk from your allowance. At tea-time
have as much tea as you like but no milk: choose
China or jasmine or any herb tea. At mid-day you
can substitute a packed lunch consisting of two
small lean lamb cutlets, two slices ham, a chicken
breast or two hard-boiled eggs with any green
salad, a Thermos of clear soup and a piece of fruit.

DAY 1

Breakfast
Fresh orange juice
1 boiled egg
1 slice lightly buttered toast
Tea or coffee with milk from day's allowance

Lunch
½ grapefruit
Slice of meat or breast of chicken
Green salad with low-calorie dressing*

Tea
China or jasmine tea with lemon

Dinner
Avocado pear with low-fat yogurt dressing
4 oz (115 g) lean grilled steak with any two green
    vegetables or green salad
Orange salad*
Coffee with little milk

Last thing
The rest of milk from day's allowance drunk warm

DAY 2

Breakfast
Fresh orange juice
1 lean slice of bacon with grilled tomato
1 slice lightly buttered crispbread
Tea or coffee with milk

Lunch
Hamburger made from 4 oz (115 g) minced beef
    and little grated onion and seasoning with egg
Mushroom salad*

Tea
China or jasmine tea with lemon

Dinner
Prawn, crab or lobster cocktail*
4 oz (115 g) roast beef or lamb with clear gravy
Any two vegetables or salad
Lemon snow*

Last thing
Warm milk

DAY 3

Breakfast
½ grapefruit
6 oz (170 g) smoked haddock
1 thin slice lightly buttered toast
Tea or coffee with milk

Lunch
Mushroom omelette (2 eggs) with mixed green
    salad and low-calorie dressing*

Tea
China or jasmine tea with lemon

Dinner
Consommé, hot or jellied
¼ chicken with braised celery and any two green
    vegetables or salad
Grapefruit meringue

Last thing
Warm milk

DAY 4

Breakfast
Fresh orange juice
Poached egg on thin slice toast, lightly buttered
Tea or coffee with milk

Lunch
2 Danish sandwiches of lightly buttered rye bread
    or crispbread with any of the following: caviar,
    lean ham, prawns, hard-boiled egg and crisp
    bacon, marinated herring or thin slice Gruyère
Watercress, thin tomato slices for garnish

Tea
China or jasmine tea with lemon

Dinner
½ grapefruit
6 oz (170 g) sole or plaice cooked in dry white wine
    with mushrooms and half a dozen green grapes
    and two green vegetables
Orange salad

Last thing
Warm milk

DAY 5

Breakfast
½ grapefruit
1 kipper
1 thin slice buttered toast
Tea or coffee with milk

Lunch
Orange and grapefruit cocktail
Chicken breast with a tomato salad and a green
   salad

Tea
China or jasmine tea with lemon

Dinner
Artichoke with yogurt dressing*
4 oz (115 g) veal cooked with one slice lean bacon
   and 1 oz (30 g) grated cheese (bake or grill)
Two green vegetables
Fresh fruit salad

Last thing
Warm milk

DAY 6

Breakfast
Fresh orange juice
Grilled lamb's kidney with 1 slice lean bacon and
   mushrooms
1 slice lightly buttered crispbread

Lunch
½ grapefruit
2-egg omelette with filling made from 1 oz (30 g)
   cheese or ham, or 2 oz (60 g) prawns, or tomato,
   or mushrooms
Green salad with low-calorie dressing*

Tea
China or jasmine tea with lemon

Dinner
Slice of melon or ½ Ogen melon
4 oz (115 g) grilled gammon with pineapple ring
Green salad with low-calorie dressing*
Yogurt

Last thing
Warm milk

Special fruit menus
Choose five of the following menus for your fruit
day and eat them at intervals throughout the day.
Leave two hours between each snack.

1. Two oranges or one orange and one grapefruit
2. Hot grapefruit meringue: whisk one egg white
   stiffly (saccharine sweetener if you wish); pile
   on a halved grapefruit and grill slowly
3. The flesh of half a grapefruit or half a large
   orange, chopped and mixed with a carton of
   fat-free yogurt
4. Grapefruit salad: arrange segments of grapefruit
   and endive and watercress, top with fine slices
   of green pepper and six spears of asparagus
5. Savoury orange salad: shredded white cabbage,
   grated carrot, chopped celery, and chopped
   orange segments tossed in a dressing made
   with orange juice mixed with a teaspoon
   vegetable oil seasoned to taste
6. Cottage cheese salad: 2 oz (55 g) cottage cheese
   with half a carton of low-fat yogurt, whisked
   with a chopped gherkin and half a segmented
   grapefruit, on a bed of lettuce
7. Wrap segments of one orange in foil with a
   little artificial sweetener and one tablespoon of
   brandy and bake in the oven
8. Squeeze the juice from two oranges, mix with a
   tablespoon of sherry and drink well chilled
9. Lemon coleslaw: chopped white cabbage, a
   little onion, grated carrot, a few raisins and
   chopped nuts, mixed with 1 dessertspoon low-
   calorie dressing and 3 teaspoons lemon juice
10. Orange and pepper salad: mix together chopped orange segments, quarter of a green and
   quarter of a red pepper in a dressing made from
   one tablespoon vegetable oil, two teaspoons
   vinegar and chopped chives. Season to taste
   and serve on a bed of lettuce.

SUMMER FRUIT DIET

It is far healthier to eat strawberries, raspberries, loganberries, blackcurrants and redcurrants on their own or with the juice of other fresh fruit such as orange, lemon or grapefruit. Covered with sugar and cream they are no longer a health food but just a mountain of calories. Here is a diet devised by Marina Andrews to bring you the maximum benefit of fresh fruit with the minimum of calories. Follow it for two days at a time and then continue with a light diet of fresh salads, lean meat and fish.
Possible weight loss: about 5 lb (2.3 kg).
Time: two days.

Breakfast
Breakfast fruit salad: 8–10 strawberries, 8–10 blackberries, 10 melon cubes – put the fruit into a small glass dish and sprinkle with the juice of a fresh orange
Yogurt health cup: pour a carton fresh natural yogurt into a tall glass full of ice cubes. Mix well together before you drink it
1 small cup of black coffee (if you wish) without milk or sugar but with half a teaspoon of honey if necessary.

Lunch
Special fruit salad: 1 cup fresh strawberries, raspberries or loganberries, 3 inch (7.5 cm) wedge of water melon, ¼ cucumber, 1 banana, 1 tablespoon blackcurrants, 2 teaspoons salted peanuts, ½ teaspoon mint jelly and 3 teaspoons lemon juice – wash and prepare the fruit and put together in a glass bowl. Mix mint jelly and lemon juice together, pour over fruit and toss. Sprinkle peanuts on top.
1 glass of yogurt health cup as for breakfast.

Supper
Exactly the same as for breakfast

During the day you may have up to two glasses more of yogurt health cup and two or three glasses of mineral water.

FIVE-DAY SUMMER SALAD DIET

This diet, devised by Marina Andrews, is based on Lebanese health salads; each dish has a very distinctive taste which comes from the herbs used. Tabbuleh – made from fresh parsley – is particularly nutritious as it is rich in vitamin C. The best liquid to drink is undoubtedly China or mint tea with a slice of lemon; you may have up to four glasses a day or six teacups without sugar.
Possible weight loss: if you are overweight you should lose 5–7 lb (2.3–3.2 kg).
Time: five days.

DAY 1
Breakfast and dinner: khosaf* with China or mint tea (an infusion of fresh mint and boiling water) with a slice of lemon
Lunch: yogurt and cucumber salad*

DAY 2
Breakfast and dinner: khosaf* with China or mint tea with a slice of lemon
Lunch: tahini salad*

DAY 3
Breakfast and dinner: khosaf* with China or mint tea with a slice of lemon
Lunch: tabbuleh*

DAY 4
Breakfast and dinner: khosaf* with China or mint tea with a slice of lemon
Lunch: Lebanese aubergines*

DAY 5
Breakfast and dinner: khosaf* with China or mint tea with a slice of lemon
Lunch: cauliflower with Taratour*

THE GREEN FOOD DIET

This is another diet by Marina Andrews. All fresh vegetables are good nutritional value but green ones are best of all. And the greener the better: the outside leaves of cabbage for instance contain more minerals than the pale inside ones.

A diet consisting of green fruits and vegetables, mostly raw, helps to build up the supply of vitamins and mineral salts essential for good health. Eat everything as fresh as possible: the vitamin content begins to deteriorate within half an hour of picking. The nutritional value can also be destroyed when fruits and vegetables are soaked in water.

For extra flavour use fresh aromatic herbs: rosemary, tarragon, basil, mint, capers. Dressings should be made with fresh lemon juice or natural yogurt and garlic to bring out the flavour of the food. Oil and salad creams not only increase the calorie content but decrease the subtle flavour of raw fruits and vegetables. You should follow this Green Food Diet for a week, varying the sample one-day menu by using fruits and vegetables from the green food list.

Possible weight loss: $2\frac{1}{2}$–3 lb (1.1–1.4 kg) with extra (see note at foot of next column); 5–7 lb (2.3–3.2 kg) if nothing is added.

Time: one week.

Breakfast
$\frac{1}{2}$ green melon cut into cubes and mixed with six greengages
1 glass mint tea (an infusion of fresh mint and boiling water)

Lunch
Large salad made from sliced avocado, watercress, green olives, spring onions, dandelion leaves, green peppers and a few capers, dressed with $\frac{1}{2}$ carton natural yogurt mixed with $\frac{1}{2}$ clove crushed garlic, juice of 1 lemon, black pepper and fresh rosemary
1 glass fresh mint tea

Dinner
Asparagus with a little melted butter
Salad of cos lettuce, finely sliced raw courgettes, spring onions and green apples chopped up and tossed in a dressing of lemon juice, black pepper and chopped mint
1 glass fresh mint tea

Green food list
Only the starred vegetables should be cooked and then only for a few minutes:

Vegetables

*artichokes	endive
*asparagus	*leeks
avocados	lettuce (particularly cos)
*broad beans	*mangetout peas
*French beans	mint
*broccoli	green olives
*Brussels sprouts	parsley
celery (including	*young peas
the leaves)	green peppers
courgettes	*spring greens
cucumber	spring onions
dandelion leaves	watercress

Fruit

green apples	green melon
green grapes	pears
greengages	

Note: If you are using this diet to slim then add nothing except a minimum of three glasses of mineral water a day. If for general health, then add up to four slices wholemeal bread lightly spread with butter or margarine, two glasses chilled white wine and three glasses of mineral water.

THREE-DAY RAW FOOD DIET

This diet, devised by Marina Andrews, concentrates on raw fruit and vegetables, since it is an established fact that cooking destroys some of the valuable nutrients in food. Peas, for example, are pleasant to eat raw and nutritionally much better for you: they are seeds and therefore living things. When cooked that living quality is destroyed. Vegetables and fruit in the vitamin B group have 35–40 per cent of their vitamins destroyed by cooking; in the vitamin C group as much as 90 per cent may be destroyed.

The effect of cooking is to cause the starch granules in vegetables to swell up and rupture the non-digestible cellulose chambers in which they, as well as the protein and fats, are contained. It is for this reason, and also because starch is more digestible cooked than raw, that cooking adds to the digestibility of vegetables, especially those high in cellulose. At the same time it relieves the organs of much of their work, thus contributing to a sluggish system.

Possible weight loss: up to 4 lb (1.8 kg)
Time: three days.

Breakfast
2 tablespoons bran, 1 chopped unpeeled raw apple, 1 chopped peeled apricot (fresh) or 2 chopped dry ones, 4 tablespoons natural yogurt, all mixed together
1 glass herbal or mint/lemon tea

Lunch
1 tablespoon fresh shelled peas or mangetout peas, 1 tablespoon chopped raw mushrooms, 1 tablespoon chopped or grated raw carrot, 1 tablespoon chopped mixed nuts, mixed together – toss the salad in a dressing made from 1 tablespoon prune juice, 1 tablespoon lemon juice, freshly grated black pepper, a pinch of garlic salt and 2 tablespoons natural yogurt
1 glass herbal or mint/lemon tea

Dinner
3 small sliced courgettes, 1 small endive, 1 large tomato and 2 hard-boiled eggs, sprinkled with capers and chopped parsley and served with 3 teaspoons of French dressing or the prune juice dressing used at lunch
1 glass herbal or mint/lemon tea

Follow this diet for three days at a time, repeating it every fortnight if you wish.

GROW YOUR OWN DIET

This diet makes use of the sprouting seeds that you can grow in your own home. They are full of protein, minerals, unsaturated oils, carbohydrates, amino acids and vitamins, and they are still growing when you eat them. To produce sprouts the seeds need to be watered regularly for several days to start the growing process. During this germination period chemical changes create a situation very favourable for human nutrition: carbohydrates are lost – burned up for growth energy by the sprouting seed – so you get a greater proportion of protein and minerals than there were before sprouting. Moreover some of the carbohydrates are changed into vitamins: A, E, K and large quantities of B and C.

Since 3000 BC the Chinese have recognized that sprouted seeds provide greater nutrition than dry seeds, and several centuries ago the Russians started adding sprouted wheat to their black bread to give extra nutrition, particularly vitamin C. More recently it has been shown that vitamin E helps athletic performance and is effective against many diseases.

Seeds from most vegetables can be sprouted and eaten – although some, tomatoes and potatoes for instance, produce sprouts that are poisonous – but they must be chemically untreated and certified edible seeds.

Here is Marina Andrews' health improved diet using alfalfa and triticale; adzuki, alphatoco, mung beans, soya, fenugreek and herbal green mint sprouts are equally good.

Possible weight loss: up to 6 lb (2.7 kg).

Time: seven days.

Breakfast

1 large glass fresh fruit juice, 1 small carton natural yogurt, ½ cup alfalfa sprouts, 1 teaspoon honey and 1 egg, whisked at high speed in a blender for 8–12 seconds; no other drinks permitted

Lunch

2 slices wholemeal bread spread thinly with margarine and Marmite and 2 medium slices Gouda cheese (the aged one is best), piled with 1 cup alfalfa sprouts and sprinkled with lemon juice and black pepper

1 large glass of lemon tea or herbal tea (no sugar)

Dinner

4 oz (115 g) any cold or hot meat *or* grilled or baked white fish *or* shellfish with health salad*

1 glass white wine *or* mineral water

Small bunch of grapes

Last thing

1 large glass hot water with 1 teaspoon honey and 1 teaspoon cider vinegar

Note: To vary the diet change the meat and fish and the sprouting seeds.

THE HONEY DIET

A diet good for almost everyone (except diabetics). The milk, fish and meat supply protein which builds and replaces damaged tissues. The fruit and vegetables give vitamin C, essential for healthy skin. The honey provides energy, contains fewer calories than sugar.

You are allowed half a pint (2.8 dl) milk a day; as much tea and coffee as you wish but only milk from the daily allowance. No sugar, artificial sweeteners if you like. Wholemeal and wheatgerm bread only. To measure the honey accurately dip the spoon in hot water first. You should lose 4–7 lb (1.8–3.2 kg) in seven days, depending on how overweight you are before you start. If you overeat one day follow with a Drastic Day and then return to the diet.

Possible weight loss: 4–7 lb (1.8–3.2 kg).

Time: one week.

OPTIONAL DRASTIC DAY

Breakfast

Honey flip: whisk 1 egg into a glass of milk and add 2 teaspoons clear honey – for a sharper taste add 1 tablespoon lemon juice (if you do not like the idea of raw egg lightly boil it but try the honey flip first – it tastes like incredibly creamy milk and is very satisfying)

Lunch

3 oz (85 g) cold meat or 8 oz (225 g) cottage cheese with any of the following: French or runner beans, beetroot, cabbage, carrot, cauliflower, celeriac, celery, cucumber, endive, lettuce, onion, radish, tomatoes, watercress

Dinner

Honey flip

Between meals

As many unsweetened drinks as you like and another ¼ pint (1.4 dl) milk for coffee and tea

DAY I

Breakfast

Half a grapefruit with 1 teaspoon clear honey

1 oz (30 g) wholewheat cereal with ¼ pint (1.4 dl) milk

Lunch
3 oz (85 g) cottage cheese
Green salad
Thin slice bread (wholemeal or wheatgerm) with
   scraping of butter

Dinner
6 oz (170 g) sole grilled with ½ oz (15 g) melted
   butter
Lemon wedges
1 grilled tomato
3 oz (85 g) runner beans
6 oz (170 g) apricots with 1 dessertspoon clear
   honey

DAY 2

Breakfast
Lemon juice with 1 teaspoon clear honey and hot
   or cold water
1 grilled rasher lean bacon
1 slice bread, scraping of butter

Lunch
2 oz (55 g) smoked salmon
Green salad
1 slice bread, scraping of butter

Dinner
Spanish omelette (i)*
6 oz (170 g) melon with 2 teaspoons clear honey

DAY 3

Breakfast
½ grapefruit with 1 teaspoon clear honey
Slimmers' French toast*
1 grilled tomato

Lunch
5 oz (140 g) herring fried in oatmeal
1 orange

Dinner
4 oz (115 g) calf's or lamb's liver braised with
   onion, 1 stock cube
3 oz (85 g) each runner beans and spinach
Baked apple*

DAY 4

Breakfast
Small glass orange juice, unsweetened
1 rasher lean bacon, grilled
1 thin slice bread, scraping of butter

Lunch
4 oz (115 g) prawns
Green salad
1 thin slice bread, scraping of butter

Dinner
Blanquette of veal*
3 oz (85 g) carrots
1 low-fat yogurt with 1 oz (30 g) sultanas,
   1 teaspoon clear honey, 1 teaspoon wheatgerm,
   1 teaspoon bran

DAY 5

Breakfast
½ grapefruit with 1 teaspoon clear honey
1 oz (30 g) wholewheat cereal with ¼ pint (1.4 dl)
   milk

Lunch
2 oz (55 g) cold, lean ham
3 oz (85 g) braised courgettes
1 thin slice bread, scraping of butter

Dinner
Kidney sauté*
3 oz (85 g) spinach
2 oz (55 g) carrots
Orange and grape jelly*

DAY 6

Breakfast
½ grapefruit with 1 teaspoon clear honey
1 boiled egg
Thin slice bread, scraping of butter

Lunch
3 oz (85 g) poached or steamed salmon
Green salad
1 thin slice bread, scraping of butter

Dinner
3 oz (85 g) lean roast beef
3 oz (85 g) green beans
3 oz (85 g) carrots
Banana snow*

DAY 7

Breakfast
Lemon juice with 1 teaspoon clear honey and hot or cold water
1 scrambled egg on thin slice toast

Lunch
2 oz (55 g) lean roast beef
Green salad
1 thin slice bread, scraping of butter

Dinner
Consommé
8 oz (225 g) chicken leg or wing brushed with German mustard and grilled
3 oz (85 g) green beans
2 oz (55 g) cauliflower
Orange bavaroise*
1 wine glass dry white wine

THE MILK DIET

Milk is an almost perfect food, providing most of the nutrients necessary for life. It consists largely of water in which proteins, lactose (milk sugar), water-soluble vitamins and minerals are dissolved or dispersed. Milk-based dairy products supply 61.8 per cent of the average person's daily calcium intake, needed for the formation and maintenance of bones and teeth, normal clotting of blood and functioning of nerves. Milk is also an excellent source of riboflavin, providing over half an adult's daily intake; remember, though, that light destroys the riboflavin content so take care not to expose it to sunlight. Vitamin A, essential for vision in dim light and for growth, is found in the carotene content of milk, giving it its creamy colour. People

on diets often neglect essential foods thinking they are fattening; to prove them wrong, here is a milk diet by Marina Andrews which, if followed for a week, could show a weight loss of up to 8 lb (3.6 kg). The diet consists of a milk cup taken in place of normal meals for four days (resulting in a weight loss of about 5 lb, 2.3 kg); for the next three days substitute the milk cup for one meal. The final weight loss should be about 8 lb (3.6 kg). The milk cup is also ideal on a once-a-week basis to maintain a health and slimming regime.
Possible weight loss: 8 lb (3.6 kg).
Time: seven days.

DAYS 1–4

One day's supply of milk cup:
1½ pints (8.5 dl) fresh milk
1 large eating apple, unpeeled
1 small carrot
1 fresh egg
1 teaspoon honey
½ teaspoon grated nutmeg
½ teaspoon Yeastamin (pure yeast extract)
Finely grate the apple and carrot and blend all ingredients together in a liquidizer, or whisk. Keep the day's supply in a jug in the fridge and stir well before drinking. It should fill five glasses to be drunk during the day.

In addition you may have three small cups of herbal or mint tea.

DAYS 5–7

Breakfast
1 lightly boiled egg
1 crispbread with a little butter
1 cup herbal or mint tea

Lunch
1 large glass of milk cup

Dinner
4 oz (115 g) grilled white fish, chicken or veal with lemon wedge
1 tablespoon any fresh green vegetable
1 piece fresh fruit
1 cup herbal or mint tea

YOGURT, GRAPES AND CHEESE DIET

A diet, devised by Marina Andrews that is pleasant to eat and easy to prepare.
Possible weight loss: 5 lb (2.3 kg).
Time: four days.

Breakfast
1 glass hot water sweetened with 1 teaspoon honey
15 large black or white grapes
2 oz (55 g) hard cheese (choose from Cheddar, Edam or Gouda)
1 small black coffee

Mid-morning
1 small carton natural yogurt

Lunch
15 large grapes, de-seeded and chopped with 2 oz (55 g) Stilton or Danish blue cheese (the salty taste of the cheese is good with the sweet grapes); put the cheese and grapes into a bowl with 1 carton natural yogurt and 6 leaves of finely chopped fresh mint; mix well before eating
1 small black coffee

Mid-afternoon
1 glass lemon tea with ½ teaspoon honey

Dinner
Iced yogurt soup*
1 small black coffee

NEW SPRING BLITZ DIET

A blitz diet to lose a few pounds quickly – but for no more than one week. It is a stringent 750 Calories a day, so take a vitamin pill with iron daily; do not make substitutions.

Breakfast
Banana blitz breakfast:
½ banana
6 fl oz (1.7 dl) skimmed milk with vitamins A and D added
1 fresh egg
2 tablespoons undiluted frozen orange juice
½ teaspoon vanilla essence
Up to the equivalent of 4 teaspoons artificial sweetener
Cinnamon to taste
Crushed ice
Combine all the ingredients in a blender and serve immediately
Coffee or tea

Lunch
4 oz (115 g) cottage cheese *or* 8 oz (225 g) low-fat plain yogurt with 1 cup strawberries *or* ½ cup tinned pineapple in natural juice (with artificial sweetener, if desired)
1 carrot
1 large stalk celery
1 medium cucumber
Coffee or tea

Dinner
8 fl oz (2.3 dl) chicken broth (skim off fat)
3½ oz (100 g) boneless, skinless chicken breast
½ cup green beans *or* ½ cup cauliflower *or* ½ cup sliced carrots *or* ½ cup spinach
1½ cups green salad with 2 tablespoons low-down salad dressing*
1 medium apple
Coffee or tea

Note: You may have as much tea or coffee – without sugar or milk – as you like, plus mineral water, sugar-free diet drinks.

TWO-DAY DRINK DIET

A diet by Marina Andrews which is high in energy yet effective for losing weight quickly. It is in the form of a drink which you can take throughout the day whenever you feel hungry.

If you follow the diet for two days every week for a month you could lose 11 lb (5 kg) providing you control your diet on other days.
Possible weight loss: 5 lb (2.3 kg).
Time: two days.

One day's supply:
1 pint (5.7 dl) fresh milk
2 fresh eggs
½ pint (2.8 dl) tomato juice
Small carton plain cottage cheese
1 level teaspoon Yeastamin (pure yeast extract)
½ teaspoon Bovril or Marmite
1 dessertspoon finely crushed peanuts or crunchy peanut butter
Blend all the ingredients and keep in a jug in the refrigerator. No other liquids or food are permitted except up to three glasses of water a day, preferably bottled.

WEEKEND WINE DIET

A two-day diet prepared by Marina Andrews.
Possible weight loss: up to 6 lb (2.7 kg).

Each day
1 bottle champagne or sparkling wine or dry white wine
As much mineral water as you like

Breakfast
Juice of 1 fresh lime and 1 fresh orange with ice cubes
1 black coffee
1 boiled egg with 1 crispbread and a little butter

Lunch
2 glasses wine
1 small poussin or ½ chicken, served with watercress and lemon wedge

Dinner
Reserve 2 glasses of wine to have with dinner, put remainder in a jug with soda, ice and lemon and drink before dinner
A good portion of grilled lobster or fresh crab or prawns or scallops
2 tablespoons spinach purée
1 small black coffee

ONE-DAY DIETS

These give your body a rest; they perform a sort of unloading job, using fruits or raw vegetables to clean out the system, which helps weight, skin and metabolism.

One-day salad diet
Make a great bowl of salad, primarily green vegetables, including celery and cucumber, and for dressing use a little olive oil and the juice of half a lemon.

One-day apple diet
Eat up to 3 lb (1.4 kg) apples, intact or juiced (put the entire fruit including peel and pips through the juicer, adding a few drops of lemon).

One-day lemon diet
Six times a day drink a glass of sparkling mineral water combined with the juice of two lemons.

One-day cocktail diet
½ pint (2.8 dl) tomato juice
½ pint (2.8 dl) vegetable juice
1 teacup natural yogurt
1 teaspoon ground almonds
Juice of 1 lemon and ½ orange
1 teaspoon finely chopped parsley

2–3 drops Worcestershire sauce
2 teaspoons medium dry sherry
Blend all ingredients well together and put them in a glass jug in the fridge. Drink this cocktail throughout the day whenever you feel hungry. With each glass you may have three sugar-lump-sized pieces of cheese (Cheddar, Edam or Gouda).

DIET IN A NUTSHELL

The principle is simple: you must replace one of the two main meals of the day with 2 oz (55 g) of peanuts, the ordinary roasted, salted kind and an orange. (Plums, grapefruit or a small handful of grapes could be substituted.) That is all.

But these important points should be watched: have a good breakfast, with a protein food – fish, egg, bacon, etc., and a small amount of starch-reduced crispbread. Have one good main meal, either in the evening or midday – it does not matter which – and this meal may include smoked salmon, prawns, melon or clear soup to start with, followed by any fish, poultry, game, meat, offal or eggs, with two green vegetables. Pudding must be replaced by fresh fruit or cheese with celery. Avoid sugar; use synthetic sweeteners. You must not eat between meals. Compulsive nibblers should have grapes or citrus fruits and/or celery at hand. Forbidden foods include everything made with flour or cornflour, root vegetables, peas, beans, cereals, pastas, all sugar, sweets, sweetened drinks. You are allowed sugar-free soft drinks, a small quantity of spirits with water, soda or sugar-free drinks, and dry wine. Keep even starch-reduced crispbreads to the minimum.

Note: Peanuts contain an average of eight grammes of protein an ounce and essential amino acids, and are so nutritionally sound that they are being used to combat undernourishment in famine areas. Boredom might be the only snag in continuing the diet indefinitely; so repeat when necessary.

BEATON 1929

EXERCISES TO SOLVE PROBLEMS

47 per cent of us need thigh exercise
30 per cent have a buttocks problem
40 per cent have a hip problem
45 per cent need stomach toning
Here are some highly effective work-outs
for the major problem spots by Lotte Berk.

1. Thighs – Stand as in picture 1a, extend the left leg, 1b, cross over the right leg keeping the toe on the floor, 1c. Swing the leg to the side; hold for a few seconds, 1d. Repeat 10 times with each leg.

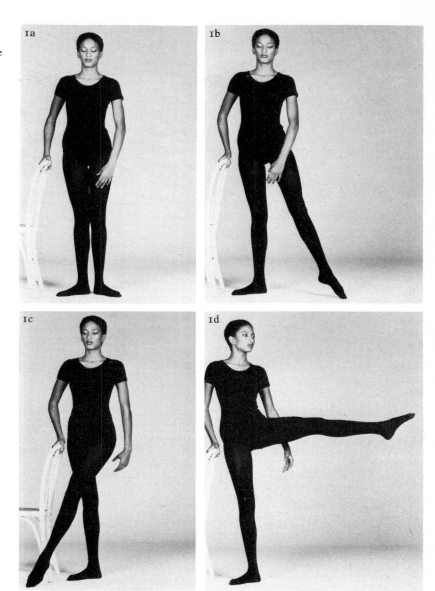

EXERCISES TO SOLVE PROBLEMS

2. Buttocks *(right)* – Lie on the stomach as in picture 2a, knees wide apart, feet touching each other. Press pelvis to floor, squeezing buttock muscles. Lift knees and thighs off floor, 2b, but don't arch back. Keep elbows touching floor, chin on hands. Hold to count of 10. Repeat until you are tired.

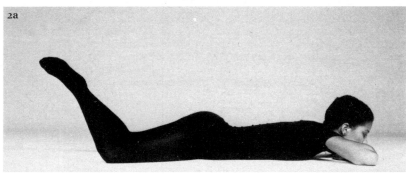

2a

2b

3. Hips and buttocks *(below)* – Stand as in picture 3a, using a chair back for balance. Bend the knees slightly and contract the buttock muscles, pressing the pelvis against the back of the chair. Bring the leg back, keeping it as straight as possible, 3b, while continuing to contract the buttock muscles; lift the leg slightly, hold and lower. Repeat 10 times with each leg.

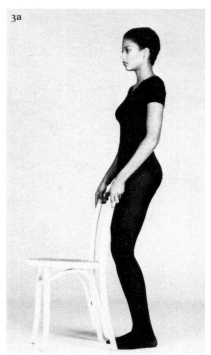

3a

3b

4. Hips and buttocks *(opposite above)* – Stand as in picture 4a, using a chair back for balance. Bend the knees slightly and press pelvis against back of chair, 4b. Bend the knee and lift leg at almost a right angle to body, 4c. Gently and slowly move the leg back and forth in a pumping motion using the buttock muscles, 4d. Repeat 10 times with each leg.

5. Stomach *(right)* – Sit as in picture 5a. Contract the buttocks and pull in the stomach, 5b. Round back and lower until waist area touches floor, 5c. Extend arms in front of you and breathe; hold, 5d. Lower 3 in (7.5 cm). Raise 3 in (7.5 cm) with waist on floor. Switch legs and repeat until you are tired.

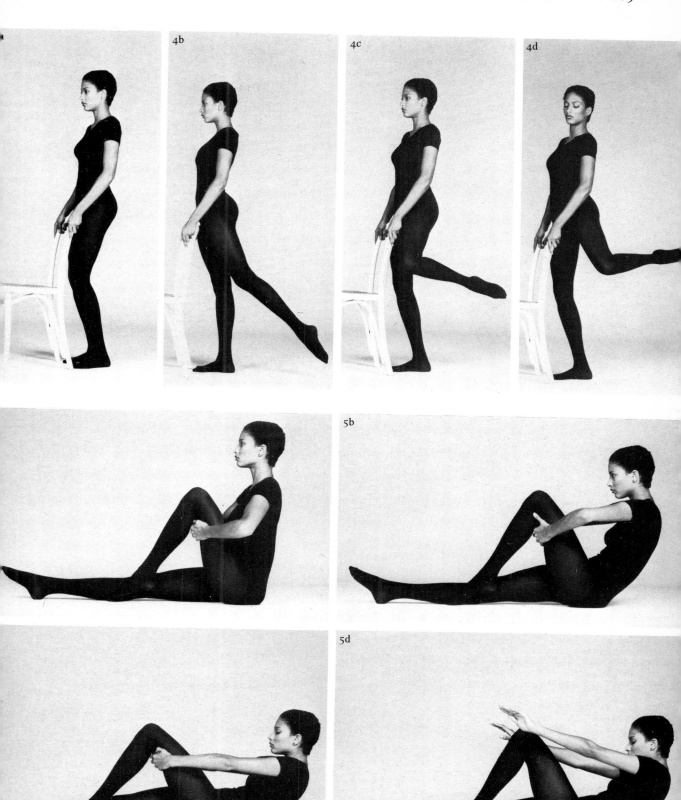

4b

4c

4d

5b

5d

EXERCISES TO SOLVE PROBLEMS

6. Stomach and abdomen (*left*) – Sit as in picture 6a. Contract the buttock muscles while you pull in the stomach. Round your back until your waist almost touches the floor, 6b. Release hands from leg and reach slowly to one side, 6c. Turn to other side, 6d. Switch legs and repeat until you are tired.

7. Stomach (*right*) – Sit as in picture 7a, elbows wide apart. Contract the buttock muscles, pull in the stomach. Round the back and lower the waist area to the floor, extending the left leg in air, 7b. Start to lift the right leg, 7c. Change hands to the right leg while lowering the left, 7d. 'Walk' with legs in air with waist area pressed to floor, 7e. Continue contracting buttock muscles, using the stomach muscles as you move your legs.

7a

7b

7c

7d

7e

SPECIAL OBJECT DIETS

Diets are not necessarily to help you slim: you can go on a diet that will give you extra energy, more vitality ... if you are feeling sluggish you could benefit from a purifying diet ... if you are having treatment for cellulite an anti-cellulite diet will be helpful. Healthy diets are automatically good for your looks but special foods can achieve a special purpose – a lack of essential minerals and vitamins is quick to show in lack-lustre hair and sallow skin.

You need calcium for good nails and teeth, iron for renewing blood cells and proteins for glowing skin. Too much fat in your diet may result in spots and pimples, but if you take too little you may be depriving yourself of essential vitamins. A diet which is too low in 'roughage' will almost certainly lead to constipation; eating too many foods with a high cholesterol content can lead to heart disease ...

THE TWELVE-DAY REGENERATION DIET

This is essentially a health plan that recharges the body as well as knocking off some pounds and inches. And it is not a bore – it is a gourmet approach to health and slimming that has been created following the basic nutrition principles of Professor Wolfgang Goetze-Claren. An integral part of his genetic therapy is his alternating three-day diet: three days of vegetables only, three days with fish or meat as well. The idea is that the vegetables help to detoxify the body. The diet should be followed for a minimum of twelve days. All food must be fresh, nothing tinned or frozen. Certain wines, as specified, are allowed, but only on the fish and meat days.

Breakfast: the same every day: muesli and tea with lemon. Muesli makes a healthy start to the day, and although made with oats it is energy-giving and not fattening when eaten raw. Mix together 1 level tablespoon oatmeal, soaked overnight in 3 tablespoons water (not the quick variety of oats, the old-fashioned rolled oats are best) and 1 dessertspoon each of lemon juice and natural honey; sprinkle on top 1 unpeeled grated apple. These quantities are sufficient for one portion.

DAY I
Lunch: cucumber and green bean salad*
Dinner: mushrooms à la grecque* with spinach à l'orange*

DAY 2
Lunch: blackberry and melon cup*
Dinner: Russian borsch* and glazed asparagus*

DAY 3
Lunch: herb salad with tomatoes and raisins*
Dinner: artichokes espagnole*

DAY 4
Lunch: chicken salad*
Dinner: lemon soup* and salmon-wrapped
   broccoli*

DAY 5
Lunch: sweetbreads in sherry*
Dinner: caviar wafers* and steak americaine* with
   spinach and bacon salad*

DAY 6
Lunch: crab and cucumber salad*
Dinner: raisin soup* and pigeon in white wine* with
   orange and olive salad*

DAY 7
Lunch: pear and watercress salad*
Dinner: sliced tomato served with mustard and
   cress and a little chopped onion; onion and
   apple casserole*

DAY 8
Lunch: health salad Pietro*
Dinner: cold cucumber soup* and onion and to-
   mato salad*

DAY 9
Lunch: stuffed tomatoes (iv)*
Dinner: aubergine and tomato pie*

DAY 10
Lunch: steak tartare* and watercress
Dinner: spinach hors d'oeuvres* and truite au bleu*

DAY 11
Lunch: chicken liver pâté* and tossed green salad*
Dinner: oysters with lemon juice and chicken
   provençale*

DAY 12
Lunch: figs and prosciutto*
Dinner: cucumber salad (i)* with calf's tongue* and
   beans

Drinks: no coffee or milk. Drink tea with lemon and
as much herbal tea as you like. Tea can be taken
after each meal. Fruit juices and carrot juice are
permitted in between.

Flavourings: it is important to use as little salt as
possible and then only sea-salt. Be herb-happy; a
liberal use can compensate for lack of salt. Pepper
is fine, garlic too. No white sugar – sweeten with
natural honey or unrefined sugar.

Dressings: this is the standard diet dressing to be
used for all salads: ¾ cup olive oil, ¼ cup vinegar,
juice of 1 lemon, 1 teaspoon grated onion, 1
crushed garlic clove, ½ teaspoon dry mustard, ¼
teaspoon paprika. Blend all together until smooth.
The dressing should be used very sparingly as a lift
to the salad. Herbs can be added if desired.

Extras: thin wafers and water biscuits can be
substituted for bread. No other extras, not even a
nut.

Wines: wine is permitted only on days when meat
and fish are included in the diet. Follow the rule of
white wine for white meats and fish, red for the
reds, but bear in mind the old saying: white wine
for lovers, red wine for dozers. So if you want more
energy, stay with the whites. The ideal is a glass for
both lunch and dinner, and it should be drunk
during the meal, not before or afterwards. (As a
liqueur, a digestive such as Fernet Branca can be
taken, with a full glass of water.)

Desserts: after each meal any citrus fruit, berries,
apple or pear – just one. *No* bananas; *no* other
dessert; *no* cheese.

Quantities: quantities have not been included in the
menus because most dishes are suitable for the
family and it is up to you to be sensible and take
small portions.

ARBOUR 1930

STATUS QUO DIET

The status quo diet-day for people who want to stay as they are: some experts believe that one day a week of light eating is good for both weight control and digestion. This diet was worked out by Swiss chemists and a London dietician.

Breakfast
Juice of 1 fresh orange and 1 fresh lemon
Thin slice of starch-reduced bread with a little butter and a small teaspoon of marmalade
Tea or coffee with not more than $\frac{1}{4}$ pint (1.4 dl) milk with synthetic sweetener

Mid-morning
Whisk an egg and add a little sweetener; heat $\frac{1}{4}$ pint (1.4 dl) milk, flavoured with two tablespoons of strong coffee to just below boiling point; pour this mixture slowly on to the egg, whisking, and drink while it is still frothy and foaming

Lunch
Tablespoonful of salted peanuts
Juice of fresh orange with soda water
Black coffee

Tea
Lemon tea, sweetened to taste

Supper
Balkan soup*
Cheese and coleslaw salad
Cinnamon-flavoured coffee

PURIFYING DIET

The important thing in this diet is not to eat between meals. Don't be concerned with measuring amounts of food: the object is to cleanse the whole system. Drink as much water as you like when you like. Follow the diet one day a week.

Morning
1 glass warm lemon water with $\frac{1}{4}$ teaspoon honey (a good source of vitamin C and energy)

Natural yogurt (for vitamins B-1, B-2, calcium and phosphorous) with a generous sprinkling of yeast. The natural bacteria of the yogurt and yeast help to clean out the system
Dandelion root – a fine blood purifier – roasted and ground is better for you than coffee. It destroys the acid in the blood and creates a better balance throughout the system

Lunch
1 glass diluted carrot juice – a rich source of vitamin A, good for vision and skin. Diluting the pure juice makes it lighter and more palatable
Wholegrain rice, rich in niacin, folic acid and B-1
1 apple – good source of vitamin C and a diuretic

Dinner
Red soya beans – rich in protein and good for the kidneys. Eat after soaking for twenty-four hours
Raw spinach – a good source of vitamins A, K, B-1, B-2, folic acid, iron and calcium; eaten with bran or wholewheat bread to provide ideal roughage

Before bed
$\frac{1}{2}$ glass lemon water

BEAUTY DIET

It is not only what you eat but the way you eat that affects your face and figure. Eat too much and the excess is stored as fat; eat too little and you are deprived of essential vitamins and minerals.

Good skin depends on good food: for instance skin may be oily because it lacks vitamin B-2 (best source, liver; good source, milk). Pimples may be the result of shortage of vitamin B-6 (pyridoxine) – good sources: pork and bananas. Taking the pill can increase the need for vitamin B-6 and folic acid (liver, green vegetables, yeast). Vitamin A is excellent for skin health (liver, eggs, milk, butter, green vegetables). Dry skins may be in need of the B vitamins, pantothenic acid and niacin (pantothenic acid is found in most fresh foods; niacin in liver, meat, yeast).

DAY 1

Breakfast
½ grapefruit
Grilled or poached kipper
2 slices bread or toast
Tea or coffee

Lunch
4 oz (115 g) roast stuffed pork* or 1 stuffed pork
    chop*
1 roast potato
Braised cabbage
Fresh fruit or yogurt

Dinner
Consommé
Cold fresh salmon
Mixed salad
Bavarian coffee*

DAY 2

Breakfast
Stewed fruit
1 boiled egg
2 slices toast
Tea or coffee

Lunch
4 oz (115 g) cold roast pork
Coleslaw
1 slice bread
1 glazed orange*

Dinner
½ grapefruit
Baked halibut with mushroom sauce*
Peas
Creamed potato
Fresh fruit salad

DAY 3

Breakfast
1 glass orange juice
2 slices grilled bacon and 2 tomatoes
1 slice toast
Tea or coffee

Lunch
Cheese omelette (2 eggs)
Green salad
1 slice bread
Fresh fruit or yogurt

Dinner
French onion soup*
Carbonnade of beef*
Vichy carrots
Jacket potatoes
Apple snow*

DAY 4

Breakfast
1 glass grapefruit juice
1 scrambled egg
1 slice toast
Tea or coffee

Lunch
2 fresh sardines
Stuffed tomatoes (i)*
1 slice bread
Rhubarb fool (ii)*

Dinner
Sweet-corn soup*
Kidney sauté turbigo*
Spinach
Creamed potato
Crème caramel*

DAY 5

Breakfast
Stewed prunes
4 oz (115 g) poached smoked haddock
1 grilled tomato
2 slices bread or toast
Tea or coffee

Lunch
Stuffed courgettes*
Runner beans, fresh or frozen
1 oz (30 g) cheese
1 water biscuit

Dinner
1 slice melon
6 oz (170 g) rump steak
Ratatouille (ii)*
Game chips
Queen of puddings*

DAY 6

Breakfast
Sliced orange
1 poached egg
1 slice toast
Tea or coffee

Lunch
Spanish omelette (2 eggs) (ii)*
Spinach
Fresh fruit or yogurt

Dinner
Liver pâté
1 grilled trout
Carrots
Sauté potatoes
Pear in red wine*

DAY 7

Breakfast
1 glass fruit juice
2 slices grilled bacon
2 tomatoes
1 slice toast
Tea or coffee

Lunch
Cottage cheese, celery and walnut salad*
1 slice bread
Baked stuffed apple*

Dinner
Oeuf en cocotte*
Chicken sauté bergère*
Runner beans, fresh or frozen
Pilaff
Lemon snow*

BODY TONING DIET

Necks tend to 'dry out' during the winter when they are constantly covered; faces become dry and dull because of diet and temperature changes. To help control excessive moisture loss use a rich moisturizer *every* day and try this four-day diet by Marina Andrews for all-over toning of the body and the face.
Possible weight loss: 7–8 lb (3.2–3.6 kg).
Time: four days.

DAY 1

Morning, noon and evening:
Two glasses – approximately $\frac{3}{4}$ pint (4.3 dl) in all – of any fresh fruit juice to which two level teaspoons of Yeastamin (yeast powder available from chemists) are added, plus three tablespoons of pure lemon juice mixed with a little hot water which you must take with each fruit juice drink. Nothing else is permitted.

DAY 2

Breakfast
Lemon juice as on first day, but with 1 level
    teaspoon Yeastamin
1 lightly boiled egg
1 thin small slice of toast with a scrape of butter
1 cup black coffee

Lunch
1 large glass vegetable juice (up to $\frac{1}{2}$ pint)
1 small carton cottage cheese
1 cup black coffee

Dinner
1 lightly boiled egg
1 thin small slice of toast with a little butter
1 small but black coffee

DAY 3
Liquid only, as for first day.

DAY 4
Same as second day.

ENERGY ON 2000 CALORIES A DAY

Many people will swear that they will get fat on a diet that yields 2,000 Calories a day: this means they are not exercising enough. To get energy you must spend energy. With exercise your circulation heightens, your vitality increases, you feel good. If you cut your food intake to avoid weight gain, you may also cut your activity level.

Never skip a meal. In particular never skip breakfast – if you do, you will be feeling tired by 10.30 a.m., and probably take sugar in your coffee or a sweet biscuit, because the sugar is what you lack. Not only that, but you will be half-way through the day before you begin taking the real food that contains your diet essentials. If you follow no-breakfast with a mid-morning snack, a hurried lunch and a big meal at night you are getting the energy you really need during the day just before going to bed: you are asking your body to bank the food energy with a food load followed by no activity.

Breakfast
Fruit or juice
Cereal and milk
1 egg cooked any way you like (or whip it raw into your orange juice)
Wholewheat toast with butter or margarine; jam if you wish
1 glass milk
Coffee or tea

Lunch
Soup or fruit juice
Meat or protein dish
Green or yellow vegetable
Green salad or tomato salad
1 slice bread and butter or margarine
1 piece fruit

Dinner
Clear soup or fruit juice
Meat, fish or poultry (lean, 3–4 oz, 85–115 g)
Potato, rice or pasta

Green or yellow vegetable, or green salad
1 slice wholemeal bread; butter or margarine if you wish
Fruit
Tea or coffee

If there is a long gap between dinner and bedtime have a glass of milk or an apple or pear.

Energy foods
Bread: one slice three times a day. Wholewheat; not sweet or fancy breads.
Cereal: one portion, hot or cold.
Eggs: three to five during the week. One each day if you love them. They are an excellent protein source but they tend to be high in cholesterol.
Fruit: twice a day or more. Citrus – for vitamin C – at least once. Fresh fruit juice counts as fruit.
Vegetables: two portions or more. Always one dark green vegetable and one yellow one for vitamin A. Salads often.
Meat, fish, poultry, cheese: two portions a day, not more than 5 oz (140 g) in all. Keep meat lean and all dishes simply prepared without rich sauces.
Sugar, fats: maximum of 4 teaspoons of each daily. Sugar includes jam, honey, syrup. Fat includes butter, oil, mayonnaise, cream.
Soups, drinks: cream soups can be very high in calories; some clear soups contain too much salt – a potential high-blood pressure threat. Drink milk once or twice a day.

Snacks
Include snacks if they are part of your energy-intake pattern, but remember that they are part of your day's diet. Choose crudités low in calories and rich in vitamins. Nuts are good basic food – but think of them as part of a meal, not just for nibbling: a dozen almonds or twenty peanuts contain 100 Calories.

Water
You have a marvellous device for regulating the correct amount of water to drink. It is called thirst. If your tissues need either more or less fluid than your thirst tells you to take, only your doctor should direct a change.

Alcohol

Bear in mind that it is high in energy and high in calories; there are about 150 Calories in a standard cocktail. If you have three they amount to 450 Calories – or over 20 per cent of your day's calorie allowance – without any protein or vitamins and hardly any minerals. If you really want a cocktail sacrifice your day's sugar allowance; do not give up bread, potatoes or milk to make room for it. Good alternatives: Perrier water with a slice of lemon, white wine with soda.

IRON-FOR-ENERGY DIET

Good sources of iron are found in lean meat. According to recent studies, the iron in eggs, beans and green vegetables is more easily absorbed when it is eaten with meat. Lack of iron, besides lowering haemoglobin (the blood substance that carries oxygen to the tissues), can cause depression and lethargy. Some people who are anaemic have no warning symptoms and those most often at risk are young children, fast growing teenagers and pregnant women. Unless you are suffering from a rare iron-storage disease (which usually only affects men) you cannot eat too much iron-containing food.

Guidelines for an eating plan high in iron levels, therefore high in energy levels

1. Have a green salad once every day, even in the coldest weather. It is just what your red cells need.
2. Vitamin C aids the absorption of iron into the blood. Fresh fruit and vegetables are good sources of vitamin C but most of it is lost during cooking. Always cook leafy green vegetables in boiling water for a few minutes only.
3. Wines, unlike spirits, are good sources of minerals and can help you to relax – essential to

good nutrition. A little – up to half a bottle of wine with dinner – can be good for digestion; a lot inflames the digestive tract.

Breakfast
Cereal
Fresh fruit or vegetable juice
Poached egg on a thin slice of lightly buttered wholemeal toast
Apple or orange
Tea or coffee

Lunch
Lean meat and a green salad whenever possible; occasionally substitute fish, cheese or poultry for the lean meat

Dinner
Meat and one green leafy vegetable
Fresh fruit

EXTRA ENERGY DIET

For more stamina, less pounds, follow this energy diet, worked out by Marina Andrews, for three days.

Before breakfast
1 cup of lemon or herbal tea with $\frac{1}{2}$ teaspoon honey and 1 multi-vitamin tablet

Breakfast
Vitality cup: take a 5 oz (140 g) carton natural yogurt, the juice of 1 orange (or 2 tablespoons thawed frozen unsweetened orange juice concentrate), 1 fresh egg and 1 teaspoon wheatgerm; whisk all ingredients together and drink at once

Lunch
These dishes are rich in iron which is essential for forming red blood cells, which help to give you energy:
1 large glass tomato juice with salt and pepper to taste

2 small lean lamb cutlets *or* 1 large lean chop *or* 2 medium slices of liver (un-floured) sautéed in a pan with a little oil, onion and garlic, and a carton of natural yogurt, added when the liver is almost cooked *or* 2–3 kidneys cooked in the same way *or* 1 medium steak cooked rare *or* 4 oz (115 g) steak tartare
Generous helping of spinach or any dark green leaf vegetable
Side salad made from fresh chopped parsley dressed with a little oil and lemon

6–8 stewed prunes with a little natural yogurt if you wish

Dinner
The same as for breakfast – the vitality cup, plus 1 cup of lemon or herbal tea

Note: In addition you may have up to $\frac{1}{2}$ pint (2.8 dl) tomato juice a day and two glasses of water. But *nothing else.*

VITALITY EATING PLAN

There is no need to change your eating plan drastically from summer to winter; but do try to incorporate all the foods in season – especially fresh fruits and vegetables which provide essential vitamins and minerals as well as a useful amount of natural fibre. As they have a high water content they are low in calories and play an important part in any weight-reducing programme.
Possible weight loss: 4–5 lb (1.8–2.3 kg).
Time: ten days.

Daily allowances: $\frac{1}{2}$ pint (2.8 dl) skimmed milk or $\frac{1}{4}$ pint (1.4 dl) ordinary milk; 1 glass dry red or white wine; artificial sweeteners in coffee and tea; as much black coffee, lemon tea, water, mineral water, low-calorie drinks and squashes as you want; not more than 1 oz (30 g) low-calorie spread.

Follow this diet for only ten days at a time, using it again if necessary after five weeks.

DAY 1

Breakfast
$\frac{1}{2}$ grapefruit
1 small grilled kipper
Coffee or tea

Light meal
Green pepper and mushroom omelette (2 eggs)
Small green salad

Main meal
Slice honeydew or $\frac{1}{2}$ Ogen melon
Ham and avocado salad*

DAY 2

Breakfast
1 glass melon vitality drink*

Light meal
5 oz (140 g) smoked trout with 1 tablespoon horse-radish sauce
1 slice wholemeal bread

Main meal
$\frac{1}{2}$ avocado with 1 tablespoon vinaigrette
3 thin slices roast beef with 1 roast potato
Large helping any green vegetables

DAY 3

Breakfast
1 glass orange juice
1 boiled egg with 1 slice wholemeal bread
Coffee or tea

Light meal
Tuna-stuffed aubergine*
Piece of fresh fruit

Main meal
Tomato juice cocktail*
Lamb kebab* and large green salad
3 tablespoons rice
1 avocado and lime cream*

DAY 4

Breakfast
8–10 fresh dates
3 oz (85 g) cottage cheese
2 crispbreads lightly spread with butter
Coffee or tea

Light meal
Crunchy avocado salad*
1 slice wholemeal bread

Main meal
1 slice honeydew melon
6 oz (170 g) grilled steak
Slimmers' ratatouille*

DAY 5

Breakfast
1 carton natural yogurt with 1 tablespoon wheat-
    germ and 2 teaspoons honey
Coffee or tea

Light meal
Large portion slimmers' ratatouille*
2 slices lean ham

Main meal
Slimmers' mussels*
Baked chicken joint
Large helping green beans
1 potato baked in jacket with avocado topping*

DAY 6

Breakfast
½ Ogen melon
1 slice wholemeal bread
Coffee or tea

Light meal
Avocado niçoise*
1 slice wholemeal bread

Main meal
Consommé
2 lamb cutlets
Large helping steamed courgettes
Large helping broccoli
Lemon sorbet

DAY 7

Breakfast
10 fresh dates
½ carton natural yogurt
1 slice wholemeal bread
Coffee or tea

Light meal
Avocado with scrambled egg
1 piece of fresh fruit

Main meal
1 slice honeydew melon
Stuffed sole in wine sauce*
2 small boiled potatoes
Green vegetables
1 portion Camembert with celery
2 water biscuits

DAY 8

Breakfast
1 orange
1 poached egg on toast
Coffee or tea

Light meal
3 oz (85 g) Parma ham, slice of melon

Main meal
½ grilled grapefruit
Pork chop (approx. 6 oz, 170 g) grilled with
    piquant sauce*
2 grilled tomatoes
Large helping spinach
Small bunch black grapes

DAY 9

Breakfast
1 glass grapefruit juice
2 well-grilled rashers of bacon
1 grilled tomato
1 slice wholemeal toast
Coffee or tea

Light meal
Slice of honeydew melon
Egg florentine*

Main meal
Consommé
Stuffed green peppers (iii)*
2 tablespoons boiled rice
1 piece of fresh fruit

DAY 10

Breakfast
½ Ogen melon
1 slice wholemeal bread

Light meal
Avocado and lemon soup*
Mozzarella and tomato salad*

Main meal
Tomato juice cocktail*
Grilled liver and bacon
Large helping green salad
Baked apple stuffed with dates*

HOLIDAY VITALITY PLAN

A holiday gives the opportunity of changing your routine: different kinds of food, different meal times, more leisure. Try Marina Andrews' Eastern Apple Diet for four days.

Eastern Apple Diet

Breakfast
1 teacup eastern apple (see below)
1 glass lemon tea (no sugar)

Lunch
2 boiled eggs with a little salt and pepper
1 teacup eastern apple
1 glass lemon tea

Dinner
2 tablespoons tuna fish or salmon with lemon juice
  and pepper, served with watercress
1 teacup eastern apple
1 glass lemon tea

Eastern apple: peel 9 crisp fresh apples and shred them into a large bowl. Mix together 1 wineglass rose-water with 4 teacups water and 1 flat teaspoon brown sugar, pour over the apples, cover and place at the bottom of the refrigerator overnight. Eat the next day.

FIBRE DIET

Start the morning with a super-charged breakfast that has enough power almost to see you through the day. In itself it provides the essential daily nutrients and vitamins; it is balanced by a lunch of fruit and vegetables only, by a dinner of vegetables for two days and including meat, fish, eggs or cheese every third day. It is a plan that stresses the value of grains and fibre foods. It can be followed regularly for health and vitality reasons; it can be adjusted to slimming by cutting down lunch to just a grapefruit (but check with your doctor first).
Possible weight loss (slimming version): 5 lb (2.3 kg).
Time: seven days.

Breakfast
1 fresh orange or apple (not just the juice)
Large bowl of raw oats soaked overnight in water.

with 1 tablespoon honey, raw nuts, sesame seeds, a small carton of plain yogurt (preferably home-nurtured) and choice of papaya, pineapple, pear or apple (in that order)
1 cup herb tea (coffee with a little milk, if you must)
1 slice wholemeal bread and a scraping of butter, topped with cheese and grilled

Lunch
For dieters: 1 grapefruit
For non-dieters: Mixed salad or fresh vegetables cooked in a little water, steamed or made into soup
1 slice wholemeal bread
1 portion any fruit

Dinner
For two days: 1 plate fresh vegetables, boiled, steamed or braised in the oven
For one day: meat, fish, eggs or cheese with fresh cooked vegetables or salad
1 portion fruit

Drinking rules
- 4 large glasses water a day.
- 2 glasses wine with dinner on protein days, 1 glass wine on vegetable days, 1 glass white wine for slimmers.
- Try to drink herb teas instead of coffee – they do not need sweetening or milk.

Bread rules
- Stick to the wholemeal varieties.
- Try to find breads made from bran.
- Do not eat more than two slices a day.

Sugar rules
- Cut it out completely, whether as a sweetener or in cakes and biscuits, etc.

Fat rules
- Vegetable oils for cooking and dressings.
- A little butter for spreading on bread.

THE FAT-MODIFIED DIET

This diet was specially prepared by the American Heart Association to reduce the risk of heart attack: it is a fat-controlled low-cholesterol meal plan. Every day you must choose foods from each of the basic food groups in lists 1–5.

1. Meat, poultry, fish, dried beans and peas, nuts, eggs
One serving: 3–4 oz (85–115 g) cooked meat or fish (not including bone or fat) *or* 3–4 oz (85–115 g) of a vegetable listed here. Eat two or more servings (a total of 6–8 oz, 170–225 g) or more daily.

Recommended
- Chicken, turkey, veal or fish in most of your meat meals for the week.
- Shellfish – clams, crab, lobster, oysters, scallop, etc. Use a 4 oz (115 g) serving as a substitute for meat.
- Beef, lamb, pork and ham less frequently. Choose lean, minced meat and lean cuts of meat. Trim all visible fat before cooking. Bake, grill, roast or stew so that you can discard the fat which cooks out of the meat.
- Nuts and dried beans and peas: kidney beans, baked beans, lentils, split peas and chick peas are high in vegetable protein and may be used in place of meat occasionally.
- Egg whites as desired.

Avoid or use sparingly
- Duck and goose.
- Heavily marbled and fatty meats, spare ribs, mutton, frankfurters, sausages, fatty hamburgers, bacon and luncheon meats.
- Offal – liver, kidney, heart and sweetbreads – is very high in cholesterol. Since liver is very rich in vitamins and iron, it should not be eliminated from the diet completely. Use a 4 oz (115 g) serving in a meat meal no more than once a week.

● Egg yolks: limit to three a week, including eggs used in cooking. Cakes, batters, sauces and other foods contain egg yolks.

● Shrimps are moderately high in cholesterol. Use a 4 oz (115 g) serving in a meat meal no more than once a week.

2. Breads and cereals (wholegrain, enriched or restored)

At least four servings daily. One serving of bread: 1 slice; one serving of cereal: ½ cup (4 oz, 115 g) cooked *or* 8 fl oz (2.3 dl) cold, with skimmed milk.

Recommended

● Breads made with a minimum of saturated fat: white enriched, wholewheat, French bread, oatmeal bread, pumpernickel and rye bread.

● Scones, muffins and pancakes made at home, using liquid oil as shortening.

● Cereal (hot and cold), rice, melba toast, matzo, pretzels.

● Pasta: macaroni, noodles (except egg noodles) and spaghetti.

Avoid or use sparingly

● Butter rolls, commercial scones, muffins, doughnuts, sweet rolls, cakes, crackers, biscuits, egg bread, cheese bread and commercial mixes containing dried eggs and whole milk.

3. Vegetables and fruit

Fresh, frozen or canned – eat at least four servings daily. One serving: ½ cup (4 oz, 115 g).

Recommended

● One serving should be a source of vitamin C: broccoli, cabbage (raw), tomatoes; berries, grapefruit (or juice), mango, melon, orange (or juice), papaya, strawberries, tangerines.

● One serving should be a source of vitamin A: dark green leafy or yellow vegetables, or yellow fruits – broccoli, carrots, chard, chicory, greens (beet, collard, dandelion, mustard, turnip), kale, peas, kohlrabi, spinach, French beans, runner beans, sweet potatoes and yams, watercress, marrow, sweet-corn; apricots, cantaloupe, mango, papaya.

● Other vegetables and fruits are also very nutritious; they should be eaten raw in salads, main dishes, snacks and desserts, in addition to the recommended daily allowances of high vitamin A and C vegetables and fruits.

Avoid or use sparingly

If you must limit your calories, use vegetables such as potatoes and sweet-corn sparingly. To add variety to your diet, one serving (½ cup, 4 oz, 115 g) may be substituted for one serving of bread or cereals.

4. Milk products

One serving: 8 fl oz (2.3 dl) skimmed milk that has been fortified with vitamins A and D.

Daily quantities: children up to twelve: 24 fl oz (6.8 dl) or more; teenagers: 32 fl oz (9 dl) or more; adults: 16 fl oz (4.5 dl) or more.

Recommended

● Milk products that are low in dairy fats: fortified skimmed (non-fat) milk and fortified skimmed milk powder and low-fat milk. The label on the container should show that the milk is fortified with vitamins A and D. The word 'fortified' alone is not enough.

● Buttermilk made from skimmed milk, yogurt made from skimmed milk, tinned, evaporated, skimmed milk and cocoa made with low-fat milk.

● Cheese made from skimmed or partially skimmed milk, such as cottage cheese, creamed or uncreamed (preferably uncreamed).

Avoid or use sparingly

● Whole milk and whole milk products: chocolate milk, canned whole milk, ice-cream, creams, including soured and whipped, and whole-milk yogurt.

● Non-dairy cream substitutes (usually contain coconut oil, which is very high in saturated fat).

● Cheese made from cream or whole milk.

● Butter.

5. Fats and oils (polyunsaturated)

An individual allowance should include about 2–4 tablespoons daily (depending on how many calories you can afford) in the form of margarine, salad dressing and cooking fat.

Recommended
Margarines, liquid oil shortenings, salad dressings and mayonnaise containing any of these polyunsaturated vegetable oils: corn oil, cottonseed oil, safflower oil, sesame-seed oil, soya-bean oil and sunflower seed oil.

   Margarines and other polyunsaturates can be identified by their label which lists a recommended liquid vegetable oil as the first ingredient and one or more partially hydrogenated vegetable oils as additional ingredients.

   Diet margarines are low in calories because they are low in fat. Therefore it takes twice as much diet margarine to supply the polyunsaturates contained in a recommended margarine.

Avoid or use sparingly
Solid fats and shortenings: butter, lard, salt pork fat, meat fat, completely hydrogenated margarines and vegetable shortenings and products containing coconut oil. Peanut oil and olive oil may be used occasionally for flavour, but they are low in polyunsaturates and do not take the place of recommended oils.

6. Desserts, beverages, snacks, seasonings
The foods on this list are acceptable because they are low in saturated fat and cholesterol. If you have eaten your daily allowance from the first five lists, however, these foods will be in excess of your nutritional needs and may also exceed your calorie limits for maintaining a desirable weight. If you must limit your calories, limit your portions as well.

   Moderation should be observed, especially in the use of alcoholic drinks, sweets and bottled drinks.

Acceptable
Low in calories or no calories: fresh fruit and tinned fruit without sugar, tea, coffee (no cream), cocoa powder, water ices, gelatine, fruit whip, puddings made with non-fat milk, low-calorie drinks, vinegar, mustard, ketchup, herbs and spices.

High in calories
Frozen or canned fruit with sugar added, jelly, jam, marmalade, honey, pure sugar sweets such as gum drops, boiled sweets, ice-cream made with safflower oil, cakes, biscuits, pies and puddings made with polyunsaturated fats, nuts, especially walnuts, peanut butter, bottled drinks, fruit drinks, wine, beer and whisky.

Avoid or use sparingly
Coconut and coconut oil, commercial cakes, pies, biscuits and mixes, frozen cream pies and cakes, commercially fried foods such as potato chips, whole milk puddings, chocolate pudding (high in cocoa butter and therefore high in saturated fat) and ice-cream.

FOR CELLULITE

This is a three-part plan: a basic reducing diet incorporating special juices and teas, an application and a friction lotion. All these working together should help disperse obvious cellulite in four weeks. It is the constant daily persistence that makes it work.

The diet
This diet has been worked out by Nevil von Stenberg, a dietician who does wonders for reshaping bodies by deftly balancing natural foods, vegetable juice and herbal tisanes. This slimming plan can be continued for a month if necessary but two weeks is the normal period.

On waking
A glass of hot water with the juice of $\frac{1}{2}$ lemon

Breakfast (to be taken twenty minutes after the initial drink)
$\frac{1}{3}$ each of cucumber, beetroot and carrot juice (the cucumber acts as a diuretic to take away excess water; the other two vegetables give energy and vitamins)
Fresh fruit salad – any fruits except banana

Lunch
Large glass of the same vegetable juice

Dinner
1 sliced ripe tomato topped with lemon juice and a drop of oil, a touch of sea-salt and basil or marjoram for flavouring. A small quantity of oil is necessary daily because some vitamins and minerals cannot be absorbed without oil)
2 steamed non-starch vegetables (string beans, cabbage, carrots, parsnips, turnips, courgettes or celery) with a very little butter
2 slices grilled liver or other lean meat

Bedtime
1 glass of vegetable juice

Drinks
Herbal tea – an infusion of equal parts couch grass roots and peppermint
No water; drink more vegetable juices if desired

The application
To be done daily. Chop leaves and stalks of common ivy and put two handfuls in $1\frac{3}{4}$ pints (1 l) water; boil for 10–15 minutes. When tepid, soak cotton-wool pads in it, place between two pieces of gauze and put on cellulitic areas, bandaging firmly into place. Leave for 20 minutes.

The lotion
To firm the flabby skin that often results from weight or cellulite reduction the lotion should be rubbed over the skin in a friction manner at least once a day. To make, pre-boil $1\frac{3}{4}$ pints (1 l) water so that the calcium precipitates and is poured off; when the water is tepid add $\frac{1}{3}$ oz (10 g) each of lavender flowers, nettle and lesser celandine. Leave for twenty-four hours, filter and use. Do not make more than 2 pints (1.1 dl) at a time; a freshly made supply is more effective.

BENITO 1929

BARKENTIN

WATER SHAPE-UPS

Your body is about two-thirds water – roughly 9 gallons (41 l) if you weigh 120 lb (54 kg), and water provides the perfect medium for shaping up. Swimming is the best all-over exerciser. Adapting floor exercises to water is another way to fitness; any movement you do in water is more effective than out, because water resists your movements, gives muscles more of a challenge. And since water seems to relieve any feeling of muscular strain, work-outs seem like play. If ever there were a lazy way to exercise, this is it. In addition you never feel sweaty. Remember that to reap these benefits, the muscles you are working on must be under the water. For these exercises, you need the side of a pool or a raft.

1. Legs and abdomen – Keep the weight on the elbows, back flat against wall, legs elevated and toes near surface, 1a. Open legs wide like scissors and close them together again, 1b. Repeat 8 times.

2. Legs and abdomen – Keep your back flat against the wall, right knee bent and foot against the wall. Lift the left foot up, swing it to the side and down. Repeat 8 times each leg.

3. Waist – Face the wall, legs together, stomach against wall. Lift both legs together and high to the right, down again, then to the left. Repeat 4 times each side.

4. Legs, arms and all-over stretching – Put feet and hands high up on pool or raft edge, knees bent as if you are ready to push off for back stroke, 4a. Keeping feet flat and hands on wall, straighten the legs, bending the body over the legs, 4b. Repeat 8 times.

5. Legs *(left)* – Hoist yourself into a Russian split with the feet resting on the pool edge. Hold for 1 minute.

6. Thighs *(below left)* – Hold on to the pool edge with the left hand, extend the right leg behind you, knee bent, and, grasping the ankle, pull your foot up towards your body. Repeat 2 times each leg.

7. Overall stretch *(below)* – Face wall, right leg straight, touching wall, and lift the left leg out behind the body and swing it to the right. Repeat 4 times each side.

8. Abdomen and thighs *(above)* – Rest on the pool or raft edge with your elbows, keeping your back flat against the wall and knees to your chest, 8a. Straighten your legs out in front, toes up near the surface, 8b. Open legs wide to the sides, keeping them straight and flexing the feet, 8c. Hold legs out with the feet flexed tight for 4 seconds. Then bring legs together along the surface, and lower to pool bottom. Repeat 8 times, and increase as the summer progresses.

9. Legs and abdomen *(right)* – Hold the edge and your partner's outer hand. Bend inside knee and press outside sole against your partner's outside sole. Now stand straight, still pressing.

10. Waist *(right)* – Hold on to the pool edge or someone's hand and place the feet at the bottom of the pool wall. Raise free arm overhead and stretch. Switch sides. Repeat 16 times each side.

11. Abdomen and fun *(far right)* – Stand back to back, elbows linked. One bends forward, lifting partner on to his or her back.

WATSON

PART II

RECIPES

SOUP

Avocado and lemon soup

1 avocado
¾ pint (4.3 dl) good chicken stock
juice of 1 lemon
salt and pepper
1–2 tablespoons natural yogurt
Serves two

Scoop the flesh from the avocado and put in blender with a little of the chicken stock until the mixture is puréed. Add more stock, blend for a few seconds and turn the mixture into a bowl: add the rest of the chicken stock, stirring all the time. Add the lemon juice and season. Chill. Before serving stir in yogurt and garnish with lemon.

Balkan soup

½ carton low-fat natural yogurt
3 tablespoons tomato juice
1 hard-boiled egg, chopped
Serves one

Mix yogurt and tomato juice together and top with the egg.

Russian borsch

4 young beetroots, peeled and coarsely grated
2 cups water
juice of 1 lemon
1 teaspoon brown sugar
freshly ground black pepper
sour cream to garnish
Serves two

Simmer the beetroot in 2 cups of water for approximately 20 minutes. Stir in lemon juice, sugar and pepper. Cook for 6 more minutes, strain. Chill the clear borsch and garnish when serving with a small blob of sour cream.

Cucumber soup

1 small onion (chopped)
1½ pints (8.5 dl) chicken stock or water
1 cucumber
1 sprig mint
1 dessertspoon cornflour
salt and pepper
green colouring
shredded mint and diced cucumber for garnish
Serves four

Simmer the onion in the stock (or water) until soft – about 10 minutes. Peel and roughly chop the cucumber. Add to the stock with the sprig of mint and simmer for 7 minutes. Put through a sieve (or electric blender). Return to the saucepan. Blend the cornflour with a little cold water, add to the soup and boil for about 1 minute stirring continuously. Season well. Leave it to get completely cold in the refrigerator. Add a little artificial colouring if necessary. Garnish with very finely diced cucumber and shredded mint.

Cold cucumber soup

1 clove garlic
1 tablespoon olive oil
dash of salt
1 cup yogurt
1 small cucumber
½ lemon
1 cup cold water
chopped mint
Serves two

Crush the garlic and mix with olive oil and salt. Beat this into the yogurt. Peel, seed and chop the cucumber and blend this into the mixture together with the juice and rind of the lemon and the cold water. Add a little chopped mint. Chill.

Egg broth

2 pints (1.1 l) meat stock or broth
4 eggs
salt and pepper to taste
chopped parsley (optional)
Serves four

Heat the broth or stock to boiling point. Beat the eggs until very light. Remove the stock from the heat and pour the egg into it, whisking well to keep from curdling. Season and serve at once. Garnish with chopped parsley.

Gazpacho

2 large peeled ripe tomatoes
¼ peeled cucumber
2 tablespoons chopped green pepper
2 tablespoons vegetable salad oil
a little salt and freshly ground pepper
1 tablespoon wine vinegar
8 fl oz (2.3 dl) tomato juice
1 teaspoon grated onion
Serves seven

Chop tomatoes, cucumber and green pepper finely. Add rest of ingredients and chill. Or put everything in the electric blender. Serve in soup cups with an ice cube in the centre.

Green garden soup

1 bunch watercress
½ head lettuce
3 spring onions
4 stalks celery
3 cabbage leaves
handful parsley
sprig of thyme and marjoram
2 pints (1.1 l) fat-free chicken broth or consommé
salt and pepper
Serves three to four

Clean and chop watercress, lettuce, onions (tops and all), celery, cabbage leaves, parsley, thyme and marjoram and put in a pan with broth or consommé. Simmer for 40 minutes, season and serve.

Lemon soup

¼ cup rice
3 cups chicken stock
yolk of 1 egg
juice of 1 lemon
grated carrot
Serves two

Add the rice (thoroughly washed) to the boiling stock and boil for 30 minutes. Beat the egg yolk with the lemon juice. Pour in 1 cup of the broth, stirring rapidly. Take the soup from the heat and stir in the egg–broth mixture. Garnish with grated carrot and serve.

Lentil soup with ham

5 oz (140 g) cooked dried lentils, drained
1 oz (30 g) carrot, finely chopped
1 oz (30 g) onion, finely chopped
1 lettuce head, finely chopped
2 oz (55 g) finely diced celery
½ bayleaf

pinch thyme
1¼ pints (7 dl) water
2 chicken stock cubes
3 oz (85 g) lean smoked ham
salt and pepper
Serves two to three

Combine all the ingredients except salt and pepper in a saucepan. Simmer 30 minutes or until the vegetables are tender and the soup has thickened. Season to taste.

Onion soup

8 oz (225 g) onions
1½ pints (8.5 dl) stock
3 level tablespoons dried milk
salt and pepper
Serves four

Slice the onions finely and boil in the stock until tender. Sieve the soup. Beat in the dried milk. Alternatively cool the soup a little, add dried milk, and put all into the electric blender. Re-heat and season to taste.

French onion soup

3 medium-size onions
2 oz (55 g) butter
1½ pints (8.5 dl) water or stock
salt and pepper
½ pint (2.8 dl) milk
4 slices bread
4 slices Gruyère cheese
Serves four

Peel onions and cut into thin slices. Put the butter into a pan, add the sliced onions, cover and simmer for 15 minutes, stirring frequently. Add stock or water, and simmer for 1 hour. Add pepper, salt and milk. Re-heat. Toast the bread and cover each slice with Gruyère and put back under the grill until bubbling. Cut each slice into eight, place in individual serving dishes and pour the hot soup over. Serve immediately.

Quick onion soup

1⅜ oz (40 g) packet onion soup
1½ pints (8.5 dl) water and skimmed milk, mixed
2 tablespoons margarine
2 tablespoons flour
2 tablespoons Cheddar cheese, grated
pepper to taste
Serves four to six

Make soup with water and skimmed milk mixture. Melt margarine in separate saucepan. Stir in flour. Slowly stir in hot liquid. Add cheese. Cook until thickened and smooth. Pepper to taste.

Orange and tomato soup

2 lb (0.9 kg) tomatoes
1 onion
1 carrot
1 bayleaf
2 pints (1.1 l) stock
6 peppercorns
thinly pared rind of 1 lemon
1 orange
salt and pepper
Serves six

Cut and squeeze the seeds from the tomatoes. Sieve these and put the liquid into a pan with the sliced onion, carrot, bayleaf, stock, peppercorns and lemon rind. Cover and simmer for 25 minutes. Sieve or put through the Mouli. Meanwhile, thinly pare the orange rind, shred and blanch it. Add the juice to the soup. Season. When about to serve, stir well and add the orange rind.

Raisin soup

1 oz (30 g) raisins
olive oil
2 oz (55 g) fresh peas
2 oz (55 g) cut string beans
1½ pints (8.5 dl) boiling water
salt and pepper

thyme
$\frac{1}{4}$ cup cooked rice
Serves three to four

Soak the raisins in water for 1 hour. Put a little olive oil into a pan with the peas and string beans. Add the boiling water, seasoning and a little thyme. Cover and simmer for 3 hours. Add the rice and the raisins. Simmer for 30 minutes.

Spinach soup

2 lb (0.9 kg) spinach, carefully washed or 2 packages frozen spinach, thawed
1 onion, sliced
1 bayleaf
2 teaspoons salt
$\frac{1}{8}$ teaspoon freshly ground black pepper
4 cups chicken stock
2 tablespoons flour
1 cup milk
1 egg yolk
Serves six

Put the spinach in a saucepan with the onion, bayleaf, salt, pepper and stock. Bring to the boil and cook over low heat for 20 minutes. Discard the bayleaf. Rub the spinach mixture through a sieve or purée in an electric blender. Return to the saucepan. Mix the flour with a little of the milk to make a smooth paste. Add the remaining milk and stir into the soup, mixing steadily until boiling point. Reduce the heat and cook over a low heat for 10 minutes. Beat the egg yolk in a bowl and slowly beat in the hot soup, stirring constantly to prevent curdling. If the soup is re-heated, do not let it boil after the egg yolk is added.

Sweet-corn soup

1 rasher streaky green bacon
1 teaspoon chopped onion
1 small chopped stick of celery
1 teaspoon chopped green pepper
1 dessertspoon diced potato
$\frac{1}{2}$ bayleaf
$\frac{1}{2}$ pint (2.8 dl) milk and water
1 level teaspoon cornflour
1 tablespoon sweet-corn kernels
chopped parsley
Serves one

Dice bacon and fry gently until turning colour. Add the onion and celery. When golden, add the pepper, potato, bayleaf and liquid. Simmer until potatoes are cooked. Blend cornflour with 1 tablespoon water, add to soup and bring to boil, stirring. Add sweet-corn, simmer a few minutes and garnish with chopped parsley.

Tomato bouillon

2 oz (55 g) diced celery
2 oz (55 g) diced carrot
2 oz (55 g) diced onion
few sprigs of parsley
1$\frac{1}{2}$ pints (8.5 dl) tomato juice
$\frac{1}{4}$ teaspoon white pepper
6 whole cloves
1 bayleaf
$\frac{1}{8}$ teaspoon thyme
$\frac{3}{4}$ pint (4.3 dl) hot consommé (chicken or beef)
Serves four to six

Simmer celery, carrot, onion, parsley, tomato juice and seasonings, covered, for 1 hour. Strain, add the consommé and re-heat. Season to taste.

Cold vegetable soup

15 oz (425 g) tin green beans with liquid
15 oz (425 g) tin asparagus with liquid
$\frac{1}{2}$ teaspoon salt
2 tablespoons lemon juice
dash of pepper
mushrooms, sliced
chopped parsley
Serves four

Combine first five ingredients in electric blender and blend. Garnish with mushrooms and parsley.

Vegetable broth

1 carrot, washed not peeled
12 fresh green beans or mangetout peas
mushroom stems if you have them
2 stalks celery
1 onion
handful spinach or watercress or parsley
Serves two

Cover the vegetables with water and simmer until they are soft. Strain, season.

This is merely an outline. Any vegetable, including potato skins, can be used.

Watercress soup

1 tablespoon corn starch or potato starch
4 cups chicken stock
1 bunch watercress, chopped
1 egg yolk
1 cup skimmed milk
Serves five to six

Mix the starch to a smooth paste with a little of the stock, then stir in the remaining stock. Cook over a low heat, stirring, until it reaches boiling point. Cook for 5 minutes. Add the watercress and cook for 2 minutes. Beat the egg yolk and milk in a bowl and slowly beat in the hot soup, stirring to prevent curdling. Return to the pan and re-heat, but do not allow to boil. Season to taste.

Jellied watercress soup

4 cups tinned jellied consommé
2 cups watercress leaves
2 dessertspoons lime or lemon juice
chopped chives

1 hard-boiled egg white
Serves four

Purée in a blender half the jellied consommé and watercress leaves. Fold in the remaining consommé and the lime juice; chill. Serve jellied, garnished with chopped chives and grated hard-boiled egg white.

Yogurt soup

1 oz (30 g) raisins
8 fl oz (2.3 dl) cold water
20 fl oz (5.7 dl) yogurt
4 fl oz (1.1 dl) skimmed milk
1 chopped hard-boiled egg
6 ice cubes
¼ finely diced cucumber
2 dessertspoons finely chopped spring onion
1 dessertspoon chopped parsley
1 teaspoon dill
Serves six

Soak the raisins in cold water till puffed. Put the yogurt in a mixing bowl with the skimmed milk, chopped egg, ice cubes, cucumber and onion. Stir well. Add raisins and the water they soaked in. Refrigerate. Serve with chopped parsley and dill.

Iced yogurt soup

5 ice cubes
1 carton natural yogurt
1 teaspoon Worcestershire sauce
juice of ½ fresh lemon
8 large grapes, de-seeded, chopped
Serves one

Put ice cubes in a bowl and add other ingredients. Mix together and serve.

EGGS

Avocado with scrambled egg

1 oz (30 g) butter
4 large eggs, beaten
a dash of Worcestershire sauce
1 tablespoon milk
salt and pepper
2 rashers bacon, rolled up
1 ripe avocado
1 spring onion, chopped
Serves two

Melt the butter in a heavy-bottomed pan. Whisk the eggs, Worcestershire sauce, milk and seasoning together. Stir into butter and continue to stir from time to time. Grill the bacon rolls. Cut the avocado in half and remove the stone. Pile the eggs on top of the avocado, sprinkle with spring onions and put the bacon on top.

Cheese custard

4 egg yolks
12 fl oz (3.4 dl) skimmed milk
5¼ oz (150 g) grated Swiss cheese
⅛ teaspoon nutmeg
a little salt
4 egg whites
Serves four

Beat the egg yolks, add the skimmed milk, cheese, nutmeg and salt to taste. Fold in the stiffly beaten egg whites. Pour into a shallow casserole and bake at 350°F (180°C) for 30 minutes.

Spicy egg curry

2 cloves garlic, finely minced
1 large onion, finely minced
1 green chilli, minced (fresh or tinned)
1 teaspoon ground coriander
1 tablespoon corn oil
½ teaspoon chilli powder
1 teaspoon poppy seeds
1 teaspoon ground cumin
2 tablespoons sesame seeds
½ teaspoon salt
8 fl oz (2.3 dl) yogurt
2 tablespoons lemon juice
8 medium eggs, hard-boiled, shelled
Serves four

Cook the garlic, onion, chilli and coriander in oil until soft (about 3 minutes). Add the chilli powder, poppy seeds, cumin, sesame seeds and salt; cook 1 minute. Add the yogurt; stir. Add the lemon juice and cook for 5 minutes. Cut the eggs in half lengthwise, add them to the sauce and heat the mixture thoroughly.

Egg foo yung

4 oz (115 g) mushrooms
1 teaspoon salt
3 tablespoons water
4 oz (115 g) bean sprouts
3 eggs
3 spring onions, finely minced

1 teaspoon soy sauce
½ tablespoon corn oil
1 vegetable stock cube dissolved in 4 fl oz (1.1 dl) water
2 oz (55 g) thinly sliced bamboo shoots
½ tablespoon cornflour
Serves two

Wipe the mushrooms with a damp cloth. Cut 1 oz (30 g) into thick slices. Heat the saucepan, add ⅛ teaspoon salt and the sliced mushrooms. Stir continuously for 2 minutes. Add 1 tablespoon water and simmer until the mushrooms wilt. Reserve for sauce. Chop the remaining mushrooms and cook as above. Blanch the bean sprouts for ½ minute; drain and rinse with cold water. Beat the eggs and 2 tablespoons water till foamy. Combine with the chopped mushrooms, ¼ teaspoon salt, the bean sprouts, half the spring onions and the soy sauce. Heat the oil in a large frying pan and spoon out the egg mixture into several small pancakes. Cook 3–4 minutes on each side.

To make the sauce: combine the sliced mushrooms, the stock, the bamboo shoots, the rest of the spring onions and the cornflour in a saucepan; bring to the boil, stirring continuously and cook until thickened.

Egg florentine

¼ oz (7 g) butter
¼ oz (7 g) flour
2½ fl oz (70 ml) milk
salt and pepper
2 oz (55 g) spinach, cooked and cooled
1 egg, soft-boiled or poached
1 oz (30 g) grated Edam cheese
Serves one

Make a white sauce with the butter, flour, milk and seasoning. Put the cooled spinach in a fireproof dish with the egg on top. Cover with the white sauce and sprinkle with grated cheese. Brown in a hot oven (400–425°F, 200–220°C) for about 10 minutes.

Slimmers' French toast

1 egg
1 thin slice wholemeal or wheatgerm bread
salt and pepper
Serves one

Beat the egg and dip the bread in it; sprinkle with salt and pepper. Place the bread on a piece of tin foil and grill on both sides.

Oeuf en cocotte

knob butter
salt and pepper
1 egg
1 tablespoon cream
Serves one

Butter a cocotte dish, sprinkle with salt and pepper and break the egg into it. Stand in a tin of water in a moderate oven for 6–10 minutes until cooked. Warm the cream, season and spoon over the egg.

Oeufs en cocotte aux champignons

4 oz (115 g) button mushrooms
½ oz (15 g) butter
2½ fl oz (70 ml) single cream
salt and ground black pepper
6 eggs
Serves six

Slice the mushrooms very thinly and fry quickly in butter. Add single cream, salt and pepper. Divide the mushrooms between 6 cocotte dishes. Break an egg into each. Bake in a bain marie for 6–10 minutes at 275°F (140°C).

Oeufs en gelée

1½ dessertspoons unflavoured gelatine
3 cups well-seasoned chicken stock
12 tarragon leaves, fresh or preserved in vinegar
6 dessertspoons finely chopped ham

6 chilled poached eggs
lettuce
Serves six

Soften the gelatine in half a cup of chicken stock. Put over a low heat and stir to dissolve. Stir in the remaining stock. Set aside to cool. Pour $\frac{1}{8}$ in (3 mm) jelly in the bottom of 6 moulds of $\frac{1}{2}$ cup capacity, and refrigerate until set, about 30 minutes. Chill remaining gelatine until almost set. Drop tarragon leaves in boiling water for 30 seconds, plunge into cold water, dry, and chill. Dip in almost set jelly, and arrange in a cross on the jelly in the bottom of each mould. Sprinkle chopped ham on top and pour in a little more jelly. Chill until set. Place an egg in each mould. Pour in the remaining jelly to cover. Chill until well set, about 1 hour. Dip in hot water for 3–4 seconds, unmould and serve on lettuce on a chilled plate.

Fluffy omelette

2 eggs (can be made with 1 egg only, but a smaller size omelette pan must then be used)
pinch of salt
1 teaspoon butter
Serves one

Heat the omelette pan over a low flame. Pre-heat the grill. Separate egg yolks and whites. Whisk the egg yolks lightly. Whisk the egg whites with a pinch of salt until stiff. Fold the beaten whites into the yolks. Increase the heat under omelette pan and melt the butter. Pour the egg mixture into the pan, leave for a few seconds until the bottom has set very lightly, then push the omelette pan under the hot grill until well risen. Serve at once, with creamed mushrooms (see p. 164) or fresh or stewed fruit.

Omelette lorraine

1 chopped shallot
1 rasher bacon
small knob butter
2 eggs

$\frac{1}{2}$ oz (15 g) finely grated cheese
Serves one

Chop the shallot and bacon finely. Fry in the butter for a few minutes. Beat the eggs and season. Add to the hot pan, stirring once or twice. When the eggs are almost set, sprinkle with cheese, fold and serve.

Spanish omelette (i)

1 teaspoon oil
1 chopped onion
1 sliced tomato
$\frac{1}{2}$ chopped green pepper
2 eggs
2 tablespoons water
pinch of dried mixed herbs
salt and pepper
Serves one

Heat the oil in a non-stick pan and lightly fry the vegetables. Remove them and keep warm. Lightly beat the eggs with the water, herbs and a little salt and pepper. Pour the egg mixture into the pan, fry lightly, add the filling, fold the omelette in half and serve.

Spanish omelette (ii)

2 tablespoons mixed vegetables
1 tablespoon peeled, seeded and chopped tomatoes
1 dessertspoon olive oil
$\frac{1}{2}$ clove garlic, crushed
1 tablespoon sliced onion
salt and pepper
paprika
2 eggs
chopped parsley
Serves one

Mix vegetables and tomatoes. Heat the oil in a small frying pan. Add the garlic and onion and fry until soft. Add the vegetables, seasoning and paprika. Heat well. Beat the eggs lightly and pour into the pan. Stir once or twice then leave until just set. Brown under a hot grill. Serve sprinkled with parsley.

Poached eggs mornay

1 pint (5.7 dl) cheese sauce (see p. 181)
8 large eggs
Serves eight

Allow 2½ fl oz (70 ml) cheese sauce for each egg.
Place the very lightly poached eggs in a heatproof
serving dish. Cover with cheese sauce and put
under a hot grill for just a few seconds, no longer,
to colour the top.

Cheese buttermilk soufflé

1 tablespoon margarine
2 tablespoons flour
dash of pepper
6 fl oz (1.7 dl) buttermilk
2 oz (55 g) grated Cheddar cheese
3 eggs, separated
⅛ teaspoon dry mustard
1 teaspoon grated onion
½ teaspoon salt
pinch of cream of tartar
Serves two

Melt the margarine and stir in the flour and pepper.
Add the buttermilk slowly, stirring until the mixture thickens. Add the cheese and well-beaten egg
yolks, and cook until the cheese melts and the
mixture is smooth. Add the mustard and onion.
Cool. Beat the egg whites, salt and cream of tartar
until stiff and fold into the cheese mixture. Spoon
into an unbuttered baking dish. Bake at 350°F
(180°C) for 25 minutes.

Mushroom soufflé

1 lb (455 g) mushrooms
1 small onion, finely diced
4 tablespoons soft margarine
2 tablespoons flour
¼ pint (1.4 dl) chicken broth or skimmed milk
a little salt
4 egg yolks
4 egg whites
3½ oz (100 g) Parmesan cheese
Serves four to six

Wash and dry the mushrooms and detach the
stems, but do not peel. Chop the stems and sauté
with the onion in 1 tablespoon margarine. Make a
sauce with 2 tablespoons margarine, the flour, the
broth or skimmed milk and the salt. Add the
sautéed mushrooms and onions; cool. Beat the egg
yolks and fold into the mixture. Sauté the mushroom caps in the remaining tablespoon margarine.
Place in the lightly greased casserole, hollow side
up. Fold the stiffly beaten egg whites into the
cooled mixture. Pour over the mushroom caps.
Sprinkle with Parmesan cheese. Bake at 375°F
(190°C) for about 30 minutes, or until puffed and
brown.

Spinach soufflé

2 tablespoons margarine
3 tablespoons flour
8 fl oz (2.3 dl) skimmed milk
1 lb (455 g) well drained, finely chopped raw spinach
  (a blender is best for this)
5 eggs, separated
¼ teaspoon white pepper
a little salt
Serves six

Melt the margarine and add the flour. Cook until
bubbly. Add the milk and cook until thickened.
Add the spinach. Cook over hot water for 30
minutes. Cool slightly. Add the egg yolks and fold
in the stiffly beaten egg whites. Grease a six-pint
(three-litre) soufflé dish with a little margarine and
pour in the mixture. Bake at 375°F (190°C) for 30
minutes.

FISH

Caviar wafers

1 oz (30 g) fresh caviar
2 slices pumpernickel bread
lemon juice
finely sliced onion
Serves one

Spread the caviar on the bread, sprinkle with lemon juice and garnish with the onion.

Baked crab meat

2 tablespoons olive oil
2 onions, finely chopped
1 clove garlic, minced
2 green peppers, finely chopped
2 tomatoes, peeled and chopped
3 tablespoons chopped parsley
1 lb (455 g) cooked or tinned crab meat, flaked
1½ teaspoons salt
½ teaspoon freshly ground white pepper
2 eggs
2 tablespoons breadcrumbs
6 stuffed green olives, sliced
Serves six

Heat the oil in a pan, and sauté the onions for 10 minutes, stirring often. Add the garlic, green peppers, tomatoes and parsley and cook over a low heat for 15 minutes. Mix in the crab meat, season with salt and pepper and cook for 5 minutes. Beat the eggs and gradually add to the mixture in the pan, stirring constantly until set. Taste for seasoning. Spoon the mixture into six individual ramekins or a large baking dish and sprinkle the top with breadcrumbs. Arrange the sliced olives on the breadcrumbs and bake at 375°F (190°C) for 10 minutes or until browned.

Crab and cucumber salad

4 oz (115 g) fresh crab meat, flaked
½ small cucumber, peeled and sliced
juice of 1 lemon
a little olive oil
ground pepper
sea-salt
parsley and celery for garnish
Serves two

Toss crab meat and cucumber together. Add lemon juice, oil, pepper and a dash of sea-salt. Garnish with parsley and celery.

Fish and bonus sauce

24 fl oz (6.8 dl) tomato juice
¼ teaspoon garlic powder
2 tablespoons dried onion flakes
1 tablespoon chopped parsley
1 tablespoon vinegar and capers
2 tablespoons basil
1 teaspoon rosemary
3 tablespoons wine vinegar

2 teaspoons lemon juice
artificial sweetener equivalent to 2 teaspoons sugar
1 lb (455 g) fish fillets cut into 1 in (2.5 cm) pieces
Serves two

Combine all except the fish in a medium saucepan. Simmer uncovered for about 20 minutes. Divide the sauce, reserve half and chill to use as a cocktail sauce. Add the fish to the remainder and simmer 10–12 minutes, or until the fish flakes.

Fish casserole

12 oz (340 g) cod, haddock or plaice
8 oz (225 g) tin of tomatoes
4 oz (115 g) button mushrooms
1 teaspoon Worcestershire sauce
salt and pepper
Serves two

Wash and flake fish into an ovenproof dish. Empty the tomatoes into the dish. Add the washed mushrooms and the Worcestershire sauce. Season to taste and bake, covered, for about 30 minutes at 350°F (180°C).

Fish with garlic

3 oz (85 g) margarine
8 oz (225 g) onions, chopped
1 clove garlic, finely chopped
1 tablespoon tomato purée
¼ pint (1.4 dl) water
juice of 1 lemon
¼ level teaspoon cayenne pepper
¼ level teaspoon ground mace
⅛ level teaspoon freshly ground black pepper
1 lb (455 g) cod fillet
2 tablespoons tarragon vinegar
Serves four

Heat the margarine in a saucepan, add the onion and garlic, cover and allow to soften slowly. Remove the lid and increase the heat to brown lightly. Add the tomato purée, water and lemon juice. Bring to the boil and simmer with lid half on for 10–15 minutes. Add both the peppers and the mace. Wash, dry and trim the fish. Place in a greased fireproof dish, moisten with water, and the tarragon vinegar, and poach for 15–20 minutes. Arrange on a hot serving dish, with a good spoonful of the onion mixture over each piece of fish.

Fish pie

8 oz (225 g) cooked cauliflower
12 fl oz (3.4 dl) chicken stock
2 teaspoons freshly chopped parsley
salt and pepper
12 oz (340 g) cooked flaked white fish
6 oz (170 g) cooked mashed potato
scraping of nutmeg
Serves two

Place the cauliflower in blender, add stock; blend until smooth. Remove from blender. Add parsley. Add salt and pepper. Fold in fish. Put in casserole; spread with potato. Sprinkle with nutmeg. Bake at 450°F (230°C) for 30 minutes or until hot and potatoes golden.

Baked halibut with mushroom sauce

1 small cutlet halibut
1 teaspoon chopped onion
2 sliced button mushrooms
½ oz (15 g) butter
1 teaspoon chopped parsley
salt and pepper
1 tablespoon cream
Serves one

Grease a piece of aluminium foil, large enough to parcel the fish and lay the halibut on it. Fry the onion and mushroom in the butter; mix in the parsley, spread over the fish and season; spoon the cream over. Enclose the fish and its sauce in foil and bake at 400°F (200°C), for approximately 25 minutes, depending on the thickness of the cutlet. Serve in the foil.

Slimmers' mussels (i)

1 pint (5.7 dl) mussels
1 small onion
pepper
chopped parsley
a few drops lemon juice
Serves one

Scrape the mussels and scrub them in several changes of water, discarding any that are not firmly closed. Put them in a pan with about 2 tablespoons water, the finely chopped onion and a sprinkle of pepper, and cover with a lid. Cook over a brisk heat, shaking the pan from time to time until the shells have opened. Discard the top shells, arrange the mussels in a dish and sprinkle with finely chopped parsley. Add a few drops of lemon juice to the liquid in the pan, adjust the seasoning (adding a little salt if necessary) and pour hot over mussels.

Slimmers' mussels (ii)

2 pints (1.1 l) mussels
½ oz (15 g) low-calorie spread
1 shallot, chopped
½ glass dry white wine
salt and pepper
chopped parsley
Serves two

Scrub and clean the mussels. Discard any that remain open and rinse in cold water until it runs clear. Melt the low-calorie spread in a pan and add the shallot; stir and cook for 2–3 minutes. Add other ingredients, cover and turn the heat on full. Shake the pan occasionally. The mussels should be ready in 5–6 minutes. Serve in their shells with more chopped parsley.

Plaice bonne femme

4 fillets of plaice
salt and pepper

4 oz (115 g) sliced mushrooms
2 fl oz (55 ml) white wine
Serves four

Place the fish in a shallow baking dish and season well. Cover with the mushrooms and moisten with wine to come not more than half-way up the fish. Bake, uncovered, until the fish is tender.

Prawns baked in foil

10–17 prawns
salt and pepper
3 spring onions, minced
1 teaspoon grated lemon
Serves one

Place prawns in foil, sprinkle with salt, pepper, onions and lemon, and seal the edges. Bake at 450°F (230°C) for 5 minutes or until the prawns are pink.

Prawn cocktail

4 tablespoons tomato juice
2 tablespoons lemon juice
2 teaspoons made mustard
2 teaspoons Worcestershire sauce
celery salt to taste
2 tablespoons yogurt
4 oz (115 g) shelled, cooked prawns
Serves two

Mix all the ingredients together except the prawns. When smooth add the prawns, put in deep glasses, and chill.

Prawn, crab or lobster cocktail

Use 2 oz (55 g) shellfish and blend with yogurt dressing (see p. 183) and a little tomato purée and Worcestershire sauce.

Salmon-wrapped broccoli

1 lb (455 g) broccoli
sea-salt
3 slices smoked salmon
sliced lemon
capers
Serves three

Prepare the broccoli by soaking in cold sea-salted water for half an hour. Drain and stand in boiling water with the flower tips above the surface; steam (water at simmering point) for 10 minutes. Wrap smoked salmon round the broccoli; serve with sliced lemon and a few capers.

Oven-baked salmon

2 fl oz (55 ml) lemon juice
1 teaspoon grated lemon peel
1 clove garlic, crushed
½ teaspoon paprika
4 salmon steaks (6 oz, 170 g, each)
1 teaspoon chopped chives
Serves four

Mix lemon juice and peel, garlic and paprika. Rub salmon with this mixture and bake at 350°F (180°C) for 20 minutes. Baste. Put under the grill to brown. Sprinkle on the chives just before serving. Serve with a twist of lemon and Swedish cucumbers (see p. 174).

Salmon mousse

Sauce:
 ¾ oz (20 g) flour
 ¾ oz (20 g) butter
 7½ fl oz (2.1 dl) skimmed milk, flavoured with bayleaf, peppercorns, a blade of mace and a slice of onion
½ oz (15 g) gelatine
3 tablespoons water
8 oz (225 g) tinned salmon
juice of 1 lemon
salt and pepper

2 egg whites
¼ cucumber
aspic jelly
parsley to garnish
Serves four

Make the sauce and allow to cool. Dissolve the gelatine in the water over a gentle heat. Flake the salmon, mix it with the cold sauce, lemon juice, seasoning and gelatine. Whisk the egg whites until very stiff and fold into the mixture when it is on the point of setting. Leave in a soufflé dish to get very cold. Decorate with sliced cucumber and aspic; garnish with parsley.

Scallops mornay

8 scallops
2½ fl oz (70 ml) dry white wine
5 fl oz (1.4 dl) water
2 slices onion
1 bayleaf
6 peppercorns
1 oz (30 g) butter
¾ oz (20 g) flour
3 oz (85 g) Cheddar cheese
2½ fl oz (70 ml) single cream
salt and pepper
2 tablespoons grated cheese for grilling
Serves four

Poach the scallops very gently in the wine and water with the onion, bayleaf and peppercorns for about 8 minutes. Make the sauce with butter, flour and poaching liquid. Add the cheese and cream. Season well. Cut the scallops into three or four pieces, arrange in the shells and spoon the sauce over them. Sprinkle with the grated cheese and brown under the grill.

Seafood casserole

4 oz (115 g) crab meat
4 oz (115 g) peeled prawns
juice of 1 lemon
black pepper

Opposite: Traeger, 1967
Overleaf: Bookbinder, 1964, 1966

8 oz (225 g) tomatoes
8 oz (225 g) pimentos
4 oz (115 g) mushrooms
1 large onion
2 tablespoons chopped parsley
2 eggs
salt and pepper
1 oz (30 g) grated cheese (half Parmesan, half Cheddar)
Serves four

Marinate the crab meat and prawns in lemon juice and pepper while preparing the other ingredients. Slice the tomatoes, pimentos and mushrooms. Peel and slice the onion in thin rings. Mix the prawns and crab meat together with the parsley, mushrooms, pimentos and tomatoes and pile into an ovenproof dish. Arrange the onion rings on top. Beat the eggs, season well and pour over. Sprinkle with cheese and bake for 25–35 minutes in a moderate oven, 350°F (180°C).

Sole casserole

6 oz (170 g) tomatoes, skinned and chopped
4 oz (115 g) mushrooms, chopped
4 level teaspoons breadcrumbs
1 level teaspoon grated lemon rind
salt and pepper
1 lb (455 g) fillets of sole
½ pint (2.8 dl) fish stock, wine or cider
Serves four

Mix the tomato with half the mushrooms, the breadcrumbs, lemon rind and seasoning. Spread on the fillets and roll up tightly. Pack close together in a casserole, cover with the rest of the mushrooms and add the liquid. Season well. Cover and cook for 20 minutes at 350°F (180°C).

Sole aux crevettes

4 large or 8 small fillets of sole
salt and pepper
white wine

1 pint (5.7 dl) shelled shrimps
chopped parsley
Serves four

Season the fillets and roll up. Poach gently in a baking dish in the oven with wine to moisten. Just before the fish is cooked, add the shrimps which may be fresh, tinned or frozen. Serve with the chopped parsley.

Sole italienne

4 fillets of sole
½ oz (15 g) butter
2 onions, finely chopped
1 tin tomatoes
2 oz (55 g) mushrooms
a pinch of mustard
a pinch of thyme
salt and pepper
1 level tablespoon arrowroot
lemon and parsley for garnish
Serves two

Brush the fillets with melted butter and grill until the fish begins to flake. Mix together the onions and tomatoes and simmer until the onions are tender. Add the sliced mushrooms and seasonings. Thicken with arrowroot blended with a little cold water. Pour over fish and garnish with lemon and parsley.

Fillet of sole en papillote

6 oz (170 g) fillet of sole
parsley
lemon juice
salt and pepper
Serves one

Put the fish on a piece of foil and sprinkle with parsley, lemon and seasonings. Bake at 350°F (180°C) for 10 minutes.

Opposite: Bookbinder, 1964

Sole voisin

Italian tomato sauce (see p. 182)
salt and pepper
4 small soles, filleted
white wine
Serves four

Make the sauce. Season the fillets and fold in half. Poach slowly in the oven (375°F, 190°C) with just enough wine to moisten. They will take 10–15 minutes depending on the thickness. If there is a little liquid left after cooking add it to the tomato sauce and pour over the fish.

Stuffed sole in wine sauce

4 small fillets of sole
4 oz (115 g) chopped mushrooms
salt and freshly ground black pepper
squeeze of lemon juice
1 glass dry white wine
1 tablespoon single cream
Serves two

Flatten the fillets. Season the mushrooms with salt and pepper and a little squeeze of lemon juice and cover each fillet of sole with the mixture. Roll up carefully and secure with a cocktail stick. Place in an ovenproof dish and pour on white wine. Bake in a medium oven, 375°F (190°C) for 20–25 minutes. Just before serving place the fillets on a hot dish. Keep warm. Boil the wine until reduced to half, remove from the heat and stir in the single cream. Pour over the fillets and serve immediately.

Truite au bleu

4 pints (2.3 l) water
¼ pint (1.4 dl) cider vinegar
2 sliced onions
2 chopped carrots
1 bayleaf
thyme
parsley
sea-salt
10 peppercorns
1 fresh trout for each person

Simmer the water, cider vinegar, onions, carrots, herbs and sea-salt for 1 hour. About 10 minutes before the end of the cooking time add 10 peppercorns. Put the trout in a deep pan and sprinkle with a little boiling vinegar. Add the boiling prepared bouillon. Reduce the heat and poach for 15 minutes. Serve with parsley.

MARTIN

MEAT AND POULTRY

Boiled beef

3 lb (1.4 kg) piece of lean silverside
1 sliced onion
1 sliced carrot
3 peppercorns
6 juniper berries (optional)
1 bayleaf
½ pint (2.8 dl) beer
water to cover
Serves six to eight

Put all ingredients in a deep saucepan and simmer for 3 hours or until tender. Remove the meat and strain the liquid. Skim off the fat and return the meat to the broth. Slice thinly and serve with the broth, seasoned to taste.

Beef patties

12 oz (340 g) minced beef
¼ teaspoon chilli powder
2 teaspoons prepared mustard
2 teaspoons horse-radish
2 teaspoons chopped green pepper
1 tablespoon dried onion flakes
2 teaspoons Worcestershire sauce
salt and pepper
Serves two

Mix well and make patties. Grill for 5 minutes. Turn and grill for 4 minutes more until done.

Carbonnade of beef

6 oz chuck steak
1 level tablespoon flour
1 small onion
½ small clove garlic
salt
1 dessertspoon dripping
¼ pint (1.4 dl) brown ale
¼ pint (1.4 dl) water
1 bouquet garni
pepper
1 slice bread, cut in 4 pieces
mustard
Serves one

Cut the meat into large squares and dust with flour. Slice the onion. Crush the garlic with the salt. Brown the meat and onions in the dripping and add the ale, water, garlic, bouquet garni and seasoning. Bring to the boil. Put into a casserole and place in the oven (300°F, 150°C) for approximately 2 hours. Forty minutes before serving, remove the bouquet garni, skim off any fat and spoon on to the bread. Spread the bread with the mustard and arrange on top of the casserole, dipping the bread into the liquid so that it is well soaked.

Put the casserole back into the oven, but without the lid, and leave until the bread has formed into a brown crust. Serve with carrots and a green vegetable.

Slimmers' cottage pie

1 large onion
1 large carrot
½ oz (15 g) fat
1 lb (455 g) minced cooked beef
2 egg yolks
¼ pint (1.4 dl) stock
pinch of mixed herbs
2 egg whites
salt and pepper
½ oz (15 g) Parmesan cheese
Serves four

Chop onion and carrot finely. Melt fat and fry meat, onion and carrot in it. Separate the eggs and add the yolks, stock and herbs to the meat and vegetables. Mix well and cook for a few minutes. Transfer to ovenproof dish. Whisk egg whites till they are stiff. Add seasoning and spread meringue over meat mixture. Sprinkle Parmesan cheese over the top. Cook in a fairly hot oven (375°F, 190°C) for about 15 minutes.

Slimmers' goulash

½ oz (15 g) butter or margarine
2 tablespoons paprika
8 oz (225 g) stewing beef
2 medium onions, sliced
1 beef stock cube
8 oz (225 g) tin tomatoes
salt and pepper
Serves two

Melt the fat in the pan, add the paprika and brown the meat evenly. Transfer the meat to an ovenproof dish. Soften the onions in remaining fat. Add to the meat. Make up the stock using the juice from the tomatoes. Add to the meat and onions. Season to taste. Cook in a cool oven (325°F, 170°C) for 2–2½ hours until the meat is tender. Add the tomatoes 15 minutes before removing from oven.

Garlic hamburger

1 clove garlic
1 teaspoon salt
1 teaspoon freshly ground black pepper
½ teaspoon Tabasco
1 lb (455 g) minced beef
Serves four

Mince the garlic and combine with the salt, pepper and Tabasco. Form meat into cakes about 1 inch thick, and press seasoning into side of each cake. Grill.

Steak americaine

4 oz (115 g) lean steak fillet
1 clove garlic
salt and pepper
olive oil
Serves one

Brush beef fillet with the juice of the garlic, season and slightly smear with olive oil. Grill under a fast heat, 2 minutes on the first side, 4 on second. Eat rare.

Steak tartare

8 oz (225 g) raw minced beef
1 egg yolk
Tabasco sauce
1 chopped onion
salt and pepper
capers
watercress
Serves two

Add the egg yolk to the beef. Blend and add a dash of Tabasco sauce, the onion, salt, pepper and capers. Form into balls; serve on watercress.

Marinaded steak

1 lb (455 g) steak, cut in portions
½ level teaspoon salt

$\frac{1}{4}$ *level teaspoon mustard*
$\frac{1}{2}$ *tablespoon red wine*
1 teaspoon Worcestershire sauce
$\frac{1}{4}$ *pint (1.4 dl) water*
Serves four

Remove fat and put the meat in a casserole. Mix the dry ingredients together and add the liquid gradually. Pour over the meat and leave it to stand for 2 hours, stirring occasionally. Cover and cook gently for 2 hours.

Carré d'agneau conti

6 fillets anchovy
1 dessertspoon chopped herbs
large finely chopped shallot
2 racks of lamb, skinned
dripping or butter for roasting
1 lb (455 g) tomatoes
1 oz (30 g) butter
salt and pepper
1 tablespoon chopped parsley
Serves six

Halve the anchovies lengthways and roll in chopped herbs and shallot. Lard the meat with the anchovies. Roast in a moderately hot oven (375°F, 190°C) for 50 minutes. Meanwhile peel the tomatoes and cut into thick slices. Melt the butter and fry, turning once. Season, draw aside. Sprinkle over any remaining herbs and the parsley. Remove the chine bone from the meat; trim bone ends. Carve in thick slices and serve with the tomatoes.

Baked lamb chops with tomatoes and cheese

4 lamb chops about 1 inch (2.5 cm) thick
1 oz (30 g) fat
2 onions
12 oz (340 g) tinned tomatoes
$\frac{1}{2}$ *level teaspoon salt*
$\frac{1}{4}$ *level teaspoon pepper*
2 oz (55 g) grated cheese
2 oz (55 g) fresh breadcrumbs
Serves four

Trim surplus fat from the chops. Heat the fat and brown the chops in it. Place in a large shallow casserole in a single layer. Put several slices of onion on top of each chop. Pour the tomatoes round and add the seasoning. Mix cheese and breadcrumbs and sprinkle thickly over the chops. Cover and bake slowly.

Grilled lamb chops with herbs

4 lamb chops or 8 small cutlets
1 level teaspoon dried basil or rosemary
1 level teaspoon marjoram
1 level teaspoon dried thyme
1 level teaspoon salt
Serves four

Trim excess fat from the meat. Mix herbs and salt and rub into each side of the chops. Cover and chill 1 hour. Grill in the usual way for 10–12 minutes or until cooked to taste.

Lamb kebabs

8 oz (225 g) lean lamb, cut into cubes
3 tomatoes, quartered
8 small onions or section of onion
small whole mushrooms
1 green pepper, sliced
lemon dressing (see p. 181)
Serves two

Marinate the lamb in lemon dressing for 2–3 hours. Drain, retaining the marinade. Put lamb, tomato, onion, mushroom, pepper, etc., alternately on skewers. Brush with marinade and grill, turning occasionally. Serve with rice and a wedge of lemon.

Roast stuffed pork

2 onions
4 oz (115 g) breadcrumbs
2 teaspoons powdered sage or 1 tablespoon finely
  chopped fresh sage

1½ oz (40 g) melted butter
pepper
salt
egg to bind
2 lb (0.9 kg) loin pork, boned
2 tablespoons dripping
½ teaspoon flour
½ pint (2.8 dl) stock
Serves five to six

Cook the onions in water until tender. Chop finely, mix with breadcrumbs, sage, butter, seasoning and sufficient egg to bind. Stuff pork. Roll and tie securely. Score the crackling. Heat dripping in the roasting tin, add the meat and roast at 375°F (190°C) for 1½–2 hours. (If serving roast potatoes, cook round the joint, basting well during cooking.) Five minutes before serving, spoon 2 tablespoons boiling water over the pork to crispen the crackling. Remove the meat and potatoes from the roasting tin and keep warm. Pour away as much fat as possible from the tin. Add ½ teaspoon flour to the remaining juices in tin and blend over gentle heat on top of stove. Stir in ½ pint (2.8 dl) stock or vegetable water. Bring to boil, check seasoning. Serve separately.

Stuffed pork chop

1 teaspoon chopped onion
knob butter
pinch sage
½ slice bread, crumbled
½ orange
salt and pepper
1 pork loin chop
cider
1 teaspoon chopped capers
1 teaspoon chopped gherkins
Serves one

Sauté the onion in butter without colouring until tender. Add sage, breadcrumbs, grated rind of ½ orange and chopped flesh. Season. Cut chop through the middle towards the bone but leaving the meat still attached to the bone. Open like a book. Spread stuffing on one side, fold over and

secure with a skewer. Place in a shallow casserole with enough cider to come ¼ inch (6 mm) up the chop. Bake at 350°F (180°C) for 1 hour. Remove the chop, take out the skewer and keep warm. Add capers, gherkins and two more tablespoons cider to casserole. Bring to the boil and serve the sauce separately.

Ham horns

8 thin slices of ham
8 button mushrooms
a squeeze of lemon juice
1 bunch watercress
Filling:
    4 oz (115 g) minced cooked chicken
    ¾ pint (4.3 dl) cold white sauce
    1 oz (30 g) butter
    chicken stock
    1 tablespoon whipped cream
    a pinch of thyme
    salt and black pepper
    watercress
Serves four

Form the ham into cornet shapes. Cook the mushrooms in a little water with the lemon juice and leave to cool. Mix all the filling ingredients together well and, using a large plain nozzle, pipe the mixture into the horns. Top each with a mushroom. Arrange on an oval dish and garnish with watercress.

Ham mousse

6 oz (170 g) minced cooked lean ham
½ pint (2.8 dl) bechamel sauce (see p. 180)
a little made mustard
½ oz (15 g) gelatine
½ pint (2.8 dl) stock
2½ fl oz (70 ml) evaporated milk
1 egg white
garnish of salad vegetables
Serves four

Mix ham, sauce and mustard. Dissolve the gelatine in hot stock. Add the sauce mixture and leave until cold but not set. Whisk the evaporated milk and fold in. Whisk the egg white stiff and fold it in. Pour into a mould or soufflé dish and leave to set. Serve in the dish or unmould. Decorate with salad vegetables.

Figs and prosciutto

2 fresh figs
2 slices prosciutto
pepper
Serves one

Peel the figs, slice and cover with prosciutto. Sprinkle with pepper.

Blanquette of veal

1 lb (455 g) stewing veal
salt and pepper
½ bayleaf
1 sprig thyme
2 onions, quartered
3 carrots
½ oz (15 g) margarine
½ oz (15 g) flour
¼ pint (1.4 dl) milk
1 egg yolk
3 sprigs parsley
Serves four

Cut up the meat and place in a saucepan. Just cover with cold water and add salt and pepper. Bring to simmering point and remove scum. Tie the herbs together and add to the meat with the onions and carrots. Cover and simmer until tender – approximately 1¼ hours. Melt the margarine and add the flour. Cook without browning over gentle heat. Add the milk and ¼ pint (1.4 dl) veal stock. Bring to the boil. Mix the egg yolk with a little sauce and return to pan. Stir over moderate heat until it thickens, but do not allow to boil. Taste and season. Strain meat and vegetables. Place on a serving dish. Pour the sauce over and sprinkle with finely chopped parsley.

Veal with pimento dressing

4 oz (115 g) cooked minced veal
1 teaspoon chilli powder
¼ teaspoon salt
1 teaspoon dried onion flakes
¼ teaspoon onion powder
dash of Tabasco sauce
¼ teaspoon paprika
1 slice bread
shredded lettuce
pimento dressing (see p. 182)
Serves one

Place the veal in a non-stick pan. Add the seasoning. Cook for 5 minutes. Toast the bread lightly. Spread the mixture on half the slice of bread, fold over and hold with toothpicks. Combine lettuce and 1 tablespoon pimento dressing and cover the veal with it.

Sauté of veal créole

1 lb (455 g) veal fillet
1 clove garlic
2 shallots or 1 small onion
1 oz (30 g) butter
1 rasher of bacon, diced
½ oz (15 g) flour
1 glass white wine
¼ pint (1.4 dl) strong stock
¼ pint (1.4 dl) tomato juice
bouquet garni
4 oz (115 g) button onions
4 oz (115 g) button mushrooms (quartered)
chopped parsley
Serves six

Cut the fillet diagonally into 1 inch (2.5 cm) thick slices. Chop the garlic and shallots finely. Sauté the veal pieces in half the butter until a good brown all over. Add the shallots, garlic and bacon, sauté for a minute or two, then add the flour. Cook for 1 minute. Remove from the heat and add the wine, the stock and tomato juice, blending the sauce smoothly. Add the bouquet garni and simmer for

40 minutes. Remove the meat, strain the liquid and reduce it by boiling to the smooth consistency of thin cream. Meanwhile, peel and simmer the onions, sauté the mushrooms in the remainder of the butter. Arrange the meat down the centre of a dish, cover with the mushrooms and onions, and spoon the sauce over. Garnish with parsley.

Calf's tongue

1 fresh calf's tongue
3 celery stalks
1 onion
4 cloves
1 tablespoon tarragon vinegar
5 sprigs parsley
8 peppercorns
sea-salt
Serves six

Boil the tongue in a large pan with just enough water to cover, with the celery, onion studded with cloves, vinegar, parsley, peppercorns and a little sea-salt. Bring slowly to the boil, skim any fatty matter off the top and simmer slowly for about $3\frac{1}{2}$ hours. Serve with fresh string beans.

Kidney sauté

4 lambs' kidneys
2 oz (55 g) mushrooms
6 very small onions
18 oz (225 g) tin tomatoes
1 bayleaf
salt and pepper
chopped parsley
Serves two

Skin and core the kidneys. Cut in half lengthways. Heat a non-stick pan and brown on both sides. Add quartered mushrooms, onions, tomatoes, bayleaf and seasoning. Cover and simmer for approximately 15 minutes until tender. Remove lid from pan and boil quickly to reduce the sauce. Remove the bayleaf. Check seasoning. Serve with chopped parsley.

Kidney sauté turbigo

6 lambs' or 4 sheep's kidneys
4 oz (115 g) mushrooms
1 oz (30 g) butter
1 small onion
1 small carrot
5 large tomatoes
bayleaf
1 rasher bacon
$\frac{1}{4}$ pint (1.4 dl) stock
salt and pepper
artificial sweetener
2 slices bread
chopped parsley
Serves two

Skin and core kidneys; cut in half lengthwise. Wash mushrooms, leave whole if small, otherwise slice. Fry the kidneys and mushrooms in butter, until browned. Remove. Add roughly diced onion, carrot, tomatoes, bayleaf, chopped bacon and stock, cover and simmer gently for $\frac{1}{2}$ hour. Rub the sauce through a sieve into a clean pan. Check seasoning and consistency. Add a little artificial sweetener if necessary. Warm the kidneys and mushrooms for 5 minutes in the sauce. Pile into a serving dish. Cut two fairly thick slices of bread. Trim away the rounded ends, leaving a square. Cut each piece into two triangles, toast. Dip the tips into chopped parsley and use as garnish.

Liver and onions with fennel

4 oz (115 g) onions, thinly sliced
$\frac{1}{4}$ pint (1.4 dl) water
1 stock cube
$\frac{1}{2}$ teaspoon Worcestershire sauce
freshly ground pepper
$\frac{1}{2}$ teaspoon paprika
6 oz (170 g) liver
salt and pepper
fennel seeds
garlic powder
$\frac{1}{2}$ oz (15 g) margarine
Serves one

Combine the onions, water and stock cube. Bring to the boil and cook until the onions are tender. Drain. Add Worcestershire sauce, pepper and paprika. Set aside. Sprinkle both sides of liver with salt, pepper, fennel seeds and garlic powder. Lightly brown each side in a hot non-stick pan. Put the onion mixture over liver, continue cooking, covered, 3–5 minutes more. Add the margarine before serving.

Liver parcels

8 oz (225 g) liver
2 lean bacon rashers
1 small onion
2 oz (55 g) mushrooms
2 medium tomatoes
Worcestershire sauce to taste
salt and pepper
4 oz (115 g) frozen peas
Serves two

Place the liver on a piece of aluminium foil. Chop the bacon and onion, slice the mushrooms and tomatoes. Layer the bacon, onion, mushrooms and tomatoes on the liver, season with Worcestershire sauce, salt and pepper. Place frozen peas on top. Carefully seal the foil in a parcel and place in a baking dish. Cook for 35 minutes at 350°F (180°C).

Liver shashlik

1 lb (455 g) liver cut in 1½ inch (3 cm) pieces
2 medium tomatoes, quartered
8 oz (225 g) small mushrooms
bayleaves
oil
vinegar
salt and pepper
chopped parsley
juice of 1 lemon
Serves four

Prepare the liver and vegetables. Take 8 long thin skewers and thread the ingredients on in the following order: bayleaf, liver, mushroom, tomato, repeating until all is used up. Put in the bottom of the grill pan and brush with a very little oil. Moisten with a little vinegar and season with salt and pepper. Leave to marinate for ½ hour. Grill for 8–10 minutes, turning once. Swill out the grill pan with a little stock or water. Boil hard in saucepan or grill pan to reduce the marinade. Add parsley and lemon juice and pour over the meat.

Sweetbreads in sherry

1 pair sweetbreads
freshly ground pepper
1 tablespoon sherry
chicken stock or water
2 oz (55 g) mushrooms
oil
juice of 1 lemon
black olives
parsley
Serves one

Blanch and drain the sweetbreads. Break into small pieces, season with pepper and put into a casserole. Mix sherry with a little chicken stock or water, pour over the sweetbreads and sauté. Slice the mushrooms and sauté in a little oil. Mix with the sweetbreads and cook in a moderate oven for 15 minutes. Drain off any excess liquid, add lemon juice, black olives and parsley.

Baked chicken and pineapple

4 portions of chicken (2–3 lb, 0.9–1.4 kg)
½ level teaspoon dried rosemary
1 level teaspoon salt
½ level teaspoon pepper
6 shallots, sliced
¼ pint (1.4 dl) unsweetened pineapple juice
¼ level teaspoon ground ginger
paprika
Serves four

Wash and dry the chicken. Combine the rosemary, salt and pepper, and rub into the chicken. Arrange, skin side up, in a shallow baking dish. Place sliced shallots round it. Combine the pineapple juice and ginger. Sprinkle paprika over the chicken and pour in the pineapple juice. Bake uncovered until tender.

Chicken and clam pancakes

1 chopped onion
4 oz (115 g) sliced mushrooms
1 oz (30 g) butter
1 heaped teaspoon cornflour
1 large tin minced clams
salt and pepper
1 chicken stock cube
a little cream or top of the milk
meat from ½ cooked chicken
4 pancakes
2 oz (55 g) cheese
browned crumbs
Serves four

Cook the onion and mushrooms in the butter. Stir in the cornflour. Add the liquid from the tin of clams to make a sauce. Then add seasoning, stock cube and cream. Chop the chicken finely and add to the sauce with the clams. Divide into four. Place the pancakes open in a fireproof dish, add filling to each one and fold over. Sprinkle with cheese and crumbs; brown under the grill.

Curried chicken with rice

8 oz (225 g) boneless, skinned chicken, coarsely diced
2 oz (55 g) onion, chopped
1 teaspoon curry powder
6 fl oz (1.7 dl) chicken stock
2 tablespoons chopped celery
8 fl oz (2.3 dl) tomato juice, reduced by half by boiling rapidly
½ medium apple, diced
2 oz (55 g) carrots, diced
½ teaspoon lemon juice
salt
3 oz (85 g) cooked rice
Serves one

Place the chicken and onion in a non-stick pan. Cook over a low heat until lightly brown. Sprinkle curry powder over the chicken and stir with a wooden spoon. Add the stock and celery. Simmer for 10 minutes, stirring. Pour in the tomato juice and add the apple, carrots and lemon juice. Simmer for another 20 minutes or until carrots are tender and the sauce is thickened. Add salt to taste. Serve with rice.

French roast chicken

5 lb (2.3 kg) roasting chicken
2 oz (55 g) butter
sprig herbs – tarragon, rosemary and bayleaf
salt and pepper
½ pint (2.8 dl) stock
1 chicken liver
watercress
Serves six

Set the oven to 400°F (200°C). Rub the chicken well with butter. Put a nut of butter and the herbs inside. Put salt and pepper into the roasting tin with half the stock. Start roasting the chicken on one side; turn on the other side, then on the breast. Should be browned on all sides. (Total roasting time 1½ hours.) Take out, joint and keep hot. Tip the remaining stock into the roasting tin. Reduce; adjust seasoning. Sauté liver in the remaining butter, slice, add to gravy and spoon over the chicken. Garnish with watercress.

Chicken en gelée

¾ pint (4.3 dl) clear chicken bouillon
1 tablespoon aspic crystals
½ cucumber
2 stalks celery
12 oz (340 g) cold chopped chicken
salt and pepper
6 lettuce leaves or 1 bunch watercress
Serves four

Boil the bouillon, leave for 1 minute and then dissolve the aspic crystals in the liquid. Leave to cool. Peel and dice the cucumber and celery and mix with the chicken. Season well. Put into the refrigerator to get very cold. When the aspic is cold but not set, add the meat and vegetables, stirring until the aspic is almost set. Pour into cocotte dishes or a ring mould. Leave to set completely. When set, turn out and garnish with watercress or lettuce.

Herbed chicken

5 lb (2.3 kg) roasting chicken
1 tablespoon olive oil
3 tablespoons lemon juice
2½ teaspoons salt
1 lb (455 g) tinned tomatoes
1½ teaspoons oregano
¾ teaspoon freshly ground black pepper
Serves six

Rub the chicken well with a mixture of the oil, lemon juice and 2 teaspoons salt. Put in a roasting pan and roast at 375°F (190°C) for 1 hour. Mix the tomatoes, oregano, pepper and remaining salt and pour over the chicken. Reduce heat to 350°F (180°C) and cook for another hour, or until the chicken is tender, basting frequently.

Chicken liver pâté

8 oz (225 g) chicken livers
water
2 sprigs parsley
bayleaf
pinch of thyme
¼ cup unsalted butter, melted
1 teaspoon mustard
pinch each ground cloves, cayenne, nutmeg
¼ cup cognac
Serves four

Place the chicken livers in a saucepan with water, and add the parsley, bayleaf and thyme. Simmer for 20 minutes. Drain, chop very finely and mix to a paste with melted butter; add mustard, cloves, cayenne, nutmeg and cognac. Chill before serving.

Skewered chicken livers

2–3 chicken livers
2 tomatoes
4 mushrooms
a few drops oil
salt and pepper
Serves two

Halve chicken livers and thread on a skewer, alternating with slices of tomato and mushroom. Brush very lightly with oil. Grill, turning frequently. Season with salt and pepper just before serving, otherwise the chicken livers will become hard.

Low-calorie chicken in the pot

1 tin chicken consommé
1 chicken breast, skinned and rubbed with lemon
1 stick of celery
3 scraped carrots
1 medium onion stuck with 3 cloves
parsley, thyme, 1 bayleaf
salt and pepper
Serves one

Empty the consommé into a saucepan. Add the chicken breast, celery, carrots, halved lengthwise, onion, herbs and seasoning to taste. Boil until the carrots are tender, about 15–20 minutes. Serve with a small green salad.

Orange roasted chicken

1 3½ lb (1.6 kg) chicken
3 dessertspoons minced spring onions
¼ teaspoon rosemary
1 dessertspoon grated orange zest
salt and freshly ground pepper
1 cup fresh or tinned unsweetened orange juice
watercress and orange segments for garnish
Serves four

Preheat oven to 300°F (150°C). Wash and dry the chicken. Place in a shallow ovenproof casserole and sprinkle with the onions, rosemary, orange zest, salt and pepper. Baste frequently with the orange juice for about 1 hour or until the chicken is brown. Garnish with watercress and fresh orange segments.

Chicken provençale

1 small poussin
salt and pepper
olive oil
4 carrots
3 small onions
1 bayleaf
sprig of thyme
4 oz (115 g) mushrooms
1 cup fresh peas
parsley
Serves two

Sprinkle the poussin with salt and pepper. Brown on all sides in olive oil, put in a heavy casserole dish with the carrots, onions, bayleaf and thyme. Cover with water and cook in a very slow oven for 1 hour. Meanwhile sauté the mushrooms, cook the peas and add to the casserole before serving. Serve sprinkled with parsley.

Chicken salad

2 chicken legs
sea-salt
½ cup cooked cauliflower
½ cup cooked green beans
1 tomato, chopped
1 hard-boiled egg
dry mustard
pepper
½ tablespoon cider vinegar
3 tablespoons olive oil
herbs
Serves two

Boil the chicken legs in slightly salted water (sea-salt). Cool; reserve stock. Dice the chicken and put

in a bowl with the cauliflower, beans, chopped tomato and the white of the egg. Crush the yolk of the egg to a paste, add a little mustard and pepper, then add cider vinegar and olive oil. Stir until smooth, then add to the dry salad ingredients. Sprinkle herbs over.

Chicken sauté bergère

1 chicken joint
½ oz (15 g) butter
small glass madeira
2½ fl oz (70 ml) stock
1 oz (30 g) sliced button mushrooms
2 tablespoons cream
Serves one

Sauté chicken in butter until cooked through but not coloured. Place on serving dish, keep warm. Pour madeira and stock into pan and cook until reduced by half. Add sliced mushrooms, simmer for 5 minutes, stir in cream. Season. Pour over chicken.

Coq au vin (i)

1 oz (30 g) butter
2 chicken pieces each about 6 oz (170 g) meat
1 onion, sliced
1 clove garlic, crushed
1 bayleaf
½ pint (2.8 dl) dry red wine
salt and pepper
4 oz (115 g) mushrooms
Serves two

Melt butter in frying pan and brown chicken pieces evenly. Transfer chicken to ovenproof dish. Fry onion and garlic in remaining fat. Add onion, garlic, bayleaf to chicken and pour wine over. Season to taste. Cover dish and cook in moderate oven (350°F, 180°C) for 1–1½ hours. Add the mushrooms and continue cooking for another ½ hour.

Coq au vin (ii)

4 10 oz (285 g) chicken portions
Marinade:
  2 tablespooons dried onion flakes
  salt and freshly ground black pepper
  1 clove garlic, crushed
  ½ pint (2.8 dl) tomato juice
  ¼ pint (1.4 dl) red wine vinegar
  ½ pint (2.8 dl) chicken stock
1¼ pints (7.1 dl) chicken stock
¼ pint (1.4 dl) red wine vinegar
bouquet garni
8 oz (225 g) button onions
8 oz (225 g) button mushrooms
Serves four

Skin the chicken joints and place in a shallow dish. Mix the ingredients for the marinade together in a bowl and pour over the chicken. Marinate for about 6 hours in a cool place. Drain the chicken and reserve the marinade. Heat a non-stick frying pan and cook the chicken until golden all over. Remove the chicken and place in a casserole. Brown the onions in frying pan and then add to the casserole with the chicken stock, vinegar and bouquet garni. Cook in a moderate oven (350°F, 180°C) for 1 hour. Wash the mushrooms and add to the casserole 20 minutes before the cooking time is completed. Meanwhile pour the reserved marinade into a saucepan. Bring to the boil and boil briskly for 5–10 minutes or until reduced slightly. Drain the chicken, mushrooms and onions and place in a serving dish. Pour the hot sauce over the top. Serve with peas.

Koulibiaca

8 oz (225 g) raw chicken meat
½ oz (15 g) butter
4 oz (115 g) onion, chopped finely
8 oz (225 g) button mushrooms, sliced
juice of 1 lemon
a little water or stock
salt and pepper

2 hard-boiled eggs, chopped
2 tablespoons chopped parsley
Serves four

Remove the skin from the chicken. Chop it into ½–1 inch (1.2–2.5 cm) pieces. Gently fry the onions and mushrooms in a large frying pan. Add the chicken, increase the heat and immediately add the lemon juice and a little stock or water. Season well, stirring continuously. Add the chopped eggs and parsley and serve at once.

Tinola

3 lb (1.4 kg) chicken cut in quarters
4 whole raw carrots
4 whole white onions
4 sticks of celery
6 oz (170 g) cooked (fresh or frozen) green beans (optional)
Serves 4

Wash chicken well. Drain. Place in a deep saucepan. Add water to cover. Add carrots, onions and celery. Simmer until the chicken is done, about 1 hour. Let it stand until the fat comes to the top. Remove and add the beans. Re-heat. Serve with vegetables and broth, and a little rice, if desired.

Duckling and turkey salad

2 bunches watercress
1 head of celery
2 oranges
8 oz (225 g) cooked duck meat
8 oz (225 g) cooked turkey meat
¼ pint (1.4 dl) aspic jelly
Salad dressing:
  2 tablespoons olive oil
  1 tablespoon lemon juice
  1 pinch mustard
  salt and black pepper
  a little artificial sweetener
  1 teaspoon chopped fresh thyme
Serves eight

Wash and drain the watercress and celery. Thinly pare the rind from 1 orange. Cut this into julienne strips and blanch for 1 minute, drain and leave to cool. Using a knife peel the oranges and cut out the segments. Chop the celery and twist the stalks from the watercress.

Cut the cold meat into strips and arrange around one side of an oval dish, alternating mounds of light and dark meat. Brush with aspic. Mix the salad vegetables with the dressing and pile down the other side keeping back a bunch of watercress to place at one end to garnish. Scatter the orange julienne over the salad and serve.

Turkey breast Singapore

4–6 lb (1.8–2.7 kg) turkey breast
1 tablespoon curry powder
1 tablespoon fines herbes, dried
1 tablespoon salt
1 tablespoon paprika
1 onion
1 carrot
1 stick celery
½ orange
8 fl oz (2.3 dl) gin
8 fl oz (2.3 dl) water
Serves sixteen to twenty

Wash turkey breast and rub dry. Mix curry powder, herbs, salt and paprika. Rub turkey inside and out with this mixture. Place in pan with vegetables and orange. Roast uncovered at 350°F (180°C) for 3 hours, or until tender. Baste with gin and water. When done spoon off all fat from juices. Serve with the pan juices (unthickened).

Pigeon in white wine

1 onion, diced
¼ clove garlic, crushed
1 stalk celery
1 rasher bacon
olive oil
1 pigeon
sea-salt
freshly ground pepper
1 cup white wine
parsley
Serves two

Brown the onion, garlic, celery and bacon in a little olive oil. Remove and brown the pigeon in the same oil. Put the pigeon in a casserole, cover with the garnish and season to taste. Pour in sufficient water to cover the pigeon and cook in a low oven for 1 hour. Remove and add a cup of white wine. Cook for further 30 minutes. Garnish with parsley.

DE LAVERERIE

PASTA AND RICE

Chop suey

24 fl oz (6.8 dl) tomato juice
1 medium green pepper, diced
2 oz (55 g) cooked mushrooms, sliced
2 oz (55 g) celery, diced
4 oz (115 g) onion, diced
½ clove garlic
2 beef stock cubes
8 oz (225 g) cooked minced beef
8 oz (225 g) cooked macaroni
salt and pepper
Serves two

Combine tomato juice, green pepper, mushrooms, celery and onion in a saucepan. Add garlic and stock cubes and simmer over low heat until the green pepper is tender. Add the beef and macaroni, season to taste, and re-heat a further 10 minutes.

Low-calorie macaroni and cheese

8 oz (225 g) low-fat cottage cheese
4 tablespoons Cheddar cheese, grated
½ pint (2.8 dl) skimmed milk
2 eggs
1 teaspoon salt
½ teaspoon pepper
¼ teaspoon dry mustard
4 oz (115 g) cooked macaroni
½ teaspoon paprika
2 teaspoons very finely chopped parsley
Serves two

Combine cottage cheese, Cheddar, milk, eggs, salt, pepper, mustard and macaroni; mix well. Pour into a two-pint (one-litre) casserole and sprinkle with paprika and parsley. Bake at 350°F (180°C) for 45 minutes.

Slimmers' macaroni cheese

2 oz (55 g) macaroni
¼ oz (7 g) cornflour
½ pint (2.8 dl) low-fat milk (separated or skimmed)
2 oz (55 g) hard cheese, grated
1 teaspoon powdered mace or cinnamon
Serves one

Cook the macaroni in boiling, salted water till soft. Drain in a colander and wash through with hot water. Put into a warmed ovenproof dish. Mix the cornflour with about 1 tablespoon milk to smooth paste. Heat the rest of the milk to just below boiling point and add to the paste, stirring all the time. Return to the pan and stir until it has thickened to the right consistency. Add half the grated cheese and stir till smooth. Pour the sauce over the macaroni. Sprinkle with mace or cinnamon and the rest of the grated cheese. Brown under a hot grill for a few minutes.

Noodles milanese

8 oz (225 g) plain noodles
1 lb (455 g) onions, chopped
2 oz (55 g) low-calorie margarine

1 lb (455g) mushrooms, sliced
1 lb (455g) tomatoes
1 pint (5.7 dl) stock
salt and pepper

Cook the noodles. Fry the onions in the margarine and add mushrooms and tomatoes. Stir in stock, season to taste and simmer for 5 minutes. Drain the noodles and mix with other ingredients.

Cold spicy noodles

2½ oz fresh Chinese noodles (Lo Mein)
2½ cups fresh bean sprouts
½ teaspoon sesame oil
1½ tablespoons wine vinegar
1½ tablespoons light soy sauce
1 teaspoon hot oil
Serves two

Drop noodles into a large quantity of boiling water, and cook until tender, approximately 5 minutes. Drain and rinse under cold water. Allow to drain again. Add oil, toss to blend, and refrigerate, overnight if possible.

Rinse the bean sprouts. Drop into boiling water and cook for approximately 30 seconds. Drain, rinse under cold water, drain again. Combine with cold noodles.

Combine vinegar, soy sauce, and hot oil. Add to the noodle and bean-sprout mixture. Serve cold.

Rice pulao

3 oz (85 g) rice
½ oz (15 g) margarine
1 teaspoon turmeric
½ pint (2.8 dl) vegetable stock
¼ teaspoon salt
4 oz (115 g) peas, cooked
1¼ oz (35 g) raisins
2 tablespoons blanched, slivered almonds
Serves four

Wash rice and soak in water to cover for 15 minutes. Drain. Melt margarine. Add rice, turmeric, stock, salt. Cover and cook until tender (about 20 minutes). Add peas and raisins. Transfer to serving dish. Garnish with almonds.

Rice salad

12 oz (340 g) cold cooked rice
3 tablespoons chopped spring onions
2 green peppers, thinly sliced
1 clove garlic, minced
3 tomatoes, peeled and diced
2 pimentos, diced
2 tablespoons chopped parsley
2 tablespoons olive oil
⅓ cup wine vinegar
1 teaspoon salt
¼ teaspoon freshly ground black pepper
Serves six

Put the rice, spring onions, peppers, garlic, tomatoes, pimentos and parsley in a bowl and toss lightly using two forks. Shake (in a screw-topped jar) or beat the oil, vinegar, salt and pepper until well blended. Pour the dressing over the salad and toss. Chill.

Spaghetti bolognaise

8 oz (225 g) wholewheat spaghetti
1 lb (455 g) chopped onions
1 oz (30 g) low-calorie margarine
8 oz (225 g) minced beef
1 lb (455 g) tomatoes
fresh mixed herbs
salt and black pepper
Serves four

Cook the spaghetti and lightly fry the onions in the margarine. Add the mince and brown. Add remaining ingredients and cook for 10 minutes. Drain the spaghetti, put on a dish and surround with the sauce.

VEGETABLES

Artichokes espagnole

2 young artichokes
6 mushrooms, sliced
1 onion, diced
¼ cup olive oil
juice of 1 lemon
thyme
1 bayleaf
coriander
1 clove garlic, crushed
freshly ground black pepper
Serves two

Trim the artichokes by discarding the tough outer leaves, then cut the remainder into quarters. Put in an ovenproof dish and cover with the mushrooms and onion. Add olive oil, lemon juice, a touch of thyme, bayleaf, a pinch of coriander, garlic and pepper. Cover; boil for about 1 minute. Transfer to the oven and cook at 350°F (180°C) for 30 minutes. Chill.

Artichoke stuffed with shrimps

1 artichoke, cooked
6–8 shrimps, cooked
chopped celery
1 dessertspoon herb mayonnaise (low-calorie mayonnaise – see p. 181 – plus 1 teaspoon minced parsley and 1 teaspoon minced herbs, tarragon, dill, chervil or ½ teaspoon dried herbs)
Serves one

Carefully pull apart the artichoke leaves and scoop out the choke with a teaspoon. Mix shrimps with celery and herb mayonnaise and fill the artichoke with the mixture.

Artichoke with lemon dressing

1 artichoke
lemon dressing (see p. 181)
Serves one

Boil the artichoke until tender. Serve with lemon dressing.

Glazed asparagus

1 lb (455 g) asparagus
Aspic:
*   1 cup stock, preferably chicken*
*   1 onion*
*   white of 1 egg, beaten*
*   finely crushed eggshell*
*   ½ tablespoon gelatine*
*   ¼ cup cold stock*
Garnish:
*   hard-boiled egg*
*   capers*
Serves four

Prepare the asparagus: wash, remove tough ends, trim stalks neatly below the tips and tie into four bundles. Use a double-boiler for cooking, half-fill the bottom with boiling water and put the asparagus into this, covering with the top of the boiler, but inverted. Asparagus usually takes about 10 minutes – be sure that the bundles stand upright so that the stalks cook in the water and the tips in the steam. Cool. Make the liquid aspic: simmer the cup of stock with the onion, the egg white and shell for 10 minutes. Let stand for 30 minutes, strain through a fine cloth, then add $\frac{1}{2}$ tablespoon gelatine dissolved in $\frac{1}{4}$ cup cold stock. Cool, pour over the asparagus and leave to set in the refrigerator. Serve on a bed of lettuce and garnish with hard-boiled egg and capers.

Asparagus vinaigrette

5–6 spears asparagus
1 teaspoon oil
$\frac{1}{2}$ teaspoon lemon juice
salt and pepper
Serves one

Wash the asparagus well and remove the woody ends of the stems. Tie into a bundle and simmer in a pan of boiling salted water for 12–18 minutes, depending on the thickness of the stems. Lift out and remove the string. Drain carefully and leave to get cold. Meanwhile make the vinaigrette with oil, lemon juice, salt and pepper. Arrange the asparagus in a dish and dress just before serving.

Baked stuffed aubergine

1 medium aubergine
1 tablespoon olive oil
1 onion, minced
4 oz (115 g) mushrooms, sliced
1 green pepper, diced
2 tomatoes, peeled and chopped
$\frac{1}{2}$ teaspoon basil
$1\frac{1}{2}$ teaspoons salt
$\frac{1}{4}$ teaspoon freshly ground black pepper
Serves six

Wash the aubergine. Dry well and cut in half lengthwise. Carefully scoop out and dice the pulp. Heat the olive oil in a pan and sauté the onion,

mushrooms, green pepper and aubergine pulp for 10 minutes, stirring often. Add the tomatoes, basil, salt and pepper and cook for another 5 minutes. Stuff the aubergine shells with the sautéed vegetables and place in a baking pan containing $\frac{1}{2}$ inch (12 mm) water. Bake at 375°F (190°C) for 20 minutes. To serve, cut each shell in three.

Lebanese aubergines

2 large sliced aubergines
oil
1 large carton natural yogurt
2 cloves fresh garlic
salt
dried mint
paprika
Serves two

Fry the aubergines in oil until lightly cooked. Whisk the yogurt until smooth, crush the garlic and add to the yogurt with salt to taste. When the aubergines are cold, lay them, overlapping, in a shallow dish and pour the yogurt over them. Garnish with dried mint and paprika.

Aubergine parmigiana

1 large aubergine
1 tablespoon olive oil
3 tablespoons grated Parmesan cheese
$\frac{1}{2}$ teaspoon dry breadcrumbs
$\frac{1}{2}$ teaspoon garlic powder
$\frac{1}{2}$ teaspoon salt
$\frac{1}{4}$ teaspoon freshly ground black pepper
8 oz (225 g) tinned tomato sauce
3 thin slices mozzarella cheese
Serves six

Peel the aubergine and cut in slices $\frac{1}{4}$ inch (6 mm) thick. Pour boiling water over the slices and soak for 5 minutes. Drain and dry thoroughly. Heat the oil in a pan and brown the aubergine on both sides. Combine the grated Parmesan cheese, breadcrumbs, garlic powder, salt and pepper, and mix thoroughly. Arrange in a baking dish layers of aubergine, cheese–crumb mixture and tomato sauce. Cover with the mozzarella cheese slices and bake in a 325°F (170°C) oven for 25 minutes.

Aubergine and tomato pie

2 aubergines
4 tomatoes
2 onions
1 green pepper
garlic, crushed
¼ cup olive oil
pepper
Parmesan cheese, grated
Serves two

Fill a shallow pie-dish with alternate layers of sautéed aubergine, tomato and onion slices and raw green pepper rings. Sprinkle the top with a little crushed garlic, olive oil, pepper to taste and grated Parmesan cheese. Bake in a moderate oven (350°F, 180°C) for 40–45 minutes.

Tuna-stuffed aubergine

1 large aubergine
2 tablespoons oil
1 large onion, chopped
1 clove garlic, crushed
8 oz (225 g) tin tomatoes, drained
1 teaspoon mixed herbs
2 tablespoons tomato purée
salt and pepper
4 oz (115 g) tin tuna, drained
2 oz (55 g) Cheddar cheese, grated
Serves two

Cut the aubergine in half lengthways. Remove the inside flesh and chop roughly. Heat the oil in a pan, brown the onion, add the garlic, tomatoes, herbs, tomato purée and aubergine, and season. Bring to the boil and cook for 15–20 minutes. Flake the tuna and stir into the mixture. Pile into the aubergine shells. Sprinkle with the grated cheese. Cover and cook for 30–35 minutes at 375°F, (190°C), until golden brown.

Avocado niçoise

4 oz (115 g) green beans, cooked
4 thick slices cucumber, diced
2 tomatoes, quartered
2 spring onions, chopped
4 oz (115 g) tin tuna
2 tablespoons French dressing (see p. 181)
1 clove garlic, crushed
salt and pepper
½ ripe avocado
1 hard-boiled egg
1 oz (30 g) tin anchovies
4 black olives
Serves two

Put beans, cucumber, tomatoes, spring onions and drained tuna in a bowl. Stir in the French dressing and garlic. Season. Cut up avocado and add to salad. Pile the mixture into a serving dish. Decorate with egg, anchovies and black olives.

Pan-fried carrots

1½ tablespoons margarine
1 lb (455 g) carrots, finely shredded
½ teaspoon salt
2 tablespoons water
1 to 2 tablespoons brown sugar
Serves four

Melt the margarine in a heavy saucepan. Add the carrots. Sprinkle with salt and add water. Cover with a tight-fitting lid. Cook until tender (6–8 minutes), stirring occasionally to prevent sticking. Add sugar; stir till melted. (This method works for cabbage, green beans and most leafy vegetables.)

Carrot pudding

6 large carrots, sliced
2 tablespoons finely chopped onion
2 tablespoons finely chopped green pepper
1 tablespoon salad oil or margarine
1 tablespoon plain flour
⅛ teaspoon artificial sweetener

little salt
8 fl oz (2.3 dl) skimmed milk
Serves four to six

Cook carrots in water until tender. Drain and mash. Sauté onion and green pepper in oil or margarine until yellow. Stir in flour and seasonings. Cook until bubbly and add the skimmed milk. Cook until thickened. Add the carrots. Pour into lightly greased three-pint ($1\frac{1}{2}$-litre) casserole and bake at 350°F (180°C) for 30 minutes.

Cauliflower with Taratour

1 large cauliflower
a little oil
Taratour sauce (see p. 182)
Serves six to eight

Cut cauliflower into flowerettes, and parboil for about 3 minutes. Cool, dry and fry in hot oil until golden brown. Leave to cool. Now make the sauce and serve with the cauliflower.

Stuffed courgettes

1 or 2 courgettes depending on size
4 oz (115 g) cooked minced beef
1 oz (30 g) butter
Serves one

Cook courgettes in boiling water for 2 minutes. Refresh with cold water. Split in two lengthwise and scoop out the seeds with a teaspoon. Stuff with well-flavoured minced beef. Bake in a casserole with the butter at 350°F, (180°C), for approximately 20 minutes, basting well.

Fresh mango with yogurt

$\frac{1}{2}$ teaspoon margarine
$\frac{1}{4}$ teaspoon black mustard seeds
1 green chilli (fresh or tinned) finely minced
1 clove garlic, finely minced
16 fl oz (4.5 dl) plain yogurt
salt to taste

pinch of sugar
3 ripe, fresh mangoes, sliced
Serves three

Melt the margarine and fry the mustard seeds until they begin to pop. Combine the seeds, chilli, garlic, yogurt, salt, sugar. Add mangoes, serve cold.

Mushrooms à la grecque

$\frac{3}{4}$ cup water
$\frac{1}{4}$ cup olive oil
juice and rind of 1 lemon
8 oz (225 g) small mushrooms, wiped clean
mustard and cress
bouquet garni:
*   1 small bayleaf*
*   pinch celery seeds*
*   4 peppercorns*
*   sprig of parsley*
* $\frac{1}{4}$ teaspoon herbs*
Serves two

Put the bouquet garni in a cheesecloth bag in a pan with the water, oil, lemon juice and rind. Boil for 10 minutes; then add the mushrooms and cook for another 10 minutes. Stand aside to cool, still in the liquid, then chill. Serve on a bed of mustard and cress.

Creamed mushrooms

4 oz (115 g) mushrooms
$\frac{1}{4}$ lemon
salt and pepper
$\frac{1}{2}$ teaspoon caraway seeds
parsley
2 cups water
1 small carton yogurt
Serves two

Clean the mushrooms. Depending on size, either halve or quarter them – if very large they should be sliced; if small, leave whole. Into a small saucepan put the $\frac{1}{4}$ lemon, pinch of salt and pepper, caraway seeds and the parsley. Add 2 cups water and bring to boil. Simmer for 5 minutes, then add the mushrooms and cook until tender. Strain through a sieve (the liquid may be used for stock, added to consommé or aspic jelly). Throw away the lemon and the parsley. Empty the yogurt into a saucepan, add the mushrooms and a little of the liquid in which they were cooked. Heat thoroughly and adjust the seasoning.

Onion and apple casserole

2 onions
3 apples
pepper
butter
cinnamon
brown sugar
Serves two

Slice onions and simmer in $\frac{3}{4}$ cup water for 10 minutes. Drain, but save the liquid. Peel, core and slice the apples. Arrange the onions and apples in alternate layers in a dish, covering the onions with pepper and a little lightly salted butter, and the apples with the cinnamon, brown sugar and a little more butter. Add some of the reserved onion liquid and bake in a moderately hot oven for 45 minutes.

Stuffed green peppers (i)

3 onions
4 oz (115 g) lean minced beef
2 tablespoons uncooked rice
1 egg, beaten
2 tablespoons cold water
2½ teaspoons salt
½ teaspoon freshly ground black pepper
6 large green peppers
1 tablespoon butter
29 oz (825 g) tin red tomatoes
4 tablespoons lemon juice
Serves six

Grate 1 onion. Put in a bowl with the beef, rice, egg, water, $1\frac{1}{4}$ teaspoons salt and $\frac{1}{4}$ teaspoon pepper and mix thoroughly. Wash the peppers. Cut a 1 inch (2.5 cm) slice from the stem ends and

reserve. Scoop out the seeds. Stuff the peppers with the beef–rice mixture and replace the reserved slices. Slice the remaining onions. Melt the butter in a heavy saucepan and sauté the onions for 5 minutes. Add the tomatoes and remaining salt and pepper. Arrange the peppers on top in an upright position, cover and cook over a low heat for $1\frac{1}{4}$ hours. Mix in the lemon juice and cook 15 minutes more, or until peppers are tender. Adjust seasoning – the sauce should have a sweet- and- sour flavour. Skim off the fat before serving.

Stuffed green peppers (ii)

6 green peppers, seeded
8 oz (225 g) mushrooms
½ teaspoon salt
2 tablespoons water
12 oz (340 g) cooked brown rice
8 oz (225 g) peas, cooked
1 tablespoon parsley, finely chopped
¼ teaspoon salt
pepper to taste
16 fl oz (4.5 dl) tomato juice
Serves six

Boil the peppers for 5 minutes; drain. Wipe the mushrooms with damp cloth; slice. Heat a saucepan and add $\frac{1}{2}$ teaspoon salt and the mushrooms. Stir continuously for 2 minutes. Add water and simmer for 2 minutes until the mushrooms wilt. Combine the rice, mushrooms, peas, parsley, salt and pepper. Stuff the peppers with the mixture. Place in a baking dish and pour tomato juice over. Bake at 350°F (180°C) for 30 minutes. Baste peppers with the liquid, adding water if necessary.

Stuffed green peppers (iii)

2 green peppers
8 oz (225 g) mince
1 tablespoon uncooked rice
1 large onion, chopped
1 tablespoon Worcestershire sauce
1 tablespoon tomato sauce

salt
1 tablespoon mixed herbs
small tin condensed soup
Serves two

Remove the tops and wash out the peppers. Mix the uncooked mince, rice, onion, Worcestershire sauce, tomato sauce, salt and herbs together and pile into the pepper. Replace the tops and put in a heavy-bottomed saucepan. Pour over the condensed soup and simmer for about 40 minutes.

Low-calorie stuffed pepper

1 green pepper
4 oz (115 g) lean minced beef
1 small diced onion
1 minced clove of garlic
pinch of parsley, cumin and paprika
2 teaspoons breadcrumbs
1 teaspoon grated Parmesan cheese
salt and pepper
1–2 tomatoes
Serves one

Having removed the seeds, parboil the pepper for 5 minutes. Sauté the beef, with the onion, garlic, parsley, cumin and paprika. Mix with the breadcrumbs, cheese and seasoning to taste. Stuff the pepper with the mixture and bake for 30 minutes at 375°F (190°C). Serve with grilled tomato.

Fenugreek potatoes

1 lb (455 g) potatoes boiled in their skins
2 tablespoons oil
½ teaspoon turmeric
2 cups fenugreek sprouts
dash cayenne
1 teaspoon salt
Serves four

Peel and chop the boiled potatoes. Heat the oil in a frying pan and add the potatoes and turmeric. Sauté for 3 minutes, stirring constantly. Add the fenugreek, cayenne and salt. Mix well and cook covered for 5 minutes.

Potatoes with avocado topping

½ avocado
1 oz (30 g) natural yogurt
salt and pepper
2 baked potatoes
Serves two

Mash the avocado with the yogurt. Beat well and season. Make a cross cut on the top of the baked potatoes, squeeze open and put a generous spoonful of the avocado mixture in each.

Quick ratatouille

tomatoes
courgettes
aubergines
chopped garlic
salt and pepper
The quantities for this can be adapted to serve as many as you want.

Arrange the vegetables in layers in a baking dish. Season with garlic, salt and pepper, and bake in a covered dish at 300°F (150°C) for 2 hours.

Ratatouille (i)

8 oz (225 g) aubergines
8 oz (225 g) courgettes
3 teaspoons salt
3 tablespoons olive oil
8 oz (225 g) onions, coarsely chopped
2 medium green peppers
2 cloves garlic, minced
1½ lb (680 g) tomatoes, seeded and coarsely chopped
2 teaspoons salt
¼ teaspoon black pepper
2 teaspoons basil
Serves four

Peel the aubergines and cut into strips. Slice the courgettes in the same way. Mix the aubergine and courgette with 1 teaspoon salt and allow to stand for 30 minutes. Drain, blot dry with kitchen paper and sauté with 2 tablespoons olive oil until lightly browned. Remove from the pan. In the same pan cook the onions, peppers, garlic in 1 tablespoon olive oil. Add the cooked aubergines, courgettes and tomatoes. Season with salt, pepper and basil. Cook in a covered pan for 20 minutes. Uncover; cook for 10 more minutes to evaporate some of liquid.

Ratatouille (ii)

½ aubergine
1 small courgette
salt
¼ green pepper
¼ onion
small clove garlic
1 dessertspoon oil
1 tomato
a pinch of coriander
Serves one

Slice the aubergine and courgette, sprinkle with salt, cover with a plate and leave to stand for 1 hour. Drain away any moisture. Remove seeds and core from the pepper and cut into slices. Slice the onion, crush the garlic and fry in oil. Add the aubergine, courgette and pepper. Season. Cover and cook gently for 30 minutes. Skin, de-seed and slice the tomato; add to the pan with the coriander and cook for another 10 minutes.

Slimmers' ratatouille

1 large aubergine
2 medium-sized courgettes
2 onions
8 oz (225 g) tomatoes
1 large pepper, finely chopped
2 cloves garlic, crushed
salt and pepper
chopped herbs – basil, parsley, etc.
a little chicken stock
Serves two

Slice the aubergine and courgettes, cut the onions into rings, skin and chop the tomatoes, slice the

pepper. Put all the ingredients into a saucepan and add a little stock. Cover and simmer until the vegetables are cooked – stir occasionally and add more stock if necessary. Adjust seasoning. Serve hot or cold.

Soya-bean loaf

9 oz (255 g) cooked and drained soya beans
1 chicken stock cube
¼ teaspoon powdered sage
½ teaspoon dried onion flakes
dash of garlic powder
1 teaspoon Worcestershire sauce
4 oz (115 g) tomato juice
2 sticks cooked celery, diced
½ medium green pepper, blanched and diced
2 oz (55 g) cooked carrots, diced
salt and pepper
1 tomato, sliced
Serves one

Preheat oven to 400°F (200°C). Put the first seven ingredients in a blender and blend until smooth. Pour into a mixing bowl. Fold in the celery, pepper and carrots. Season to taste. Turn into a non-stick loaf tin, top with tomato slices and bake for 45 minutes. Serve with mushroom sauce (see p. 182).

Spinach hors d'oeuvres

8 oz (225 g) spinach
parsley
½ onion, chopped
a tarragon leaf
2 hard-boiled eggs
2 sardines
1 anchovy fillet
salt and pepper
pumpernickel bread
Serves two

Combine the washed spinach with a little parsley, the onion and the tarragon leaf. Cook quickly for 5 minutes without water. Drain and combine with the hard-boiled eggs, sardines and anchovy, all neatly chopped. Purée in blender, season with salt and pepper to taste. Spread on a shallow dish or baking sheet and chill. Serve on slices of pumpernickel.

Spinach italienne

2 lb (0.9 kg) spinach
½ cupful breadcrumbs
1 tablespoon butter
salt and pepper
1 teaspoon lemon juice
2 hard-boiled eggs
Serves four

Wash and cook spinach in as little water as possible. Brown the breadcrumbs in butter. When spinach is cooked, drain and toss in salt, pepper, lemon juice and the diced whites of eggs. Place in dish and sprinkle with breadcrumbs and sieved egg yolks.

Spinach à l'orange

1½ lb (680 g) small leaf spinach
sea-salt
4 dessertspoons olive oil
½ clove garlic, crushed
nutmeg
2 mandarins or 1 orange
grated Parmesan
Serves two to four

Boil the spinach in salted water for 6–8 minutes. Drain well. In a heavy pan heat the oil with the garlic, toss in the spinach and sprinkle with the nutmeg: stir well over a low flame until the liquid is absorbed. Peel the mandarins or orange, divide into segments (cut the segments in half if you are using an orange) and toss into the cooked spinach. Serve with a little grated Parmesan.

Baked tomato with spinach purée

1½ lb (680 g) fresh spinach
1 tablespoon chopped onion

4 fl oz (1.1 dl) skimmed milk
salt and white pepper
2 medium tomatoes, cut in half
Parmesan cheese or chopped mushrooms or capers
Serves four

Wash the spinach and place in a saucepan with the onion. Heat only until the spinach has wilted. Drain dry, add half the milk and blend at high speed until finely chopped. Place in saucepan with the remaining milk and simmer for 5 minutes. Season. Bake the tomatoes at 375°F (190°C) until tender. Pile the spinach high on top, sprinkle with Parmesan cheese or chopped mushrooms or capers and return to the oven until hot.

Tomato and fennel casserole

1 onion
3 cloves garlic
4 bulbs fennel
½ cup olive oil
i large tin Italian tomatoes
salt and freshly ground black pepper
½ cup wholewheat breadcrumbs
3 tablespoons grated Cheddar cheese
grated rind of ½ lemon

Chop onion and garlic. Halve the fennel and cut into wedges. Heat the oil in a heavy casserole. Sauté onions and garlic until soft and add the fennel. Cook until the fennel starts to brown, stirring from time to time. Add the tomatoes and seasoning. Lower the heat and simmer for 5 minutes. Sprinkle with breadcrumbs, cheese and grated lemon rind and bake in a hot oven until the topping is crisp.

Sorbet de tomates

2½ lb (1.1 kg) ripe tomatoes, peeled, seeded and cut up
2 anchovies
1 tablespoon olive oil
2 teaspoons lemon juice
1 teaspoon grenadine
2–3 dashes Tabasco sauce

2–3 teaspoons Worcestershire sauce
salt and freshly ground pepper
¼ *cup dill or basil, trimmed of stems*
optional garnish – additional sprigs of fresh dill or basil
Serves six

Blend all the ingredients in a liquidizer till smooth, stopping after a few seconds to push down with a spatula any pieces clinging to the side of the bowl; then blend for a few seconds longer. The mixture should be smooth with consistency of thin pancake batter. Taste and correct seasoning, remembering that very cold food can be more highly seasoned than usual. Freeze. Spoon into stemmed glasses and serve, decorated, if you like, with sprigs of fresh herbs. If the sorbet is frozen solid break it up, replace in the liquidizer and blend (adding 1 or 2 more teaspoons grenadine to preserve the colour as it tends to lighten during blending) until just soft enough to spoon into glasses. If there is any left over turn it into a gazpacho-like soup by stirring in half the amount of yogurt and adding a bit of chopped cucumber.

Stuffed tomatoes (i)

2 large or 4 small tomatoes
cucumber
mint
French dressing (see p. 181)
Serves two

Slice the tops off the tomatoes, scoop out the seeds with a teaspoon, being careful not to break the skin, and turn the tomatoes upside down to drain. Fill with a mixture of finely diced cucumber, chopped mint and a tablespoon of French dressing.

Stuffed tomatoes (ii)

4 large or 8 small tomatoes
1 lettuce
1 small tin tuna fish
juice of 1 lemon
1 tablespoon chopped parsley
salt and pepper
Serves four

Cut a slice off the top of the tomatoes and scoop out the flesh. Wash the lettuce and keep back some leaves on which to serve the tomatoes. Shred the remainder finely and mix with the well-drained tuna fish, lemon, parsley and seasoning. Fill the tomatoes with this mixture and replace the tops. Arrange on the lettuce leaves and serve chilled.

Stuffed tomatoes (iii)

2 large or 4 small tomatoes
2 oz (55 g) peeled shrimps
2 oz (55 g) cottage cheese
salt and pepper
lettuce
watercress
Serves two

Cut a slice from the top of each tomato. Scoop out the flesh and allow to drain. Chop the shrimps and mix with the cottage cheese and seasoning. Fill the tomatoes, top with the lids and arrange on a bed of lettuce and watercress.

Stuffed tomatoes (iv)

1 large or 2 small tomatoes
1 hard-boiled egg, mashed
1 radish, chopped
2 spring onions, chopped
salt and pepper
¼ *cucumber, chopped and seeded*
mayonnaise
watercress
Serves one

Slice the tops off the tomatoes. Remove the flesh, push it through a sieve and add the egg, radish, spring onions, seasoning and cucumber. Blend with a little mayonnaise. Fill the empty tomatoes with this mixture and serve with watercress.

Tomato and vegetable aspic

4 cups tinned tomatoes
2 stalks celery

1 sliced onion
1 bayleaf
artificial sweetener
1 teaspoon salt
½ teaspoon freshly ground black pepper
¼ teaspoon marjoram
2 tablespoons plain gelatine
1 tablespoon lemon juice
1 lb (455 g) cooked mixed vegetables, diced
shredded lettuce
Serves four

Put the tomatoes in a saucepan with the celery, onion, bayleaf, sweetener, salt, pepper and marjoram. Cook over a low heat for 20 minutes. Rub through a sieve and then strain through cheesecloth. Soften the gelatine in a little cold water and stir into the hot tomato liquid. Stir until dissolved. Add the lemon juice and taste for seasoning. Cool or stir over ice until the aspic is on the point of setting. Mix the vegetables into the aspic and pour into a three-pint (1½ litre) mould which has been rinsed with cold water. Chill until set and firm, then carefully unmould onto a cold serving dish. Serve on shredded lettuce.

Turnips with cheese and garlic

2 lb (0.9 kg) turnips
2 onions
1 clove garlic
1½ cups milk
½ cup cream
salt and freshly ground black pepper
½ cup grated Cheddar cheese
Chopped parsley or chives for garnish
Serves four

Peel and slice the turnips; chop the onions and slice the garlic. Put all ingredients except the cheese into a heavy casserole and bring to the boil. Simmer for 3 minutes, stirring all the time. Grease a dish with a little butter, put in the mixture and cover with grated cheese. Bake in a moderate oven for 45 minutes. Sprinkle with chopped parsley or chives before serving.

Vegetables with bean-curd sauce

Bean-curd sauce:
  3 tablespoons sesame seeds
  1 cake bean curd ('tofu' in oriental stores)
  1 tablespoon sugar
  2 teaspoons soy sauce
8 oz (225 g) turnips, peeled
4 medium carrots, peeled
2 oz (55 g) bamboo shoots
1 stock cube
1 teaspoon soy sauce
½ teaspoon salt
½ teaspoon sugar
1 pint (5.7 dl) water
8 oz (225 g) spinach, washed, de-stemmed
Serves four

To make the sauce, toast the sesame seeds in an ungreased frying pan until golden. Blend the bean curd, sugar and soy sauce and add to the sesame seeds.

Cut the turnips, carrots and bamboo shoots into julienne strips. Add the stock cube, soy sauce, salt and sugar to the water and bring to the boil. Add all the vegetables. Cover and cook for 5 minutes. Drain, add sauce and mix lightly. Serve immediately, with bean-curd sauce.

SALADS

Crunchy apple salad

2 apples
2 tablespoons lemon juice
2 sticks celery
3 medium carrots
1 green pepper
Serves four to six

Core the apples and slice them thinly. Toss in the lemon juice. Thinly slice the vegetables, mix together with the apple and serve.

Avocado salad (i)

1 medium cucumber
1 small avocado
2 tomatoes
2 cups any bean sprouts
1 tablespoon French dressing (see p. 181)
1 teaspoon chopped chives
Serves six

Finely slice the cucumber without peeling. Peel and slice the avocado. Slice the tomatoes. Mix all ingredients with French dressing and sprinkle with chives.

Avocado salad (ii)

12 oz (340 g) white cabbage or Chinese leaves, shredded
1–2 tablespoons grated onion
4 carrots, peeled and julienned
2 oz (55 g) roughly chopped walnuts
4 chopped tomatoes
1 large avocado
4 tablespoons French dressing (see p. 181)
salt, pepper and parsley
Serves four to six

Put the first six ingredients into a large bowl. Season to taste, add dressing and toss well. Decorate with parsley.

Crunchy avocado salad

Iceberg lettuce (heart only)
½ avocado, sliced
4 rashers bacon
lemon dressing (see p. 181)
Serves two

Wash and dry the lettuce and put into a bowl with the avocado. Grill the bacon until crisp and crumble over the lettuce and avocado. Heat a little lemon dressing and pour over.

Savoury banana salad

1 lettuce
4 bananas
4 tomatoes
Serves four

Make a nest of lettuce in a salad bowl. Peel and slice the bananas. Pile in the centre of the lettuce and surround with sliced tomatoes.

Corned beef and lettuce salad

1 tablespoon finely chopped onion
½ oz (15 g) butter or margarine
½ level tablespoon plain flour
1 level teaspoon dry mustard
2½ fl oz (70 ml) stock
1 tablespoon vinegar
4 oz (115 g) corned beef
salt and pepper
1 teaspoon Worcestershire sauce
1 small lettuce
a few cooked peas or other salad vegetables to garnish
Serves four

Fry the onion in the butter or margarine. Add the flour and mustard mix and cook for a few minutes. Add stock and stir until it boils. Boil for a few minutes. Add vinegar, chopped corned beef, seasoning and Worcestershire sauce and leave to become cold. Line a bowl with the lettuce leaves or arrange on individual plates. Pile the filling in the centre. Garnish with the green peas or other salad vegetables.

Cold roast beef salad

1 teaspoon hot mustard
¼ teaspoon dried tarragon
1 dessertspoon oil and vinegar dressing
3 oz (85 g) cold roast beef, sliced
¼ cup cold cooked green beans
1 small tomato, quartered
1 dessertspoon chopped parsley
lettuce
Serves one

Mix the mustard and tarragon into the dressing, and toss with the roast beef and green beans. Marinate ½ hour, then mix in tomatoes and parsley; serve on lettuce.

Marinated beetroots

8 oz (225 g) freshly cooked beetroots
4 fl oz (1.1 dl) red wine vinegar

1 piece fresh dill
1 whole onion
a few drops artificial sweetener
Serves four

Combine the ingredients and refrigerate for as long as you wish.

Caesar salad

3 heads Romaine lettuce
2 cloves garlic, minced
2 tablespoons olive oil
2 slices white toast, trimmed and cut into small cubes
¼ teaspoon dry mustard
1 teaspoon salt
½ teaspoon freshly ground black pepper
5 tablespoons lemon juice
1 egg, boiled for 1 minute
3 tablespoons grated Parmesan cheese
4 anchovy fillets, shredded
Serves six

Wash the lettuce and remove the large outside leaves. Dry well on kitchen paper and chill until needed – the crisper the lettuce, the better the salad will be. Combine half the garlic with the oil, pour over the toast cubes and toss until well coated. Tear the chilled lettuce into a salad bowl. Sprinkle with the mustard, salt, pepper and remaining garlic and toss lightly. Mix the lemon juice and remaining oil, pour over the lettuce and toss. Break the egg over the lettuce and toss until egg is thoroughly mixed in. Add the cheese and anchovies and toss again. Sprinkle the salad with the toast cubes.

Cottage cheese, celery and walnut salad

1 stick celery
6 walnuts
1 tablespoon cottage cheese
Serves one

Chop the celery and walnuts and mix lightly with cottage cheese just before serving.

Chicken and mushroom salad

8 oz (225 g) cooked diced chicken
4 oz (115 g) cooked or tinned mushrooms
8 oz (225 g) diced celery
French dressing (see p. 181) to moisten
salt and pepper
1 lettuce
Serves four

Mix the first five ingredients together and serve in a nest of lettuce leaves.

Salad Clementine

2 oz (55 g) anchovies
1 lb (455 g) tomatoes
6 sliced hard-boiled eggs
2 oz (55 g) capers
1 tablespoon chopped parsley
Dressing:
   juice of 1 lemon
   2 tablespoons tomato ketchup
   salt and pepper
Serves eight

Soak the anchovies in warm water to remove some of the oil. Drain well. Peel the tomatoes by plunging them first into near-boiling water for 8 seconds then straight into cold to loosen the skins. Halve them. Place sliced eggs in an oval dish. Cover with mixed capers and parsley. Place tomato halves cut side down on the capers. Cut the anchovies longways into thin strips. Lattice them across the tomatoes. Cover this with the dressing just before serving.

Apple coleslaw

Dressing:
   1 carton natural low-fat yogurt
   1 teaspoon lemon juice
   ¼ teaspoon salt
   1 tablespoon chopped olives
2 cups finely shredded white cabbage
2 large grated carrots

6 leaves chopped mint
2 diced apples
Serves four to six

Combine the ingredients for the dressing. Mix the salad and toss in the dressing.

German coleslaw

1 head red or white cabbage
2 tablespoons finely chopped onion (optional)
2 fl oz (55 ml) cider vinegar
3 dessertspoons vegetable salad oil
freshly milled pepper
Serves four to six

Shred cabbage as fine as possible. Cover with boiling water for 5 minutes. Drain dry. Add the rest of ingredients and toss lightly. Serve warm.

Cucumber salad (i)

1 cucumber, peeled and finely sliced
8 fl oz (2.3 dl) Japanese seasoned rice wine vinegar
2 teaspoons sugar
salt and pepper to taste
2 spring onions, thinly sliced
Serves two

Place the cucumber in a bowl. Combine the rest of ingredients. Add to the cucumber. Marinate for at least 1 hour.

Cucumber salad (ii)

small tin tuna fish
½ pint (2.8 dl) yogurt
1 cucumber (diced)
juice of ½ lemon
black pepper and salt
chopped parsley
Serves four

Flake the tuna fish and mix with the rest of the ingredients. Season well. Sprinkle with chopped parsley.

Jellied cucumber salad

1 tablespoon unflavoured gelatine
1 fl oz (30 ml) cold water
1 tablespoon grated onion
3 oz (85 g) coarsely grated cucumber
6 tablespoons prepared horse-radish
6 tablespoons vinegar
lettuce
Serves four

Dissolve the gelatine in cold water. Melt over hot water and add the rest of the ingredients. Pour into individual moulds. Refrigerate; serve with lettuce.

Cucumber and green-bean salad

4 oz (115 g) green string beans
sea-salt
½ unpeeled cucumber, finely sliced
6 radishes, finely sliced
low-calorie dressing (see p. 181)
1 hard-boiled egg, chopped
Serves one

Boil the beans in a little sea-salt and water; leave to cool. Combine with the cucumber and radishes. Toss with salad dressing and sprinkle with chopped hard-boiled egg.

Swedish cucumbers

2 cucumbers, peeled and very thinly sliced
white wine vinegar to cover
6 spring onions, thinly sliced
½ teaspoon dried or few fresh sprigs of dill
¼ teaspoon artificial sweetener
Serves four

Place all the ingredients in a bowl. Cover and refrigerate for several hours.

Esqueixda salad

½ cupful flaked cod
onion, grated

2–3 anchovies, chopped
4 stuffed olives
1 chopped green pepper
2 sliced hard-boiled eggs
salt and pepper
lettuce or endive
olive oil
lemon juice
Serves two

Boil, flake and cool cod. Add the onion, anchovies, olives, pepper, hard-boiled eggs, salt and pepper and toss with lettuce leaves or curly endive. Serve with olive oil and lemon juice.

Sliced fruit and cottage cheese

1 fresh pear
lime juice
1 orange
4 oz (115 g) cottage cheese
¼ teaspoon celery seeds
lettuce
Serves one

Peel, core and slice the pear; dip in lime juice. Peel and slice the orange. Mix cottage cheese and celery seeds. Serve with sliced fruit on lettuce.

Tossed green salad

1 head Romaine lettuce
½ chopped green pepper
5 raw sliced mushrooms
garlic
watercress
mustard and cress
low-calorie dressing (see p. 181)
Serves one

Rub a salad bowl with garlic and put all the ingredients into it. Toss with salad dressing.

Ham and avocado salad

1 green pepper, de-seeded and sliced
2 sticks celery chopped

1 small onion
3 oz (85 g) ham, shredded
1 apple, cored and sliced
½ ripe avocado
2 tablespoons French dressing (see p. 181)
1 hard-boiled egg, chopped
Serves two

Put the pepper, celery, onion, ham and apple in a bowl. Add sliced avocado. Stir in the French dressing. Pile the mixture into a serving dish and sprinkle with chopped egg.

Health salad

½ cup alfalfa
½ cup triticale
½ bunch watercress
½ fresh orange
4 crushed walnuts
2 spring onions, chopped
2 tablespoons French dressing (see p. 181)
Serves one

Mix the first six ingredients together and toss in French dressing.

Health salad Pietro

3 young carrots
2 apples
2 celery stalks
juice of 1 lemon
Serves one

Grate the carrots, apples and celery into a salad bowl. Cover with the lemon juice.

Herb salad with tomatoes and raisins

1 tablespoon each of
 thyme, basil, fennel, tarragon, marjoram and chives
1 oz (30 g) raisins
3 tomatoes
Dressing:
 2 tablespoons olive oil

juice of 1 lemon
 1 teaspoon French mustard
 1 teaspoon brown sugar
 pinch sea-salt
 freshly ground black pepper
Serves one

Chop the herbs and raisins. Peel and quarter the tomatoes, add the raisins and sprinkle with the herb mixture. Toss with dressing.

Lentil salad

2 tablespoons olive oil
1 tablespoon wine vinegar
2½ oz (70 g) finely minced onion
2 tablespoons finely minced parsley
salt and pepper
8 oz (225 g) cooked lentils
4 tomatoes
1 cucumber
Serves four

Mix oil, vinegar, onion, parsley, salt and pepper. Add lentils and toss. Serve cold with sliced tomatoes and cucumber.

Mozzarella and tomato salad

2 large tomatoes
2 oz (55 g) mozzarella cheese
2 tablespoons lemon dressing
fresh basil, finely chopped
freshly ground pepper
Serves two

Skin and slice the tomatoes. Slice cheese thinly. Arrange an overlapping layer of cheese and tomatoes on a plate. Add the dressing, chopped basil and pepper.

Mushroom salad

1 cup sliced raw mushrooms
1 cup bean sprouts (any kind)
½ cup fresh peas

1 small potato, scrubbed and thinly sliced
2 cups alfalfa sprouts
French dressing (see p. 181)
Serves four

Mix all the vegetables in a bowl and serve with French dressing.

Mushroom and tomato salad

4 oz (115 g) fresh mushrooms
2 tomatoes
French dressing (see p. 181) to moisten
4 crisp lettuce leaves
Serves one

Wash the mushrooms and tomatoes. Peel and slice the mushrooms finely. Slice the tomatoes and mix in the mushrooms. Add a little French dressing to moisten, toss and serve in the centre of the lettuce leaves.

Onion and tomato salad

1 onion
4 tomatoes
chives
dill
celery seeds
ground pepper
Serves two

Thinly slice the onion. Peel and thickly slice the tomatoes; arrange in bowl with the onions at the bottom. Sprinkle with chives and dill, a few celery seeds and ground pepper. Chill.

Orange salad

4 oranges
chopped tarragon and chervil
2 tablespoons oil
1 tablespoon vinegar
2 teaspoons lemon juice
watercress or lettuce
Serves four

Peel the oranges and remove the pith. Slice thinly, removing all pips. Sprinkle with the chopped herbs. Mix oil, vinegar, and lemon juice and pour over the oranges. Leave to stand for a while. Surround with watercress or lettuce.

Orange and olive salad

sliced orange
2 slices onion
6 black olives, stoned
low-calorie dressing (see p. 181)
Serves one

Cut orange slices into sections, add the slices of onion and the olives. Toss with dressing.

Parisian salad

8 oz (225 g) cold cooked veal
4 small boiled potatoes, diced
2 small onions, parboiled and chopped
2 hard-boiled eggs, sliced
4 tomatoes, sliced
French dressing (see p. 181) to moisten
1 small lettuce or a few leaves
2 teaspoons chopped parsley
Serves four

Cut the meat in thin strips. Mix the meat, potatoes, onions, eggs and tomatoes. Combine with the dressing. Add the lettuce torn roughly or left whole if the leaves are small. Sprinkle with parsley and serve.

Pear and watercress salad

1 pear
½ bunch watercress
Serves one

Peel and halve pear. Chop watercress into fine pieces and toss with a little dressing. Arrange the pear on a bed of cress, leaving a little to decorate the hollow of the pear.

Opposite: Scavullo, 1975
Overleaf: Chatelain, 1978

Roast pepper salad

4 green peppers
2 red onions, sliced
2 cucumbers, peeled and sliced
3 tomatoes, peeled and sliced
2 tablespoons olive oil
3 tablespoons cider vinegar
2 tablespoons water
1 teaspoon salt
¼ teaspoon freshly ground pepper
Serves six

Wash the peppers and dry on kitchen paper. Place on a long fork one at a time, and hold over gas flame until the skin browns and wrinkles. Peel and cut into 1 inch (2.5 cm) strips. Cool for 1 hour. Put the pepper strips in a bowl with the onions, cucumbers and tomatoes. Beat the oil, vinegar, water, salt and pepper until well blended and pour it over the vegetable salad. Mix lightly. Chill 1 hour before serving.

Pineapple and lettuce salad

4 large lettuce leaves
4 rings fresh pineapple
¼ medium cucumber
1 oz (30 g) watercress to garnish
Serves four

Wash, drain, and dry the lettuce leaves. Put one on each plate, put a pineapple ring on each. Chop the cucumber, pile it in the centre of the pineapple, and decorate with watercress.

Prawn salad

4 oz (115 g) French beans
4–6 sticks celery
½ cucumber
½ bunch watercress
¼ avocado
juice of 1 lemon
4 oz (115 g) peeled prawns

1 tablespoon chopped parsley
salt and black pepper
Serves four

Top, tail and blanch French beans. Wash and chop the celery sticks. Peel and dice cucumber. Wash the watercress and twist the leaves from the stems. Peel and slice the avocado. Sprinkle with lemon juice. Combine all ingredients except the watercress. Season very well with salt and black pepper. Garnish with watercress.

Relish salad bowl

1 tin artichoke hearts, cut in half
8 oz (225 g) sliced raw mushrooms
4 tomatoes peeled and quartered
1 cucumber sliced thin (optional)
toasted sesame seeds
1 head Romaine lettuce broken into pieces
wine vinegar dressing (see p. 183)
Serves four

Toss salad ingredients lightly together and sprinkle with wine vinegar dressing.

Salade niçoise

1 green pepper
2 oz (55 g) cooked green beans
fennel
1 tomato
1 hard-boiled egg
2 oz (55 g) tuna fish
low-calorie salad dressing (see p. 181)
Serves one

Chop pepper, beans and fennel. Slice tomato and egg and mix all together with tuna fish. Dress with low-calorie salad dressing.

Soya-bean salad

2 tablespoons olive oil
1 tablespoon lemon juice

Opposite: Reinhardt, 1972

salt and pepper to taste
8 oz (225 g) cooked soya beans
3 spring onions, chopped
1 teaspoon fresh dill, chopped
pinch of mint
lettuce leaves
4 tomatoes
1 cucumber
Serves four

Combine the olive oil, lemon juice, salt and pepper and blend thoroughly. Add the soya beans; toss lightly. Add the spring onions, dill, mint; mix. Serve on lettuce leaves with tomato wedges and sliced cucumber.

Spicy salad

2 cucumbers, peeled and finely diced
2 tomatoes, seeded and finely diced
2 green peppers, seeded and finely diced
Dressing:
   2 fl oz (55 ml) lemon juice
   2 tablespoons honey
   2 teaspoons sugar
   $\frac{1}{2}$ teaspoon cayenne
   $1\frac{1}{2}$ teaspoons salt
Serves six

Place chopped vegetables in a bowl, alternating layers; lightly salt each layer. Mix the dressing and add to the vegetables. Chill for at least 1 hour.

Spinach salad

8 oz (225 g) spinach
8 oz (225 g) mushrooms, raw, sliced thin
2 tomatoes, cut in wedges
low-calorie salad dressing (see p. 181)
2 hard-boiled eggs, sliced
thin slices of Spanish onion
Serves two

Wash spinach, remove stems, and cut into bite-size pieces. Combine spinach, mushrooms and tomatoes. Toss with dressing. Garnish with egg and onion slices.

Spinach and bacon salad

1 lb (455 g) fresh small-leaf spinach
low-calorie dressing (see p. 181)
2 slices chopped, well-grilled bacon
Serves two

Wash and drain the spinach and remove the stalks. Toss with salad dressing and sprinkle with the bacon.

Spinach and mushroom salad

1 lb (455 g) crisp raw spinach
3 oz (85 g) sliced raw mushrooms
2 tablespoons pine nuts
salt
tarragon vinegar
Serves four

Sprinkle the vegetables and pine nuts with salt and a little tarragon vinegar; toss.

Jellied spring salad

1 packet lime jelly
12 fl oz (3.4 dl) hot water
2 tablespoons vinegar
8 oz (225 g) finely chopped celery
4 oz (115 g) finely shredded cucumber
2 oz (55 g) chopped pimento
green salad
Serves four to six

Dissolve the jelly in hot water; cool. Add the next four ingredients. When it begins to congeal, pour into a ring mould. Refrigerate for several hours. Unmould on to a green salad and serve with yogurt dressing (see p. 183).

Tabbuleh

$\frac{1}{2}$ cup fine burghul (cracked wheat)
8 oz (225 g) tomatoes
1 small onion finely chopped
10 oz (285 g) parsley

I very small bunch fresh mint
⅓ cup lemon juice
½ cup olive oil
salt and pepper to taste
Cos lettuce
Serves two

Soften the burghul with a little hot water and set on one side. Chop the tomatoes and onion. Wash the parsley, pick off the leaves, squeeze out all the moisture from the leaves and chop very finely. Do the same with the mint leaves. Put all these in a salad bowl, dress with lemon juice, olive oil and seasonings, and blend well. Garnish with upright leaves of Cos lettuce all around the bowl.

Tahini salad

I lb (455 g) tomatoes
I cucumber
3 tablespoons tahini paste (available from Greek and Turkish grocers)
3 tablespoons cold water
juice of I lemon
I tablespoon garlic seasoning
Serves two

Dice tomatoes and cucumber. Dilute tahini paste with equal amount of cold water until it is fairly thin. Add lemon juice and garlic seasoning and pour the dressing on the vegetables.

Waldorf salad

4 eating apples
4 tablespoons chopped walnuts
4 stalks of chopped celery
16 lettuce leaves
Serves four

Core the apples but leave the skin on. Cut in small dice. Mix with the walnuts and celery, keeping a little apple for garnishing. Put the mixture in a nest of lettuce leaves and decorate with pieces of apple.

Yogurt and cucumber salad

I carton natural yogurt
I teaspoon garlic salt
½ cucumber
I teaspoon dried mint leaves
Serves two

Stir the yogurt with a whisk until smooth and season with the garlic salt. Slice the cucumber very thin and add to the yogurt. Garnish with dried mint.

FISH 1920

SAUCES AND DRESSINGS

Aspic jelly

1 calf's foot (or pig's trotter)
1 knuckle of veal (or ¼ calf's head minus the brains)
small quantities of fish, meat or fowl
1 medium onion
2 carrots
parsley, including some root
salt, peppercorns
thyme
2 cloves
lemon peel
1–2 bayleaves
½ tumbler wine vinegar
4 pints (2.3 l) water
juice of 1 lemon
1 egg white plus the egg shell

Chop the calf's foot and the knuckle of veal (or alternatives) into convenient pieces and put them in a saucepan with the meat or fish, onion, carrots, parsley, salt, peppercorns, thyme, cloves, lemon peel, bayleaves and vinegar. Cover with the water. If you have a chicken carcass (or some chicken giblets) add this as well. Bring to boil and simmer very slowly (no skimming) until the meat literally falls from the bone, about 4–5 hours (considerably less in a pressure cooker). Strain the liquid into a bowl and leave to set. When set, remove all the fat – this must be done very thoroughly. Put the jelly in a saucepan and heat. In a bowl whisk together the egg white, lemon juice, about 1 ladleful of the melted, but not yet hot, jelly and the crushed egg shell. Bring the remaining jelly to boil and stir in the egg-white mixture. Bring to boil without stirring, then lower the heat at once. Cover the saucepan with a lid and leave on very low heat for 15 minutes – no stirring. Strain the liquid through a cloth previously wrung out in cold water, taking care not to stir up the sediment. If necessary, strain again.

Bechamel sauce

1 pint (5.7 dl) milk
1 shallot
small piece carrot
a small piece of celery
a piece of bayleaf
10 peppercorns
2 oz (55 g) butter
2 oz (55 g) plain flour
salt
4 tablespoons single cream
Serves four

Put the milk, prepared vegetables and seasonings into a pan. Bring to the boil, remove to a warm place and infuse for 5 minutes; strain. Make a roux with the fat and flour, add the milk, blend and cook 5–10 mins. Just before serving add the cream.

Bonus sauce

See p. 141.

Cheese sauce

1 oz (30 g) butter
1 oz (30 g) plain flour
a pinch of dry mustard
salt and pepper
1 pint (5.7 dl) milk
3 oz (85 g) grated cheese
Serves eight

Make a roux with the butter and flour. Add mustard and seasoning. Slowly add the milk to make a smooth sauce; add the cheese.

Egg-yolk dressing

1 hard-boiled egg yolk (use the white in a salad)
3 dessertspoons white-wine vinegar
¼ teaspoon salt
freshly ground black pepper
pinch each of dried dill and basil
⅛ teaspoon dry mustard
Serves one

Mash the egg yolk thoroughly or put it through a sieve. Mix well with the vinegar, salt, pepper to taste, dill, basil and mustard.

   This could also be made with a raw egg yolk: beat the vinegar into the lightly beaten yolk, and then mix in the seasonings.

French dressing

3 tablespoons oil
a pinch of pepper
artificial sweetener
1 tablespoon vinegar (wine, tarragon or other herb)
mustard

Mix the oil, seasonings and sweeten to taste; add the vinegar. Stir before using.

Lemon dressing

freshly squeezed juice from 3 lemons
zest from 1 lemon

½ clove garlic, crushed
4 finely sliced spring onions
2 tablespoons sour cream or natural yogurt
freshly ground black pepper
salt
Serves six

Place all the ingredients in a bowl and combine thoroughly. Allow to stand for an hour or so.

Low-calorie dressing

2 tablespoons vegetable oil
1 tablespoon vinegar
artificial sweetener
½ teaspoon salt
pepper
herbs – chopped mint, parsley, chives, etc.

Use whatever herb or herbs you like. Mix all the ingredients together.

Low-calorie mayonnaise

1 egg yolk
½ teaspoon dry mustard
½ teaspoon salt
dash cayenne
1 dessertspoon vinegar
¾ cup oil
Makes about one cup

Beat the egg yolk and stir in the seasonings and vinegar. Continue beating while adding the oil a drop at a time. The mixture will thicken as the oil is added. Chill until ready to serve. To reduce the calorie count beat in an equal amount of skimmed milk just before spooning over the salad.

Low-calorie salad dressing

2 teaspoons cornflour
1½ teaspoons sugar
1 teaspoon salt
¾ teaspoon paprika
6 fl oz (1.7 dl) water

1 tablespoon salad oil
3 tablespoons wine vinegar
½ teaspoon Worcestershire sauce
2 tablespoons tomato ketchup
pepper and extra salt to taste
pinch of garlic
Makes one cup

Mix cornflour, sugar, salt and paprika. Stir in water slowly and cook gently for 5 minutes or until thickened. Cool. Stir in remaining ingredients.

Low-down salad dressing

1 cup V-8 juice
¼ cup wine vinegar
½ chopped green pepper
1 clove minced garlic
1 teaspoon dry mustard
1 teaspoon Worcestershire sauce
¾ teaspoon salt
pepper
artificial sweetener to taste
2–4 tablespoons chopped parsley or spring onions

Combine all the ingredients, except the parsley or spring onions, in the blender until the green pepper is puréed. Add chopped parsley or spring onions and keep in a refrigerator.

Mushroom sauce

8 oz (225 g) tomato juice
4 oz (115 g) beef stock
2 oz (55 g) chopped onion
dash of garlic powder
¼ bayleaf
1 teaspoon vinegar
salt and pepper
2 oz (55 g) sliced mushrooms
artificial sweetener to equal ½ teaspoon sugar
1½ teaspoons chopped fresh parsley
a few drops of brown food colouring

Combine the ingredients in a saucepan. Simmer uncovered until reduced to about half.

Pimento dressing

7 oz (200 g) jar pimentos
2 tablespoons vinegar
1 tablespoon prepared mustard
artificial sweetener
Makes one cup

Put the ingredients in the blender and blend until smooth. Store in a refrigerator.

Piquant sauce

2 tablespoons soured cream
1 tablespoon moutarde de Meaux
a dash of Tabasco

Mix and heat gently. Do not boil. Serve with chops or steak.

Piquant sauce for green vegetables

1 tablespoon salad oil
1 onion peeled and thinly sliced
a few drops of Tabasco
freshly ground black pepper
2 tablespoons chopped parsley
2 fl oz (55 ml) red wine

Heat the oil in a pan. Separate the onion rings and add; cover and cook until limp. Add seasonings and parsley. Add the wine while cooking and let it evaporate.

Taratour sauce

4 oz (115 g) pine kernels
juice of 1 lemon
1 clove garlic

Grind the pine kernels finely and add a little cold water and lemon juice. Add the crushed clove of garlic and grind once or twice more until you have a thick sauce, the consistency of mayonnaise. This sauce is excellent served with cauliflower (see p. 164) and with grilled sea bass.

Italian tomato sauce

2 tablespoons olive oil
2 onions finely chopped
small tin of tomato purée
pinch of thyme
1 pint (5.7 dl) water
salt and pepper
Serves four

Heat the oil in a small pan and fry the onions for 5 minutes. Add the tomato purée and cook for a few minutes, stirring all the time. Add the thyme and water, cover, and simmer gently for about 25 minutes or until of the desired thickness. Season to taste. Strain if necessary.

Wine vinegar dressing

4 fl oz (1.1 dl) red wine vinegar
2 tablespoons vegetable salad oil
½ clove garlic, crushed
1 tablespoon chopped parsley
pinch of oregano or tarragon

Put all ingredients in a bottle and shake well. Use sparingly on salads or cooked vegetables.

Yogurt dressing (i)

½ teaspoon made mustard
½ teaspoon castor sugar
1 teaspoon finely grated Parmesan
juice of ½ lemon
1 carton low-fat yogurt

Mix all the ingredients together and chill for 1 hour before serving.

Yogurt dressing (ii)

2 egg yolks, hard boiled and sieved
2 raw egg yolks
1 teaspoon dry mustard
¾ pint (4.3 dl) yogurt
2 teaspoons lemon juice
salt

Add raw eggs to sieved egg yolks with the mustard. Beat in the rest of the ingredients slowly. Keep in the fridge.

Yogurt remoulade

8 fl oz (2.3 dl) yogurt
½ oz (15 g) chopped parsley
½ teaspoon tarragon
2 tablespoons finely chopped onion
1 teaspoon prepared mustard
1 tablespoon chopped capers

Mix all the ingredients and refrigerate. Good with all seafoods.

DE LAVERERIE

PUDDINGS

Baked apple

1 cooking apple
1 teaspoon clear honey
Serves one

Core the apple and cut a circle just through the skin round the middle of the apple. Stand the apple on a baking tin or ovenproof dish, put the honey into the hole left by removing the core and pour a little water round the apple. Bake at 350°F (180° C) for $\frac{1}{2}$–1 hour depending on the size of the apple. Ensure the apple is thoroughly cooked.

Baked apple with dates

2 large Bramleys
10 stoned, fresh dates
1 teaspoon honey
pinch cinnamon
a little fresh orange juice
Serves two

Wash and core the apples and score the skins about a quarter of the way down. Mix the dates, honey and cinnamon, and fill each cavity with the mixture. Spoon a little orange juice over each one and bake at 375°F (190°C) for 40–45 minutes. Serve hot or cold.

Baked stuffed apple

1 cooking apple
1 oz (30 g) raisins
1 oz (30 g) soft brown sugar
a small knob of butter
2 tablespoons water
Serves one

Wash and core the apple, cut a circle round it just through the skin and place on a baking tin. Fill the hole with raisins and sugar, and dot with butter. Pour 2 tablespoons water round the apple. Bake at 350°F (180°C) for about 45 minutes.

Apple cakes

a medium green apple
artificial sweetener to taste
2 oz (55 g) non-fat milk powder
3–4 cloves or $\frac{1}{4}$ teaspoon ground cloves
Serves two

Stew the apple in a very little water and add the other ingredients. Make into 12 flat pancakes. Bake on a flat tin in moderate oven (350°F, 180°C) until brown.

Apple cream

1 lb (455 g) cooking apples
$\frac{1}{2}$ pint (2.8 dl) water
artificial sweetener
$2\frac{1}{2}$ fl oz (70 ml) double cream
2 bananas
$\frac{1}{4}$ pint (1.4 dl) yogurt
cinnamon
Serves six

Peel, core and simmer the apples in the water and sweetener until soft. Leave to cool. Whip the cream and mash the bananas. Mix them with the apple and yogurt. Pile into individual glass bowls and decorate with a pinch or two of powdered cinnamon.

Apple snow

1 egg white
2 rounded tablespoons sweetened apple purée
blanched almonds
angelica
Serves one

Whisk the egg white until stiff. Beat in the apple purée a little at a time. Serve piled in a glass dish with thin spikes of almond and angelica as garnish.

Apple and pear snow

2 pears and 2 eating apples
¼ pint (1.4 dl) water
artificial sweetener
2 egg whites
Serves four

Peel and core the fruit. Slice and simmer in the water until soft. Purée and sweeten to taste. Leave to cool. Whip the egg whites until stiff; while still beating gradually add the purée. Pile into a glass bowl or individual dishes.

Apple scallops

4 oz (115 g) eating apples
¼ pint (1.4 dl) water
grated rind of 1 orange
artificial sweetener
½ oz (15 g) dried skimmed milk
Serves one

Peel, core and roughly chop the apples. Bring the water to the boil. Add the orange peel and apples and sweeten to taste. Boil quickly until the apples are soft but not shapeless. Pile the apple into

scallop shells. Make the skimmed milk and cover the apple with it; grill until golden brown. This will take 3 or 4 seconds under a hot grill. Serve hot.

Stewed apples and mandarin oranges

4 apples
½ lemon sliced thin
16 fl oz (4.5 dl) water
artificial sweetener
Serves four

Peel and quarter the apples. Add with the peelings and lemon to the water and sweetener. The peelings give a pretty pink tinge to the fruit. Simmer until tender. Cool and strain. Serve warm or cold with tinned mandarin orange sections.

Use these apples, sprinkled with prepared horse-radish, as an accompaniment to grilled chicken.

Avocado and lime cream

1 ripe avocado
3 drops liquid sweetener
3 tablespoons lime juice
¼ pint (1.4 dl) double cream, whipped
pistachio nuts
Serves two

Remove the skin and stone from the avocado and mash the flesh. Add the sweetener and lime juice and fold in the whipped cream. Pile into individual dishes and decorate with cream and pistachio nuts.

Avocado whip

¼ pint (1.4 dl) double cream
2 tablespoons top of milk
½ teaspoon finely grated lemon rind
2 tablespoons castor sugar
1 ripe avocado
1 tablespoon lemon juice
2 egg whites
Serves four

Whip the cream and milk together until thick but not too stiff. Fold in the lemon rind and sugar. Peel and mash the avocado, mix in the lemon juice and then fold in the cream. Whisk the egg whites until stiff and fold in. Serve in individual dishes and chill for up to an hour before serving.

Banana soufflé

¾ oz (20 g) butter
¾ oz (20 g) flour
¼ pint (1.4 dl) skimmed milk
2 bananas
artificial sweetener
3 eggs
Serves six

Heat the oven to 380°F (190°C). Melt the butter, remove the pan from the heat and stir in the flour. Add the milk gradually and stir until smooth over a low heat. Simmer for two minutes. Mash the bananas and sweeten to taste. Separate the eggs. Beat the yolks into the banana mixture. Whisk the whites until stiff and fold into the mixture. Pour into a two-pint (one-litre) soufflé dish. Bake for 20–25 minutes.

Banana snow

1 large egg white
1 large banana
1 tablespoon clear honey
1 teaspoon lemon juice
Serves one

Stiffly whisk the egg white. Mash the banana with the honey and lemon juice. Fold the banana into the egg white. Eat within 1½–2 hours.

Bavarian coffee

¼ oz (7 g) gelatine
1 tablespoon water
1 egg, separated
1 oz (30 g) castor sugar
¼ pint (1.4 dl) milk
strong coffee essence
¼ pint (1.4 dl) cream
Serves two

Soak the gelatine in a tablespoon of cold water. Cream the egg yolk and sugar until almost white. Bring the milk to boil, whisk into egg yolk and sugar and return to a low heat, stirring constantly until it thickens. Remove from the heat, add the gelatine and stir until it dissolves. Flavour with coffee essence. Strain and allow to cool. Fold in half the lightly beaten cream, then the stiffly beaten egg white. Set in a mould. Turn out and decorate with the remaining cream.

Blackberry and melon cup

1 cantaloupe melon
a few blackberries
lemon juice
Serves one

Halve the melon and remove the seeds. Remove the pulp and make into small balls, combine with the blackberries and use to fill the melon shell. Sprinkle with lemon juice only.

Blackcurrant crêpes

¼ oz (7 g) arrowroot
a little water
8 oz (225 g) frozen blackcurrants
artificial sweetener
2 tablespoons kirsch or brandy
12 pancakes
Serves twelve

Blend the arrowroot with water. Bring the blackcurrants slowly to the boil and add the arrowroot immediately. Stir until thick. Remove from the heat. Sweeten to taste and add half the kirsch or brandy. When the blackcurrants are cold, place a dessertspoon of the mixture on each crêpe and roll up. Arrange in rows in a fireproof dish, cover and put to heat in a hot oven. Meanwhile, gently warm the remainder of the brandy. When ready to serve, pour over the crêpes and light. Serve immediately.

Blackcurrant fool

¾ pint (4.3 dl) skimmed milk
3 eggs, separated
1 pint (5.7 dl) blackcurrant purée
artificial sweetener
Serves eight

Bring the milk to the boil; beat the egg yolks; pour the hot milk on to the egg yolks, stirring vigorously, and return to the pan, heating gently until the custard thickens. Do not boil. Leave to cool. Whip the egg whites until stiff. In another bowl mix the purée, custard and sweetener. Fold in the egg whites. Pour into a glass bowl or individual dishes.

Cheesecake

6 eggs
2 tablespoons lemon juice
2 teaspoons vanilla essence
4 teaspoons soft margarine or vegetable oil
artificial sweetener to taste
2 lb (0.9 kg) cottage cheese
cinnamon
Serves eight

Blend thoroughly the eggs, lemon juice, vanilla essence, margarine and sweetener. Then add the cottage cheese. Blend until very smooth. Pour into a narrow, long tin, such as a large loaf tin. Top with cinnamon. Bake in pre-heated oven 350°F (180°C) for 45 minutes or until firm. Turn off the oven, leaving the cake there with the door open for about 1 hour; then chill. Overnight refrigeration will add to the flavour.

Chocolate bavaroise

3 egg yolks
¼ pint (1.4 dl) skimmed milk
½ oz (15 g) cocoa powder
½ oz (15 g) gelatine
3 tablespoons water
artificial sweetener
3 egg whites
Serves six

Make a custard with the yolks, milk and cocoa (the cocoa should be boiled together with the milk), taking care not to curdle it by overheating. Leave to cool. Dissolve the gelatine in the water and add to the custard. Sweeten to taste. Fold the stiffly beaten egg whites carefully and thoroughly into the mixture. Pour into a mould and leave to set.

Instant chocolate and orange mousse

4 eggs
¼ oz (7 g) cocoa
juice and grated rind of 1 orange
artificial sweetener
1 teaspoon browned flaked almonds
Serves six

Separate the eggs. Dissolve the cocoa with the orange juice in a double boiler. Stir this for about 1 minute to form a smooth cream. Remove the top pan from the heat and immediately add the egg yolks and sweeten to taste, stirring all the time to prevent overcooking. Whisk the egg whites stiffly and fold into the chocolate mixture. Return the pan to the heat and continue to fold in for about another 30 seconds. Pile into a soufflé dish and scatter with flaked almonds. Serve within 1 hour.

Hot coffee soufflé

2 oz (55 g) butter
2 oz (55 g) flour
¼ pint (1.4 dl) skimmed milk
¼ pint (1.4 dl) strong black coffee
½ oz (15 g) powdered cocoa
3 egg yolks
artificial sweetener
4 egg whites
Serves six

Set the oven at 325°F (170°C). Grease a deep two-pint (one-litre) soufflé dish. Melt the butter, add the flour and allow to cool. Slowly stir in the milk.

When smooth, add the coffee and cocoa and bring to the boil, stirring continuously. Boil for 1 minute. Leave on one side. Beat the yolks into the coffee mixture. Add the sweetener. Whip the whites to a snow and fold into the mixture with a metal spoon. Fill the soufflé dish to within 1 inch (2.5 cm) of the top and bake for 20–25 minutes. Serve immediately.

Crème caramel

4 oz (115 g) sugar
2 tablespoons water
1 teaspoon lemon juice
3 eggs
1 pint (5.7 dl) milk
artificial sweetener
Serves four

Put sugar, water and lemon juice in an aluminium pan and cook gently until mixture turns a light brown and is as thick as treacle. Pour into a mould and turn the mould round and round until the inner surface is completely lined with the caramel. Whisk the eggs thoroughly, and at the same time bring the milk to scalding point. Sweeten the milk to taste and pour it over the eggs. Return the mixture to the pan and warm through thoroughly, stirring all the time; do not allow it to come to the boil. Strain the custard into the mould and cover with a piece of buttered greaseproof paper. To finish, you can either steam the custard or cook in the oven. When using a steamer be sure that no water falls into the custard and cook slowly for about 35–40 minutes. If cooking in the oven put the mould in a basin of hot water and cook at 300°F (150°C) for about 30 minutes.

Crêpes aux pêches

4 oz (115 g) flour
1 egg and 1 yolk
8 oz (225 g) skimmed milk
½ level teaspoon salt
artificial sweetener

8 peaches
corn oil
Serves twelve

Make a batter with the flour, eggs and milk (this will make twelve 7 inch, 18 cm, pancakes). Add the salt and sweeten to taste. For the filling, stone and peel the peaches. Chop roughly and purée using a liquidizer or sieve. Heat the pan until smoking hot. Using a little corn oil for each pancake, pour in enough batter to coat the base of the pan, turn with a knife or spatula and cook quickly. Keep warm in a clean cloth. Divide the filling into fourteen and spread each pancake to its edge. Dilute the remaining purée with very little (2 or 3 teaspoons) water and serve as a sauce.

Slimmers' custard

1 oz (30 g) custard powder
1 pint (5.7 dl) low-fat milk
artificial sweetener
Makes 1 pint (5.7 dl)

Mix the custard powder to a smooth paste with about 3 tablespoons cold milk. Heat the rest of the milk to just below boiling point and then pour the milk on the paste. Return the custard to the saucepan to thicken. Add sweetener to taste.

Floating islands

½ pint (2.8 dl) skimmed milk
¼ teaspoon grated nutmeg
2 eggs, separated
artificial sweetener
¾ tablespoon gelatine
vanilla essence
Serves two

Put the milk and nutmeg into a large saucepan. Whisk the egg whites until stiff, add sweetener to taste. Heat the milk and, when simmering, drop in 2–3 teaspoons meringue mixture. Cook for 3–4 minutes, turning once. Remove with a slotted scoop and drain on absorbent kitchen paper.

Continue until all the meringue is cooked. Allow the milk to cool, then whisk in the egg yolks. Sprinkle in the gelatine and stir until dissolved, add the vanilla essence. Strain the egg custard into a serving dish and float the meringue 'islands' on top. Chill until set.

Gooseberry jelly

1 lb (455 g) fresh gooseberries
¾ pint (4.3 dl) water
¾ oz (20 g) gelatine
artificial sweetener
green colouring
2½ fl oz (70 ml) double cream
mint sprigs
Serves six

Top, tail and stew the gooseberries in ½ pint (2.8 dl) of the water until soft. Add the gelatine to the remaining ¼ pint (1.4 dl). Heat this very gently until all the crystals have dissolved. Sieve the gooseberries or put them through a Mouli. Add to the purée the sweetener, gelatine and enough colouring to give a delicate green. Pour into a wet mould and leave to set. Whip the cream with a hand whisk until it becomes thicker but will still pour. Turn out the jelly, pour the cream over it and decorate the top with mint sprigs.

Khosaf

1 lb (455 g) dried apricots
1 lb (455 g) dried prunes
3 tablespoons orange flower water or 1 tablespoon rose
   water
honey
pine kernels
Serves six

Cover the dried apricots and prunes with water and add the orange flower water or rose water and enough honey to sweeten. Sprinkle a few pine kernels so they float on top of the water. Soak overnight. Next morning your khosaf is ready to eat; it keeps well in a cool place or refrigerator.

Lemon ice

1½ pints (8.5 dl) water
artificial sweetener
6 fl oz (1.7 dl) lemon juice
1 tablespoon grated lemon rind
Serves six to eight

Mix together and freeze in the refrigerator tray. Take it out when partially frozen and whip by hand or in an electric blender.

   For orange ice, use 1 pint (5.7 dl) orange juice, 2 fl oz (55 ml) lemon juice, the grated rind of 2 oranges and sweetener to taste. For lime ice the method is the same as for lemon.

Lemon snow

2½ fl oz (70 ml) cold water
1 rounded teaspoon powdered gelatine
½ oz (15 g) castor sugar
1 lemon
1 egg white
Serves two

Measure the water into a saucepan and sprinkle in the gelatine. Add the sugar and thinly pared lemon rind. Stir over a low heat until the sugar and gelatine have dissolved. Do not boil. Allow to cool. Add the lemon juice and egg white and whisk until it thickens. Pour into serving dishes and chill.

Mint and grape mould

½ oz (15 g) gelatine
juice of 1 lemon made up to ½ pint (2.8 dl) with water
artificial sweetener
2 tablespoons chopped mint
green colouring
8 oz (225 g) white grapes, skinned and de-seeded
lettuce
Serves two

Dissolve the gelatine in hot lemon and water. Add sweetener, mint and green colouring. Cool on ice. When about to set, add grapes. Pour into a ring mould to set. Turn out and serve with crisp lettuce.

Oatmeal biscuits

1 egg
2 dessertspoons soft butter
¼ cup finely packed brown sugar
¼ cup buttermilk
1 cup flour
½ teaspoon baking soda
½ teaspoon salt
5 dessertspoons honey
1½ cups rolled oats
2 dessertspoons chopped walnuts
Makes about four dozen

Beat together the egg, butter, brown sugar, and buttermilk until thoroughly blended. Sift the flour with the baking soda and salt. Add to the butter mixture with the honey. Fold in the rolled oats and chopped nuts. Drop teaspoonfuls on a lightly greased biscuit sheet. Bake in a preheated oven (375°F, 190°C) for about 10 minutes until delicately brown. In the freezer these biscuits will keep for several months.

Hot sweet soufflé omelette

4 eggs, separated
a few drops liquid sweetener
1 drop vanilla essence
⅛ oz (3 g) fat
Serves two

Beat egg yolks with sweetener and essence. Beat egg whites until stiff. Fold the egg whites into the yolk mixture. Melt the fat in the pan and let it get hot. Pour in the egg mixture and let it cook for a couple of minutes without stirring so that the base cooks. Transfer to a hot grill for 2–3 minutes or until the top is golden brown. Fold in half and serve at once.

Orange bavaroise

1 orange
½ pint (2.8 dl) milk
1 egg yolk

1 tablespoon clear honey
2 level teaspoons gelatine
2 tablespoons water
Serves three

Pare the rind from the orange with a potato peeler, taking care not to remove any white pith. Add to the milk. Cream the egg yolk with the honey and pour on to the milk. Return to the pan and heat gently, stirring all the time, until mixture thickens. Leave to stand in a warm place for ½ hour. Soak the gelatine in water and dissolve over hot water. Strain the milk and add to the dissolved gelatine. Allow to cool. Remove all pith and skin from the orange and put the flesh in the base of three sundae glasses. When the gelatine mixture starts to thicken divide between the three glasses and leave in a cool place to set.

Glazed orange

1 orange
1 oz (30 g) sugar
3 tablespoons water
1 teaspoon orange liqueur
1 tablespoon orange juice – fresh, tinned or frozen
angelica leaf
Serves one

Remove the skin and pith from the orange. Dissolve the sugar in water over a low heat, bring to the boil and cook rapidly for about 3 minutes until the mixture is syrupy. Stir in the liqueur and orange juice. Spoon over the orange. Chill, and baste orange occasionally while syrup is cooling. Decorate with an angelica leaf before serving.

Orange and grape jelly

juice of 3 oranges
juice of ½ lemon
2½ fl oz (70 ml) water
1 tablespoon honey
3 teaspoons gelatine
1½ oz (40 g) black grapes
Serves four

Place the juice from the oranges and lemon in a bowl. Heat the water, stir in the honey and sprinkle the gelatine over the water. When the gelatine has completely dissolved stir into the orange and lemon juice. Cut the grapes in half, remove the pips and cut in half again; add to the mixture. Pour into a serving dish and leave in a cool place to set.

Oranges juliennes

4 large seedless oranges
1 pint (5.7 dl) water
6 drops red vegetable colouring
2 drops yellow vegetable colouring
½ level teaspoon arrowroot
artificial sweetener
Serves four

Thinly pare 2 oranges, leaving the pith. Cut the rind into needle-thin strips about 1½ inches (4 cm) long. Put into a saucepan with the water and colouring. Boil steadily until the liquid is reduced to ½ pint (2.8 dl) and the peel is soft. Blend the arrowroot with a dessertspoon of water and pour on the boiling peel liquid. Return to the pan to cook the arrowroot for about 1 minute. Leave to cool. Meanwhile cut the pith off all the oranges, slice horizontally and place in serving dish or dishes. Sweeten to taste. Spoon the juliennes on to the oranges and pour the syrup over.

Pear in red wine

1 oz (30 g) sugar
4 tablespoons red wine
2 tablespoons water
a strip of lemon peel
a small piece of cinnamon
1 pear
toasted almonds
Serves one

Put the sugar in a pan with the wine, water, lemon peel and cinnamon. Dissolve the sugar slowly and then boil for 1 minute. Peel and core the pear, and poach in liquid in a moderate (350°F, 180°C) oven until tender. Serve with a few toasted almonds.

Pear mousse

1 envelope unflavoured gelatine
2 oz (55 g) cold water
2 oz (55 g) boiling water
1 ripe medium pear, peeled
2 oz (55 g) dried skimmed milk powder
½ teaspoon almond extract
artificial sweetener to equal 6 teaspoons sugar
6–8 ice cubes
5 oz (140 g) strawberries
Serves two

Sprinkle gelatine over cold water to soften; add boiling water. Pour gelatine mixture into blender, add three-quarters of the pear and the milk, almond extract and sweetener. Blend until smooth. Add the ice cubes, one at a time, blending after each. Dice the remaining pear finely and fold into the mixture. Divide the mousse between two dishes. Serve topped with strawberries.

Pineapple ice-cream

1 large pineapple
¼ pint (1.4 dl) yogurt
artificial sweetener
Serves four

Cut the top off the pineapple, leaving about 1 inch (2.5 cm) of the fruit attached to the leaves to form a lid. Scrape out the pulp from the body of the pineapple without damaging the case. Remove any core. Purée the pulp and mix it with the yogurt and sweetener. Pour into a freezing tray and put into the freezing compartment turned to its coldest. When the mixture is slushy, mash or whisk it to break down the large crystals. Return to the freezing compartment until it is frozen. Spoon it into the pineapple case. Replace the pineapple lid and serve immediately.

Pineapple japonaise

1 egg
2 tablespoons orange juice
1 small pineapple

12 oz (340 g) clementines
¼ pint (1.4 dl) double cream
Serves six

Beat the egg and put in a double saucepan with the orange juice. Heat slowly, stirring continuously until the mixture thickens. Leave to cool. Peel, core and slice the pineapple. Peel and pip the clementines. Arrange in a shallow glass dish. Half whip the cream, add the egg mixture and spoon over the fruit.

Pots de crème

3 egg yolks
8 fl oz (2.3 dl) skimmed milk
vanilla essence
1 teaspoon instant coffee (optional)
artificial sweetener
Serves four to six

Beat the egg yolks until lemon-coloured. Beat in the skimmed milk with vanilla and instant coffee. Sweeten to taste. Pour into pots or ramekins. Cover and bake in pan three-quarters full of water for 1 hour at 325°F (170°C).

Queen of puddings

¼ pint (1.4 dl) milk
½ oz (15 g) butter
1 egg, separated
½ oz (15 g) sugar
1 oz (30 g) cake crumbs
½ lemon
1 teaspoon warmed jam
1 oz (30 g) castor sugar
Serves two to three

Boil milk with butter and pour on to the egg yolk and sugar. Place cake crumbs and grated lemon rind in a fireproof dish, strain milk mixture over and bake in a pan of hot water in a moderate oven (350°F, 180°C) until set, approximately 30 minutes. Spread with jam. Beat the egg white until stiff, fold in the castor sugar and pile on to pudding. Brown in a hot oven (425°F, 220°C).

Raspberry and blackcurrant mould

1 oz (30 g) gelatine
1 dessertspoon lemon juice
¼ pint (1.4 dl) low-calorie ginger ale
¼ pint (1.4 dl) blackcurrant purée
1 lb (455 g) raspberries (fresh or frozen)
artificial sweetener
sprigs of fresh mint
Serves six

Heat the gelatine gently in the lemon juice and ginger ale until all the crystals are dissolved. Mix into the blackcurrant purée. Add the raspberries (if using fresh raspberries, purée half) and sweeten to taste. Pour into a mould. If a ring mould is used the centre can be filled with additional fresh raspberries. Allow at least 3 hours to set in the refrigerator. Garnish with sprigs of fresh mint.

Raspberry cream

8 oz (225 g) frozen or fresh raspberries
¼ pint (1.4 dl) yogurt
1 teaspoon lemon juice
artificial sweetener
scant ½ oz (15 g) gelatine
2½ fl oz (70 ml) water
2½ fl oz (70 ml) double cream
Serves four

Purée and sieve the raspberries and add the yogurt and lemon juice, and sweeten to taste. Slowly dissolve the gelatine in the water. Half whip the cream. Combine everything and when the mixture begins to thicken pour into glass dishes and chill.

Rhubarb fool (i)

rhubarb
artificial sweetener
yogurt

Cook rhubarb with a very little water until it is a thick pulp and sweeten to taste. Sieve or beat with a wooden spoon to a smooth purée. Mix with an equal quantity of yogurt and chill.

Rhubarb fool (ii)

2½ fl oz (70 ml) milk
1 egg yolk
1 teaspoon sugar
2½ fl oz (70 ml) rhubarb purée (rhubarb stewed and sieved)
Serves one

Make a custard using the milk, egg yolk and sugar. Allow to cool. Lightly combine the custard and purée and serve in a glass dish.

Three-fruit sorbet

12 fl oz (3.4 dl) orange juice
6 fl oz (1.7 dl) lemon juice
3 mashed bananas
24 fl oz (6.8 dl) water
16 fl oz (4.5 dl) skimmed milk
artificial sweetener

Garnish:
*   orange sections*
*   green leaves*
Serves six

Mix all the ingredients and freeze in the refrigerator tray. Take out when partially frozen and whip by hand or in an electric blender.

The sorbet can be frozen and then packed in a mould to make it more decorative. Turn out on a silver tray and decorate with the garnish.

Zabaglione

3 egg yolks
2 tablespoons marsala
artificial sweetener
Serves four

Whisk all the ingredients in a double saucepan over gentle heat, increasing the heat as it thickens. Pour into small goblets. Serve immediately.

FISH

DRINKS

Alfalfa cocktail

1 cup alfalfa sprouts
1½ cups pineapple juice
1 ripe banana
honey to taste
pinch of salt to taste
Serves two

Blend all the ingredients for 2–3 minutes and chill.

Bloody shame

Worcestershire sauce
2½ fl oz (70 ml) tomato juice
pepper
ice
Serves one

Mix the Worcestershire sauce into the tomato juice, add the pepper and pour over the ice.

Bonus milkshake

8 fl oz (2.3 dl) liquid skimmed milk
½–¾ teaspoon flavouring (any)
artificial sweetener to taste
3 ice cubes
1 fresh peach
Serves one

Put all the ingredients in a blender for about 30 seconds or until the mixture froths.

Bouillon on the rocks

1 tumbler beef bouillon
ice
lemon juice
Worcestershire sauce
Serves one

Pour the bouillon over the ice and season with lots of lemon juice and a dash of Worcestershire sauce.

Spiced cider

2 pints (1.1 l) natural, unsweetened cider
4 or 5 cloves
a pinch of mace
1 cinnamon stick or ¼ teaspoon cinnamon
¼ teaspoon nutmeg
4 or 5 thin slices lemon
Serves four

Simmer all the ingredients for ½ hour. For non-dieters add a jigger of dark rum per glass.

Cocktail refresher

¾ pint (4.3 dl) tomato juice
2 tablespoons parsley sprigs
1 teaspoon dried onion flakes
1 small stalk celery with leaves, diced
2 slices lemon with peel
artificial sweetener
Serves two

Put everything into blender and run at high speed until all vegetables are liquefied. Allow to stand for 20 minutes before serving.

Jamaica orange

1 glass low-calorie sparkling orange
1 large teaspoon rum essence
ice
a slice of lemon
Serves one

Add the rum essence to the orange. Serve with ice and a twist of lemon.

Lemon juice and soda on the rocks

Try adding a dash of angostura bitters.

Melon vitality drink

1 slice honeydew melon, quartered
3 oz (85 g) natural yogurt
a little skimmed milk
1 teaspoon wheatgerm
Serves one

Put all ingredients into blender and liquidize for a few seconds. If the mixture is too thick add more skimmed milk. If extra sweetness is required add $\frac{1}{2}$ teaspoon of honey.

Plantation punch

pot of strong tea, cooled
5 cups unsweetened grape juice
2 cups unsweetened apple juice
green and purple grapes for garnish

Mix tea and juices. Serve iced, garnished with the grapes.

Tomato juice cocktail (i)

$\frac{1}{2}$ pint (2.8 dl) fresh or tinned tomato juice
1 tablespoon vinegar
1 tablespoon lemon juice
$\frac{1}{2}$ teaspoon Worcestershire sauce
1 teaspoon grated or finely chopped onion
$\frac{1}{4}$ level teaspoon celery salt
2 level teaspoons sugar
$\frac{1}{4}$ bayleaf
Serves four

Mix all ingredients together and leave to stand in a cool place for 15 minutes. Strain through muslin or a fine nylon or plastic strainer. Chill and serve in small glasses.

Tomato juice cocktail (ii)

8 fl oz (2.3 dl) tomato juice
dash of Worcestershire sauce
dash of Tabasco sauce
juice of 1 lemon
salt and pepper
ice
a slice of lemon
Serves two

Combine all ingredients except the last and mix well. Garnish with the slice of lemon.

Tomato juice frappé

1 pint (5.7 dl) tomato juice
Worcestershire sauce
salt and pepper
Serves four

Season the juice to taste with salt and pepper and Worcestershire sauce. Pour into a freezing tray and freeze to a mush, stirring once. Mash up with a fork before serving in small glasses.

ALL ROUND EXERCISE PLAN

You need three kinds of exercise for real fitness – stretching, strengthening, and endurance. Work gradually up to fifteen minutes of stretching and strengthening daily for good posture and a good figure. And up to twenty minutes of endurance exercise, at least three times a week. (Plan devised by Dr W. Nagler, New York Hospital, Cornell Medical Center.)

Knee kiss – Stand with feet together and bring left knee to chest and hug it, using both arms. Repeat with right knee.

SAWYER

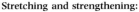

Stretching and strengthening:
● Build up gradually to 15–20 times for each exercise. Left-right counts as one. Don't force or bounce as you might sprain a muscle or tear a tendon.
● Never exhaust yourself. Don't exercise to the point of hurting or shaking. Ease into your routine over a period of weeks.
● Check with your doctor before plunging into an exercise programme, especially if you are out of condition.

1. Front bend (*above*) – Stand with the feet 12 ins (30 cm) apart, knees slightly bent, 1a. Bend from the waist, touch fingers to floor, 1b. Rise and stretch.

2. Side bend (*above right*) Stand with feet apart, hands behind neck, 2a. Bend from waist to left side, 2b, and back to centre. Repeat to right side.

3. Neck (*right*) – Place hand against right side of face and press head against resistance. Hold for 5 seconds Repeat on left side.

4. Arm circles (*left*) – Windmill left arm, making large circles, in both directions (towards front, then back).Repeat with right arm.

ALL ROUND EXERCISE PLAN

5a 5b

7

5. Chest muscles *(opposite above)* – Lie on back, on a mat, with arms out, weights in hands, 5a. Bring arms up and together, 5b. Lower.

6. Upper back *(opposite centre)* – Lie on stomach, a pillow underneath you, and close hands behind neck, 6a. Arch head and trunk up, without raising feet, 6b. Hold for 5 seconds.

7. Lower back *(opposite below)* – Keep trunk down and raise legs. (Not for those with back problems.)

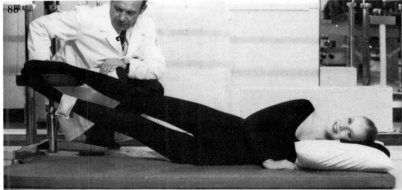

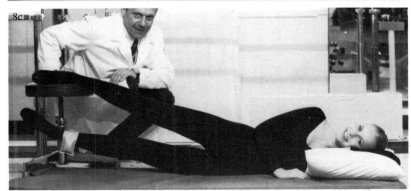

8. Inner thigh *(right)* – Lie on left side, legs straight. Place right foot on chair seat, 8a. Raise left leg to meet right one, 8b. then lower, 8c and 8d. Repeat on other side. This exercise is best done with a weight around the ankle of the moving leg.

ALL ROUND EXERCISE PLAN

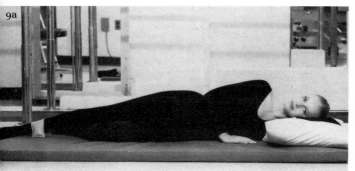

9. Outer thigh *(above)* – Lie on left side, left leg slightly bent, upper leg straight, 9a. Raise right leg up, 9b, then down (best if weighted). Repeat on other side.

10. Knees *(right)* – Lie on back, pillow under knees. Straighten right leg. Lower. Repeat with left leg. A weight on the leg adds resistance.

11. Sit ups *(below)* – Lie on back, knees bent, hands behind head, 11a. Feet should be held down or placed under a piece of furniture. Curl up slowly, breathing out. Bring right elbow to left knee, 11b. Lower. Repeat on other side.

12. Cat back *(bottom)* – Get on hands and knees, back straight, 12a. Arch the back, pulling in the abdominal muscles, breathing out, 12b. Hold for 5 seconds.

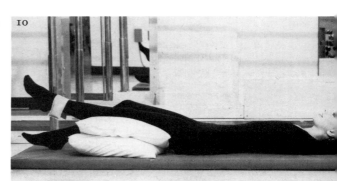

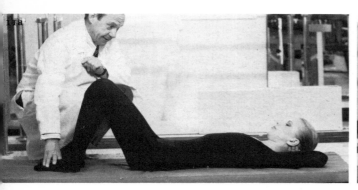

13. Feet *(right)* – Walking on heels, 13a, then toes, 13b, helps to strengthen the feet. (But it will not prevent or cure flat feet.)

13a

13b

Endurance:

● To build up endurance you must bring your heart beat up to 130–140 (see p. 204) by using major muscles over a period of time – running, bicycling, swimming, dancing, playing tennis, or fast walking are all good ways to do this.

● Before each stint, warm up for at least five minutes to limber muscles and joints, and to raise the pulse. Never stop short; cool down to avoid faintness, nausea. Do stretching exercises as part of warm-up and cool-down.

● Exercise has to be progressive. Run further at the same speed, for example, or run the same distance but faster.

14. Jogging on the spot *(below)* – Good shoes are essential. Do leg stretches before and after. Build up to 20 minutes.

15. Skipping *(below right)* – Work up to doing it fast, with a twirling flick of the wrist, keeping the upper arms close to the body. Do this for 3 minutes, take 1 minute's rest, then continue for another 3. This exercise is also good for the calves and ankles.

14a

14b

15a

15b

ELGORT

PART III

GLOSSARY AND CHARTS

DIET GLOSSARY

AEROBIC EXERCISE

Swimming, jogging, walking, cycling, skipping: these are aerobic – 'with oxygen' – activities. While isometrics, calisthenics and weight lifting are useful muscle-toning exercises to combine with aerobics, usually they do not raise your heart rate significantly. When you exercise aerobically your heart rate is pushed up to between 70 and 85 per cent of its maximum capacity and if it is done regularly this strengthens and enlarges the cardiac and pulmonary systems. The ultimate objective is to lower your resting heart rate and increase its stroke volume so that more blood reaches more tissues – in short, aerobic training increases your heart's efficiency so that it has a built-in protection against strain during activity.

Each of the following exercises is equivalent to the others in its aerobic training effect – any one of them, done two or three times a week, would give you all the exercise you need:

- Running one mile in less than eight minutes
- Swimming six hundred yards in less than fifteen minutes
- Cycling five miles in less than twenty minutes
- Stationary running for a total of twelve and a half minutes.

How to take your heart rate

First, find a pulse point you can feel easily. The radial pulse is located on the inside of the wrist, just below the hand on the thumb side. The carotid pulse is slightly below the jawbone, about half-way between the chin and the ear. Use your third and fourth fingers, and touch firmly, but without applying heavy pressure. Count your pulse beat for exactly fifteen seconds and multiply by four to get heart beats a minute. Then compare with chart.

Age	Threshold for training (70% of maximum predicted beats a minute)	Limit not to be exceeded for peaks (85% of maximum predicted beats a minute)	Maximum predicted beats a minute
20–24	140	170	200
25–29	140	170	200
30–34	136	165	194
35–39	132	160	188
40–44	128	155	182
45–49	124	150	176
50–54	119	145	171
55–59	115	140	165
60–64	111	135	159

The limits for people over fifty must be rigidly applied; the over-sixties should not exceed 130 beats a minute, although this is actually less than 85 per cent.

The following is a good running programme for an at-home regime; use your heart rate as a barometer to determine the intensity of the work-out. After one and a half to two minutes of exercising, count your pulse beat. The chart opposite will tell you whether you are working too hard or not hard enough. The precise timing of the exercise and the effort exerted to reach the 70 per cent level will vary with each person. The speed at which you run and the height to which you raise your knees will also affect your heart rate. An initial trial-and-error period will be necessary to establish your own level of exercise. The ideal programme is three days of exercise followed by one day of rest, then two days of exercise followed by one day of rest.

Weeks 1 and 2 – six minutes:
Run for 2 minutes (at least 70 per cent maximum heart rate)
Walk on the spot for 1 minute
Run for 2 minutes (at 70 per cent)
Walk on the spot for 1 minute

Weeks 3 to 6 – eight minutes:
Run for 3 minutes (at 70 per cent)
Walk on the spot for 1 minute
Run for 3 minutes (at 70 per cent)
Walk on the spot for 1 minute

Weeks 7 and 8 – nine minutes:
Run for 2 minutes (at 70 per cent)
Run for 1 minute (at 85 per cent)
Run for 1 minute (at 70 per cent)
Walk on the spot for one minute
Run for 3 minutes (at 70 per cent)
Walk on the spot for 1 minute

Weeks 9 and over – fifteen minutes:
Run for 2 minutes (at 70 per cent)
Run for 1 minute (at 85 per cent)
Run for 1 minute (at 70 per cent)
Walk on the spot for 1 minute
Repeat the entire cycle three times.

ALCOHOL

Alcohol is the enemy of dieters for two reasons: it contains calories (a lot) and it undermines will-power. The more you drink the less you care about calories and getting fat. Most people drink as an accompaniment to food – which probably already supplies all the calories required – so the calorie content of the alcohol is surplus. If you try to restrict your daily calorie intake and substitute alcohol for some food then you must make sure that what you eat is really nutritious or you could find yourself with another problem – lack of essential nutrients.

People drink for many reasons. Miss A drinks to be sociable: will-power is her only problem. She can perfectly well drink Perrier or soda water with a twist of lemon and ice (which looks like gin and tonic), or low-calorie ginger ale (which could pass for whisky) or a spritzer (half dry white wine, half soda water – 35 Calories) and still look like a drinker.

Miss B really likes and thinks she really needs the lift that alcohol gives. A few drinks remove enough of her inhibitions to enable her to enjoy herself. Unfortunately they also remove any ideas about keeping to a diet. Alcohol is a quick pick-up but also a quick let-down. The answer for Miss B might be to switch to high-protein foods: often loading your body with protein decreases the desire for alcohol. So Miss B should eat meals which include plenty of lean meat, fish and cottage cheese, and, between meals, have protein snacks or a piece of cheese. Before going to a drinks party she could drink iced tea or coffee (without milk) to give an extra lift.

Although alcohol appears to be a stimulant it does in fact have a depressant effect on the central nervous system and only removes tension and inhibition by numbing certain parts of the brain. As the Porter in Macbeth says, 'It provokes the desire but it takes away the performance.'

The speed at which alcohol takes effect and the length of time it lasts depends on several things. If you drink on an empty stomach the alcohol is absorbed quickly into the blood stream; if you have recently eaten a good meal the absorption of the alcohol is delayed until it reaches the intestine. The faster you drink the faster you will get drunk; if you drink slowly the absorption is slow. Carbon dioxide gas in drinks such as soda water, fizzy lemonade or the bubbles in champagne push the alcohol rapidly from the stomach to the intestine where absorption is quickest.

ANOREXIA

Every year more and more people go into hospital in advanced stages of malnutrition but not as a result of a deprived economic situation for their starvation is a purposeful act. They are suffering from what psychiatrists call a 'distorted body image' – the disease known as anorexia nervosa. While their weight falls to as little as 60 lb (27.2 kg) they still refuse food, still believing that they are fat.

Anorexia nervosa was first recognized by William Gull in 1874 as a 'peculiar form of disease' involving a refusal to eat and extreme emaciation. He attributed it to a 'morbid mental state'. Since then the disease has been variously labelled 'hysteria', 'neurosis', 'starvation sickness' or merely 'fading away'. It was not until 1929 that the disease was taken seriously and although anorexia is now greatly on the increase – five times greater than it was ten years ago in Britain and the US – this is partly because of more accurate medical diagnosis. At one time most GPs just did not recognize anorexia nervosa even when they saw their patient literally fading away before their eyes.

Another difficulty is that one of the symptoms of anorexia is the patient's refusal to accept help – genuinely believing that she does not need it. She becomes very devious in hiding how little she is eating and hides her emaciated figure in loose, bulky clothes. Fortunately her family or close friends usually insist that medical assistance is necessary, otherwise the patient literally starves to death. The anorexic often develops bizarre eating habits, sometimes eating huge quantities of low

calorie or low-carbohydrate foods such as salads and spinach, or sugar by the spoonful, or éclairs. Often linked with these episodes is habitual vomiting which gradually becomes involuntary and is done in secret.

Over 90 per cent of anorexics are female, and the majority are between fourteen and twenty-two. They almost always have amenorrhea caused either by the starved nutritional state or induced psychologically through the subconscious desire to avoid womanhood. The teenage anorexic tries to keep her childlike figure by removing all fat from it. The start of menstruation – the visible sign of the onset of puberty – appears to be affected by a critical weight level of 104 lb (47 kg).

Many adolescents who do not receive medical treatment may have a period of anorexia behaviour and recover from it. Patients who have suffered from the disease for less than five years usually recover after treatment and go on to lead a full and normal life. Once the disease has been established for more than ten years the chances of full recovery are poor.

When the body weight is dangerously low hospitalization is necessary. Quick nourishment is essential to prevent further weight loss and then intensive psychotherapy to help the patient make the transition from hospital to the outside world.

Various methods of force-feeding have been tried but it is useless to try to increase the weight without dealing with the underlying psychopathology. For the treatment to be successful the patient must be willing to cooperate; much encouragement is needed and reassurance that the weight gain will be controlled and not too fast.

BABY FAT

Babies are born thin, with little fat under their skin but usually, during the first few months, they quickly become rounder and fatter. This is completely natural and like most natural things there is a reason for it: in the early days of man a fat baby had a better chance of survival. The fat not only protected against the cold but when food was scarce the fat baby was less likely to die of hunger. Thus a fat baby is generally regarded as a healthy baby. This is fine when the baby *is* a baby but the fat child is less healthy than a thin child and will, unless the eating pattern is changed, become a fat adult. Fat is stored in cells and the child who habitually lays down a lot of fat will continue to do so when he grows up. Once a pattern of fatness is established it becomes a vicious circle. The fat child is unlikely to enjoy exercising because he gets hot, breathless and uncomfortable. So he avoids exercise and as a result probably has fewer friends and compensates by doing the thing he enjoys most – eating (and getting fatter).

BREAKFAST

One of the first things a doctor does when he treats an overweight patient is to put her on a diet that begins the day with 'a good breakfast'. This surprises many people, who claim that they only eat one meal a day anyway – that may be true but there are a number of small snacks in between.

Breakfast is important because it comes after the body has had its longest period without food, probably twelve hours. So breakfast lifts the energy level ready for the day's activity. It has been demonstrated beyond all doubt that people – especially children – who go without breakfast become less efficient both mentally and physically by mid-morning. Studies show that factory workers who skip breakfast are involved with more accidents than those who have eaten. What is more the effects of not eating breakfast are accumulative. Although the efficiency levels of the non-breakfasters increase after lunch they still do not quite catch up with the proficiency of the breakfast-eaters.

Breakfast is important for everybody, and particularly for dieters: if you eat all, or most of, your daily food intake in one meal you are more likely to put on weight than if it is divided into three or four equal-sized meals.

Nevertheless there are some people who simply cannot eat a big breakfast. If you are one of these it is no good forcing yourself – this is true of all meals.

What is a good breakfast? Here are a few examples:
- A boiled or poached egg on wholemeal toast thinly spread with butter and a glass of orange juice (250 Calories).
- 1 oz (30 g) muesli soaked in 2 fl oz (55 ml) each of milk and fruit juice with a freshly chopped piece of fruit (220 Calories).
- Porridge made with 1 oz (30 g) oats and water and a little sea-salt (115 Calories).

CALORIES

Most people know about counting calories but at least 50 per cent do not have the least idea what they are counting. A calorie is a measure of heat: the amount of heat required to raise the temperature of one gramme of water by one degree centigrade.

Food is measured in units of 1,000 calories, or a kilocalorie – written kcal for short or Calorie (with a capital C) as in this book. All foods contain calories, with the exception of salt, but in varying degrees. At one end of the scale come boiled marrow and celery with only 2.5 Calories an ounce, and at the other potato crisps with 165 Calories an ounce and margarine and butter both with 220 Calories an ounce.

If you take in more calories than your body burns up the excess is stored as fat. Apart from surgery, the only way to remove surplus fat is to consume fewer calories than are being used so that the body is forced to draw on its reserve supply. It takes approximately 3,500 Calories to produce a pound of surplus fat. It seems an enormous amount but a piece of chocolate cake every other week, for example – if taken over and above your daily required amount of calories – could do it in six months.

To put weight on – or take it off – the calories need not be balanced out, so if you consume 500 Calories more than you need on Monday and 500 less than you need on Tuesday your weight will remain the same.

It is practically impossible to get rid of all surplus fat by exercising, though it helps. And one of the advantages is that it takes the same amount of calories to run a mile in ten minutes as it does to run it in five – so however overweight you are it is worth trying. Most people put on fat slowly over a period of years and this is the best way to take it off: even an ounce a week adds up on a long-term basis.

Sport	Calories per minute	Calories per hour
badminton	6	350
cricket	2–8	very variable
cross-country running	10–12	600–700
cycling	7–15	400–900
football	5–12	300–700
golf	4–7	250–400
hockey	7–9	400–550
riding	3–10	200–600
skiing	5–18	300–1,100
squash	10–18	600–1,100
swimming	5–15	300–900
tennis	6–8	350–500
walking	3–5	200–300

This table gives the approximate Calories per minute used in various sports; they can only be approximate since two people playing a game of tennis can use up very different amounts of energy.

CARBOHYDRATES

Carbohydrates provide a convenient source of energy and few people in western countries suffer from a deficiency. A balanced diet should contain all nine of the following carbohydrates, but not in excess:

Ribose: a component of RNA and coenzymes; found in meat and liver

Deoxyribose: a component of DNA, the substance on which life is based and the means by which characteristics are passed on from one generation to the next.

Glucose: a source of energy found in animal and plant starch; in the absence of glucose, proteins and fats become the chief sources of energy

Fructose: can be converted to glucose in the liver; found in fruits

Galactose: the liver converts it to glucose; breasts synthesize it to make lactose, found in milk

Maltose: produced by digestion; found in malts

Lactose: produced by digestion; found in milk

Sucrose: produced by digestion

Starch: produced by digestion; found in flour and vegetables.

The most important carbohydrates are starch, sugar and fibre. The staggering rise in the amount of sugar in western diets – 126 lb (50 kg) per head compared with 4 lb (2 kg) per head a hundred years ago – is partly due to the amount of sugar added to various processed foods (dried soup, peanut butter, baked beans, mustard, etc) simply to satisfy the demand for sweetness. On the other hand the amount of starch in western diets is decreasing: 40 per cent compared with over 95 per cent at the beginning of the century. Fibre (e.g. husks of wheat) is made up in such a way that we cannot digest it and was once regarded as of no importance except as roughage. Today some nutritionists claim that it protects against heart disease and piles. Certainly nobody suggests that it does any harm and it is easily obtainable as bran or in wholemeal bread.

CELLULITE

The trouble with cellulite is that no one knows how or why it develops so no one knows exactly how to treat it. It is not like ordinary fat and though obese people usually have problems with cellulite quite thin people may have it too. The wrinkled 'orange peel' skin that denotes cellulite can appear on neck, arms, thighs, legs and even breasts.

It develops in three stages: fluids from blood and lymph infiltrate the septa between the fat lobules which become charged with fat. The cells become waterlogged, the fibrous tissue increases, the walls of the blood vessels swell slowing down the circulation. The skin hardens and sclerosis sets in.

The problem was first recognized and treated in Latin countries where women are physically less active but it is increasing in the UK and has become more noticeable since women have been wearing tight trousers and jeans. It mattered less when skirts were down to the ankles and bathing suits to the knees.

Circulation problems are almost certainly a contributory cause and probably hormones have something to do with it – especially the female hormone oestrodiol. Cellulite is essentially a female affliction. Over-eating and alcohol seem to increase the likelihood of cellulite and there seems to be an emotional aspect too as it has been known to appear after an emotional shock.

Treatment

Diet: if overweight follow a low-carbohydrate reducing diet, cut out sugar and drink plenty of water. If the weight is normal follow a healthy diet with lots of fresh fruit and vegetables. Be wary of internal treatments which can include the use of hormones and cortisone derivatives: they often have unpleasant side-effects and until the cause of cellulite is established the efficacy of drugs is suspect.

Exercise: as much and as strenuous as possible (cellulite is rare in athletes and ballet dancers) – all sports, brisk walking, preferably uphill, and bicycling are excellent.

Massage: helpful as long as it is done by an expert. Massage that stimulates the circulation must be good but rough pummelling can only make the condition much worse. Correct massage, with an oil or cellulite cream, helps improve the look of the skin and generally tones the muscles. Many salons use a vibrator which is also helpful.

Friction: again the object is to improve the circulation; treatment can be undertaken at home under a doctor's supervision or at a salon.

Salon treatments: injections and a special electrical treatment known as iontophoresis are also possible; usually about twenty treatments are

necessary and it can be a lengthy and expensive process.

Do-it-yourself methods: some people believe in cold showers following a hot bath to close the pores; or a scrub in the bath with a soft brush or loofah; or using rough salt on a loofah glove on the cellulitic areas; or using special anti-cellulite creams (usually containing ivy) rubbed into the skin. Certainly these can do no harm.

CHOLESTEROL

Cholesterol is a special kind of fat, present in everybody's blood and a natural and important constituent of the body. It is made in the liver and transported via the blood to the tissues that need it; we also get it in the foods we eat and this is known as dietary cholesterol. The amount in the blood tends to go up with increasing age and it has been established that people suffering from heart disease generally have a high level of blood cholesterol. There is, however, controversy about whether cholesterol concentration is in itself a cause of heart disease and many people think that a high cholesterol level is an indication of an underlying condition rather than a cause in itself. Cholesterol has nothing to do with weight and it is untrue to say that to lose weight you need to lower your cholesterol level, although any effective slimming diet would automatically do so.

Hard fats – saturated fats – such as butter, meat fat, increase the amount of cholesterol in your blood. Most liquid fats – unsaturated fats – such as olive oil, corn oil, lower the cholesterol level. Therefore the less hard fats we consume the more we are likely to replace them with liquid fats and the more likely it seems that our blood cholesterol will stay at its ideal level.

COLOUR

Many market research organizations and psychologists have carried out studies to see to what extent colour influences appetite. For instance, red stimulates the desire to eat; orange is often considered the ideal food colour; orange-brown increases appetite, especially when connected with drinks and roast and baked foods. The strength of drinks – for example, coffee, beer – is related to the depth of colour. All these factors are being considered with a view to producing new kinds of slimming diets.

Before the Second World War white was considered a symbol of purity and hygiene: thus white bread and white flour. Even today in Mexico poorly refined cornflour is considered inferior to white flour.

Today the preference for 'natural' foods has led us to associate brownness with goodness so we want wholemeal bread and brown eggs. In fact brown colouring is often added to bread along with synthetic minerals and vitamins to replace those lost in milling; brown eggs are in no way better for you than white eggs – their colour is largely determined by the breed of bird that lays them.

Adding colour to make food more attractive has been done for centuries: probably turmeric and saffron were the first. With large-scale food processing the use of dyes and colourings rapidly increased but recent evidence of cancer-producing side-effects has resulted in all but about half a dozen synthetic dyes being banned in Europe. Food colourings must now be almost exclusively made of animal or vegetable products. Carotene – from a variety of plants and animals – produces orange and yellow colourings for sauces. Anatto – from a Central American plant – produces a pale yellow colour used in processed cheese. Chlorophyll – from plant leaves – is used for colouring processed vegetables. Caramel – probably the most widely used of all – colours things like Colas, bread and flavouring cubes.

EATING HABITS

Nobody sets out to be overweight deliberately. But it is easy to overeat until it becomes a habit. As children we are taught to eat everything on our plates. Ice-cream and sweets are offered as bribes

for good behaviour – a reward pattern that continues into adulthood. The prettiest girls are taken to the best restaurants and seduced with expensive food and drink.

For good eating habits it is necessary to unlearn some of the things we were taught in childhood:

- Eat less at each meal. Take smaller mouthfuls, smaller portions and eat more slowly than you usually do. Leave something on your plate deliberately.
- Never eat between meals except for fresh vegetable snacks: a carrot, a stick of celery, radishes, a tomato.
- Substitute fresh fruit for all puddings, cakes and pastries.
- Have potatoes only twice a week.
- Drink mineral water instead of Colas, bitter lemon, etc.

FASTING

If you are in general good health fasting within limits – for one to three days – is not dangerous and some people find it a most effective way of losing weight. Under medical supervision fasting for several weeks has been used to treat cases of severe obesity. It is possible to lose up to 4 lb (1.8 kg) on a one-day fast and up to 10 lb (4.5 kg) in a weekend. As with all diets the amount you lose depends on how overweight you are before you start – the more overweight you are the more you lose. After an initial fast you should be able to lose a further 2 lb (0.9 kg) a week on a daily diet of under 1,500 Calories.

Fasting means eating absolutely nothing but drinking as much water as you wish: a minimum of 4 pints (2.3 l) is recommended.

Fasting may be criticized as a way of losing weight on the grounds that it upsets the bodily rhythm – an 800 Calorie a day diet for a longer period is a much safer and more certain way of slimming.

FAT

Fat accounts for 15 per cent of body weight in the average person and up to 50 per cent in an obese one. The fat lies in the fat cells in the layer of adipose tissue just beneath the skin. Its function is to conserve heat, act as an insulator and perform a complicated chemical conversion between protein, carbohydrate and fat.

Obesity is a major health problem in the western world. We know that obese people not only have bigger, fatter fat cells than people of average weight but they also have more of them – and it is not fully understood why. It is thought that the number of fat cells is determined at an early stage in infancy so that an overfed baby has a greater number of fat cells which will lead to an over-weight problem throughout life. It is certainly true that fat babies tend to grow into fat adults.

When obese people lose weight it is entirely due to shrinkage of each cell and not reduction in their number. This is probably why really fat people find it so difficult to slim: they have a greater number of fat cells each sending a 'feed me' message to the brain.

Heredity may also be a factor but it's more likely that obesity tends to run in families because the children of fat parents follow the same pattern of family eating – or overeating. Get into the habit of seeing yourself as a thin person, imagining the kind of clothes you will wear when you are a stone thinner. Everyone can lose weight provided they eat and drink less than their minimum food requirement. But that minimum can seem alarmingly low at first.

FATS

Basically there are two kinds: saturated and un-saturated. It is easy to distinguish them – saturated fats like lard and butter are solid at room temperature; unsaturated fats like cooking and salad oils are liquid. People trying to slim often say they have cut out all fats – by which they usually mean they do not eat butter or oil and cut off the bits on bacon

and beef. But they are still consuming fat in the form of milk, cheese, eggs, fish, nuts and even bread. In an average diet half the daily average of around 3.9 oz (110g) of fat is consumed in these hidden forms. Of all the 'fatty acids' three are essential: linoleic, linolenic and arachidonic and like the essential amino acids the body cannot manufacture these itself.

As a slimming aid there is no point in switching from butter to margarine – the calorie content is the same – unless you choose a margarine that specifically states that it is low-fat.

FIGURE ANALYSIS

Figures can be divided into three basic types: endomorphs, mesomorphs and ectomorphs.

Endomorphs are plump people with round heads and pear-shaped bodies.

Mesomorphs are well-muscled, athletic people, basically medium in build but able to put on fat easily. The hallmark of a mesomorph is sturdiness, whereas that of the endomorph is softness.

Ectomorphs: are the naturally slender people, often thin and fragile looking, with long, slim, poorly muscled extremities. They have delicate bones and the women have small bosoms.

The *morph* is seldom pure, however, and the vast majority of people are a mixture of all three in varying ratios. The type is recorded in a series of three numerals, each of which indicates the approximate strength of one of the primary components of a person's physique. The first numeral always refers to the degree of *endo*, the second to the *meso*, the third to the *ecto*. So when a seven-point scale is used the most extreme endomorph is shown as 7–1–1, the most extreme ectomorph as 1–1–7. One of the most pleasing combinations is 2–3–5 which, in a woman, indicates an endomorph's rounded bosom, the slim waist and legs of an ectomorph and the lightly muscled look of a mesomorph. A more common type might be 4–3½–1, or 4–4–4. The 4–3–3– subject would be tall, well-built, slender, with rounded limbs – the most often painted and photographed type. You could be almost any combination, with one factor predominating. Only a trained doctor or physiotherapist can analyse you completely but there is one way of establishing a fairly accurate picture of yourself; undress, stand in front of a mirror and analyse your figure bit by bit, truthfully.

It is now thought that temperament may be quite closely related to physical condition.

Endomorphs are extroverts, usually cheerful and sociable; they love parties and physical proximity with others. They enjoy food, relax easily, and have relatively weak muscles and connective tissue. Because they are basically lazy they find dieting a penance and often increase their body weight by 50 per cent between the ages of 20 and 50. But they can slim if they put their mind to it.

Mesomorphs are active athletic people. They are direct, often noisy and pushy. Because they are well-muscled they can get a bulky look where fat is laid down over muscles and unless they are careful they can put on 20 per cent in body weight between the ages of 20 and 50. They need constant exercise, not only games but walking, hurrying, running, swimming.

Ectomorphs are often introverts. Usually quiet and restrained, they may also be highly-strung and sensitive. They do not like parties and hate drawing attention to themselves; they need solitude. They often look younger than they are and stay slim and youthful-looking into old age. Dieting is no problem to them, on the contrary they have to take care to keep up their appetite, unlike the other types who turn to food for consolation.

These descriptions apply, of course, to the trait when it is dominant. Most people are not 'pure' types but it should be possible to spot your dominant characteristic and to eat – and exercise – accordingly.

JOULES

The move towards world unification of scientific standards is leading to the use of joules (J) to measure energy. (Joules are named after the man who measured the work output of horses and found there was a definite ratio of heat to work, thus proving work and heat to be interconvertible). One calorie is roughly 4.2 joules. A unit of 1,000 joules is called a kilojoule (kJ) and a unit of a million joules is called a megajoule (MJ).

KETOSIS

A condition that results from a too-low carbohydrate diet. On such diets the lack of carbohydrates forces the body to substitute proteins and fats as sources for energy. Ketones – fragments of fat waste – are chemically formed and the kidneys have to work overtime to dispose of them. Weight is lost, most of it water weight.

MINERALS

Essential daily requirements:
Calcium, sodium, potassium, phosphorus,
    chlorine, magnesium: 500–2,000 mg
Iron, zinc, copper, manganese: 2–20 mg
Molybdenum, nickel, iodine, fluorine, cobalt,
    selenium, cadmium: about 500 microgrammes
Water: 1,000–2,000 g
Proteins, fats, sugars: 50–100 g
Many minerals essential to life are injurious to living tissue but when combined as chlorides or sulphates the injurious properties disappear. Most essential minerals are widely dispersed in our foods and there should be little difficulty in obtaining adequate amounts. The trouble only arises in a western diet that relies too heavily on refined sugar, white flour and excessive salt.

Calcium: our bodies contain up to 3.3 lb ($1\frac{1}{2}$ kg) of calcium but half enters and leaves the bones every day. We probably get one-fifth of our daily requirement from hard water, the rest from dairy produce.

Chromium: needed to maintain adequate glucose levels in the blood and protect against diabetes. Most of the chromium in our bodies is present at birth and the amount tends to decline as we get older. The best sources are brewers' yeast and black pepper. Other good sources are hard cheese, calf's liver, wheatgerm, wholewheat bread, brown sugar, molasses. Chromium is lost in sugar refining and softened water.

Cobalt: lack of cobalt causes anaemia and lassitude. We can store several months' supply in the liver. Best source: liver.

Copper: the distribution of copper and iron is much the same, therefore a diet low in iron tends to be low in copper too. Good sources: red meat and fruits with a high vitamin C content.

Fluorine: necessary to the teeth. When there is a lack of fluorine sugar produces decay more easily. In natural water an adequate amount is present; tap water can have fluorides such as sodium fluoride added but it has yet to be established whether these have harmful side-effects.

Iodine: a lack of iodine results in various goitres; women are more vulnerable than men. Iodine is an essential component of hormones from the thyroid gland and therefore particularly important for stability of mood. Good sources: all seafood; other sources: dairy produce. Iodized salt is easily obtainable.

Magnesium: an important constituent of bones. Alcohol can cause a lack which may result in muscle tremors or even convulsions. Sources: cereals and fresh vegetables.

Manganese: essential to sexual development; it also helps build the enzymes which aid oxidization of sugars and provide energy. Lack of manganese results in bone abnormalities and low growth rate. Babies have little reserve and it is essential they get enough (lack of it is almost certainly a cause of rickets) at the right time. Good sources: nuts, wholewheat bread, cereals and leaf vegetables; other sources: dried fruits, fresh fruit, non-leaf vegetables and poultry.

Phosphorus: important in the structure of bones and teeth and the storage of energy in muscles. Deficiency is unlikely except in a diet relying heavily on refined foods. Sources: proteins, meat, fish and dairy products.

Potassium: lack of potassium causes weak muscles, poor heart function and irritability. It is linked to salt and foods high in sodium can cause an imbalance. There are adequate supplies in meats and vegetables.

Selenium: increases the effect of vitamin E which is essential for growth, tissue health and fertility. Much is lost in the water when vegetables are cooked. A good source of active vitamin E is wheatgerm.

Sodium chloride: salt is essential but an excess causes an imbalance of other minerals.

Sulphur: an essential component of proteins: if the protein intake is adequate the sulphur intake will be too. Sources: meat, fish, eggs, beans and cereals.

Zinc: helps heal wounds and burns and keeps the respiratory waste products of the blood stream at an acceptable level. A deficiency causes lack of growth; also insomnia, anxiety, loss of skin elasticity, hair, taste and smell. Zinc levels fluctuate, falling rapidly under stress. People on a low zinc diet should not make matters worse by taking vitamin pills which contain high levels of copper and iron as these antagonize zinc. Good sources: red meat; other sources: wholewheat bread, potatoes.

MUSCLES

Although the skeleton establishes the basic inner structure of the figure it is the muscles that actually determine the body shape. When muscles are weak the figure sags and posture is poor. Most women in western countries have poor muscles especially in the back, abdomen and shoulder areas. Tummy flab is often a jelly-like mass of muscle.

Healthy muscles are smooth to the touch, resilient and springy. They are never slack and they support the internal organs and body frame all the time. Apart from water, they are composed mainly of protein, which needs to be replaced constantly – hence the need for a high protein content in the diet. Muscles are also composed of a number of individual fibres; the number of fibres never changes but when muscles are poor they become very thin. Good exercise makes them plump.

The important muscles are:
- Abdominals, usually weak in women; these determine whether the stomach is flat or full
- Pectorals, beneath the breasts
- Dorsal muscles or the trapezius in the back, which lead to poor posture when weak
- Erector muscles in the lower back.

Muscles exert power by contraction and the energy for this comes from compounds of phosphorus which form a kind of muscle energizing system. This is kept going through respiration which is why deep breathing is essential to the efficient working of muscles. As the heart beat rises the waste products of muscular activity – carbon dioxide, etc. – are removed by being excreted from the body.

NATURAL OILS

The importance of natural oils in our diet has yet to be satisfactorily explained but it is known that they contain the essential fatty acids (EFA) linoleic and linolenic. These two acids, together with arachidonic acid, are essential to maintain good health: without them growth is retarded and skin health suffers.

The composition of fat beneath the skin depends on the composition of the fats you eat. If you eat mainly saturated fat then the fat will be hard and unyielding, if fats of the EFA type then the fat will be more supple.

Oils that are good for you include olive, sunflower-seed, safflower and wheatgerm. Oils to avoid are those containing erucic acid – mustard seed and wallflower seed.

Olive oil contains mostly oleic acid, non-essential but unsaturated.

Sunflower-seed oil contains linoleic acid and considerable amounts of vitamin E.

Safflower oil contains linoleic acid and other polyunsaturated materials.

Wheatgerm oil is a good source of polyunsaturated acids and has an excellent vitamin E content.

These oils are all excellent for cooking; for salad dressings use sunflower, safflower or wheatgerm.

OBESITY

Obesity has been called the twentieth-century disease. It is the most common nutritional disorder of modern western society and affects around 50 per cent of the adult population – but there is argument about the exact meaning of the word. The *Oxford Dictionary* merely says 'corpulent', but it is generally defined as being 10–15 per cent over normal ideal weight.

Most people judge their weight by standing on the bathroom scales and assuming that anything over their ideal weight is excess fat. In most cases this is true.

But what is 'ideal' weight? The tables most people use are based on those published by the Metropolitan Life Insurance Company of the United States. These were originally related to no more than height and weight and had to be considerably revised when it was found that the United States military authorities were rejecting most of their top athletes as being overweight. (In this case muscle rather than fat was accounting for the excess.)

Another easy method is the skin-fold test – which can be very accurate in the hands of an expert. This is based on the measurement of skin-fold thickness at biceps, triceps, under the shoulder blade and the side of the waist. Doctors do this with precision calipers.

Fluid retention – when the body tissues accumulate excessive water – accounts for some over-weight. Many women temporarily gain several pounds due to retained fluid just before a period; it is also thought to be one of the causes of cellulite. It can be due to excessive salt in the diet, an underactive kidney or to a congenital defect. It can be helped by keeping salt to the minimum and by drinking at least four glasses of water a day: this helps the elimination of salt and other minerals that require water in order to leave the body. Fluid retention is usually worse in heavy alcohol drinkers.

POSTURE

Good posture cannot affect how much you weigh; but it does affect the way you look. There are two kinds of upright posture: active and alert, which most people have to learn; and inactive slouching, which comes to most people naturally.

Posture is closely associated with mood: the inactive slouchers have hunched shoulders, downcast expressions and look depressed. The active alert people look confident, walk with a spring, head up, shoulders back.

Since man started moving about on two limbs instead of four he has had to contend with the changed effect of the force of gravity. When you are standing properly gravity's downward pull on internal organs and joints is lessened.

To achieve good posture stand with the weight evenly distributed on the heels and the outer sides of the feet, gripping the ground with the toes; the knees slightly flexed and acting as shock absorbers; the buttocks tucked under, the pelvis tilted; shoulders lifted and relaxed, slightly forward; head held so that the contraction of one group of muscles at the back of the neck balances the ones in front. Chin tucked in and the back of the neck held straight and lifted so that the top of the head is as if attached to the ceiling.

By making the feet a firm base you are able to act quickly and the internal organs are well supported in the pelvic basin by the balanced contraction of the abdominal, back and buttock muscles. Good posture allows the lungs to be expanded to the full, ensuring balanced action between the muscles of the abdominal wall and the diaphragm. The whole process is like a bellows, removing waste products from the bottom as well as the top of the lungs.

Flexible, lifted shoulders neutralize gravity's pull on upper limbs, shoulder and neck muscles. The blood flows freely to the brain, carrying oxygen to counteract fatigue, poor memory and headaches.

PROTEINS

There are hundreds of different kinds of protein and they are made up by the fusing of a varied assortment of substances called amino acids. Eight of them are essential: valine, leucine, isoleucine, threonine, lysine, phenylalanine, tryptophan and methionine. From these eight the body can make the other important amino acids: glycine, alanine, serine, aspartic acid, glutamic acid, ornithine, arginine, histidine, tyrosine, systeine, proline, hydroxyproline. The different proteins we eat can be of more or less value to the body, depending on whether they have the essential amino acids in the proportions in which our body needs them. Two foods only are perfect in this respect: human milk and the hen's egg. But other good sources are meat, fish, cereals, grains, legumes, and dairy produce.

In any reasonable diet there is little likelihood of a lack of protein: all living material contains it, which means most food. But while a lettuce contains perhaps only 1 per cent protein, legumes – which are seeds storing protein for the next generation – can contain 25 per cent. Meat and fish – often called the protein foods – can contain up to 30 per cent. Obviously a growing child, building flesh and blood and tissues, needs plenty of protein foods. So does a pregnant woman or nursing mother. Adults need them because of the constant breakdown and replacement of cells: the exact amount required is a matter of controversy. In the United States the National Academy of Sciences, in 1974, recommended a minimum daily allowance of 1.9 oz (55 g) for men, 1.6 oz (46 g) for women. Other recommended daily allowances vary from 1.4–1.9 oz (40–55 g) for women; 1.4–2.3 oz (40–65 g) for men. But as with all nutrients there is no advantage in taking more than you need.

SUGAR

In the year 1800 the average person in Great Britain would have eaten about 4 lb (2 kg) of sugar a year; today the figure has gone up to around 126 lb (57 kg). This huge amount of sugar is far in excess of what our bodies can use and they therefore do their best to store it as fat. This stems from the ancient animal reflex to store food for the lean times ahead. The trouble is that for western man the lean time never comes. And eating – with its consequent high blood sugar level – has a tranquillizing effect not dissimilar to alcohol. We have developed an addiction for sugar which has made us eat more and more, even when we do not need it. Jams, cakes, ice-creams, biscuits and sweets are all high in calories and some people can eat them indefinitely without feeling satisfied.

THERMODYNAMICS

This is the study of the convertibility of forms of energy. Joule discovered that there is a fixed ratio of heat to work that is true of any form of energy or any form of heat. Our fuel is food and we use it up in work – chemical, mental, muscular and nervous – and also by radiating heat from our body. The amount of heat we lose when sitting and resting is called the basal rate. This rate is lower for women than for men and tends to get lower as we get older. Fat people have a lower basal rate than thin people and tend to conserve more food as fat than thin people.

VEGETARIANISM

No vegetarian will eat meat but most include eggs, milk and cheese in their diet and some also include fish. This is a nutritionally sound diet; there is no evidence to prove that it is superior to a well-balanced meat diet for promoting health and beauty. Any restricted diet is fraught with danger. The strict vegetarians – the Vegans – who eschew all animal foods will run into trouble with serious deficiencies in vitamin B-12 (not found in cereals, vegetables or fruits) and possibly vitamin D. Without vitamin B-12 anaemia results and without sufficient vitamin D bone malformation can occur – particularly dangerous in growing children and pregnant women. Few vegetarians have a weight problem – possibly because they have usually thought seriously about food and avoid sugary junk foods as well as meat.

The almost completely vegetarian Okinawans of Japan and the Otomi Indians of Mexico show few signs of overweight, heart disease or cancer. And a study of two Roman Catholic orders of monks showed that the largely vegetarian Trappists had lower cholesterol levels than their meat-eating Benedictine brothers.

Becoming a vegetarian does not necessarily mean that you will live longer or that you will achieve instant health and beauty. Someone who consumes huge quantities of bread and cakes instead of meat will finish up both overweight and ill. Also, while fruits and vegetables are excellent sources of vitamins and minerals they may not provide enough protein, the vital substance the body needs for skin, organs, muscles and bones.

Proteins are made up of chemicals called amino acids and meat proteins contain the eight essential ones. However, while plant proteins lack one or another of the amino acids what one vegetable lacks, another contains and it is therefore possible to get adequate nutrition from a combination of vegetables.

VITAMINS

Vitamins became fashionable in the thirty years between 1915 and 1945 when over fifty were identified – most of them incorrectly.

The first indications had come in the eighteenth century when James Lind cured the British Navy of scurvy with a compulsory ration of lemon juice. Later a Dutchman, Christian Eijkman, discovered he could produce the disease in chickens by removing the husks from the rice on which they were fed. Then a Polish biochemist, Casimir Funk, suggested that the vital link was a chemical called an amine. He called it the vital amine – or 'vitamine' and the name stuck.

When vitamins were found to be either fat soluble or water soluble they were termed A and B. Soon C, D and E were added and the family of Bs had to be numbered 1 to 20. These have now been reduced in number and have alternative names, e.g. vitamin C – ascorbic acid. Although nearly 400 tonnes of vitamin tablets are sold in Britain each year in tablet form there is seldom any real need for them. If your diet lacks vitamins it almost certainly lacks some food that is essential to good health and cannot be turned into a diet that is good for you just by adding a few vitamin pills; the diet needs to be changed, not supplemented.

Just as a car runs no better with ten gallons of petrol in the tank than it does with one so it is unnecessary – and sometimes even harmful – to overfill your body with vitamins. Unlike a car your body has no tank to store the surplus until it is required (the vitamins are lost in the urine), and most vitamins need to be replenished daily.

What is more, by trying to increase the amount of one vitamin you add extra quantities of another which may have an antagonizing effect on something else. Far better to eat widely and well: wholewheat bread rather than white, no refined sugar, vegetables cooked for the minimum time in a small amount of water and eaten as fresh as possible – some start to lose their vitamin content within thirty minutes of being picked.

Vitamin A (carotene or retinol)

Essential to a healthy skin, which becomes dry and wrinkled when vitamin A is lacking. Also necessary for good sight, steady growth and energy. Severe deficiency can result in blindness. Low-fat diets can be deficient in vitamin A. Good sources: red and yellow coloured vegetables, particularly carrots and tomatoes; dairy produce; liver; meat; some fish. It is toxic in excess as it is stored in the liver. It is not destroyed by cooking.

Vitamins B

All essential to the body's molecular machinery.

B-1 (thiamine): It is lost from the body in the urine so it must be replaced daily. Essential for the health of the nerves – a deficiency commonly results in nervous diseases. People on a high carbohydrate diet are at risk. Good sources: wholemeal cereal, liver, heart, kidney, brewers' yeast, pork, pulses. Destroyed by overcooking.

B-2 (riboflavin): An essential energy-making vitamin, necessary for skin health and resistance to infection. Good sources: cheese, eggs, liver, kidneys, Indian tea and fresh vegetables. Riboflavin is destroyed by sunlight.

B-3 (niacin): Crucial energy-forming vitamin; an inadequate supply causes mental disorder. Essential to skin health. Good sources: brewers' yeast, lean meat, liver and wholemeal grain.

B-5 (pantothenic acid): Essential to nerve health and the adrenal glands, and to the production of the hormones which balance the levels of minerals and water in the tissues. Emotional shocks always upset these balances. Pantothenic acid also aids the burning of fat for energy. Good sources: eggs, kidneys, liver, yeast, beef and milk. Fifty per cent is lost from grains when they are refined and a little from vegetables when they are cooked.

B-6 (pyridoxine): Lack of this vitamin has been related to nervous disorders; the first signs are irritability and stomach upsets. Alcohol slows down its absorption. Good sources: brewers' yeast, whole grains, liver, milk, eggs and green vegetables. It is available at some level in most foods.

B-12 (cyanobalamin): Lack of this vitamin seriously affects the nervous system: anaemia is one of the first symptoms. It is absent from plant produce and therefore vegetarians are sometimes at risk although it can be stored in the liver for up to a year. Good sources: milk, meat, eggs, liver and kidneys. There is evidence that bacteria in the intestines can produce B-12.

Bc (folic acid): Insufficiency causes blood disorders. Good sources: fresh leaf vegetables, egg yolk, oysters, kidney and liver. It is sensitive to heat and quickly lost in cooking.

Vitamin C (ascorbic acid)

Water soluble, so lost in the urine; it is essential that it is replaced constantly otherwise blood levels fall and infection becomes a danger as the cells can be more easily penetrated; varicose veins form; depression is common. One massive dose cannot restore the balance. In states of stress and infection extra vitamin C is required. Good sources: fruit, especially citrus fruit (1 orange provides the daily requirement of 60 mg), and fresh vegetables. Much lost in cooking.

Vitamin D (calciferol)

The chief function is to aid the absorption of calcium – without it bone malformation can occur, i.e. rickets in babies and brittle bones in old people. Vitamin D is synthesized by the skin in summer sunshine. This does not mean that you should bare the entire body for hours in hot sunshine for even the face can produce a good quantity of vitamin D. Good sources: eggs and most animal fats. It is toxic in large amounts but it can be stored in the body.

Vitamin E (tocopherol)

There are three closely related E vitamins which, for convenience, are referred to as vitamin E. They are fat soluble and stored in the fatty parts of the tissues. They help to keep the lungs healthy and guard against air pollutants. Essential for the health of the blood cells and fertility. The need for vitamin E increases as the intake of polyunsaturated oils and fats is increased: another example of the importance of balance in diet. Good sources: eggs, meats, liver, fish, whole grain and wheat-germ oil.

Vitamin H (biotin)

Essential in the removal of waste protein from the body. Bacteria in the intestines makes all that is necessary and deficiency only arises when antibiotics are taken. Good sources: egg yolk, liver, kidneys, tomatoes and yeast.

Vitamin K (menadione)

Main function of vitamin K is to ensure the clotting of the blood. Bacteria in the intestines makes much of this vitamin and it is widely distributed in our food. Vitamin K deficiency has been known in children and adults treated with antibiotics; as green vegetables are a major source of supply a lack may occur in the winter when fresh greens are difficult to obtain.

Essential daily requirements:
Vitamin A (retinol or carotene): 0.75 mg
Vitamin B-1 (thiamin): 1.3 mg
Vitamin B-2 (riboflavin): 1.4 mg
Vitamin B-3 (nicotinic acid, niacin): 17 mg
Vitamin B-5 (pantothenic acid): 10 mg
Vitamin B-6 (pyridoxine): 2 mg
Vitamin B-12 (cyanabalamin): 0.005 mg
Vitamin Bc (folic acid): 0.4 mg
Vitamin C (ascorbic acid): 60 mg
Vitamin D (calciferol): 0.01 mg
Vitamin E (tocopherol): 30 mg
Vitamin H (biotin): trace
Vitamin K (menadione): not established

WEIGHT WATCHERS

This is the world's best-known group of slimming clubs: there are about 15,000, mainly throughout the USA and Europe. It was the brainchild of Berenice Weston who explains her success by saying that she taught 'Thought for Food' rather than 'Food for Thought'. Weight Watchers are trained to think before they buy, before they prepare and before they eat.

As with most clubs there is a fee for joining, and a fee for each weekly session. To quote Mrs Weston 'the togetherness of people with the same overweight problem not only helps the individual to lose weight but is the prime ingredient for maintaining the correct weight once the goal has been achieved. Very practical and sincere advice is given by both the lecturer and other members of the group on how to deal with real problems such as summer holidays, Christmas celebrations, invitations to dinner, hungry children who think "chips" are a way of life and the ever-rising price of food.'

Undoubtedly it is easier to do something – even slimming – if you know a lot of other people are similar to you and encouraging you. And in situations where loneliness is as real a problem as obesity Weight Watchers can serve a dual purpose.

There is no calorie counting in the Weight Watchers' levelling plan and high-calorie, low-nutritious foods are banned. Members are given menu plans and lists of foods that are permitted in limited, unlimited and moderate amounts, and forty items that are banned completely: these include all alcoholic drinks and beer, butter, olive oil, soup, nuts, raw fish, raw meat, sugar, cakes, biscuits, chocolate, sweets and all fried foods. It is bad luck if you do not like fish – which *must* be taken five times a week – and loathe liver, which you *must* have at least once a week.

ZEN MACROBIOTIC

This sounds as if it is the ancient eating regime of the Zen Buddhists but in fact it is the 'concept for living' presented by Georges Ohsawa who died in 1965. In a macrobiotic diet (*macro* – great; *bio* – energy) food is divided into *yin* (acid) and *yang* (alkaline). To achieve the correct balance you should eat five parts *yin* to one part *yang*. Brown rice is the ideal food because it is both *yin* and *yang* in these proportions. Apart from the actual *yin* and *yang* foods there are *yang* factors: heat, time, pressure, salt. Most foods are eaten but there is great emphasis on grains and vegetables and the more macrobiotic you become the less you eat until you are down to nothing but wild rice.

Yin

bananas	mushrooms	pork
butter	oranges	potatoes
cream	peanuts	spinach
cucumber	pears	yogurt
honey	peas	
melon	pineapple	

Yang

apples	duck	salmon
carrots	herrings	sardines
cherries	lettuce	strawberries
chestnuts	onions	watercress
chicory	pheasant	

BLACKADDER 1931

TAI CHAI

The movements are performed as slowly as possible, and are continuous. Relax but use a positive although nearly zero amount of muscle contraction, and breathe gently. If you find yourself becoming tense with effort, return to the neutral position. Learn each of the seven forms separately, preferably one each day. There is nothing to be gained by rushing the learning process. A general rule of breathing is exhale as you extend, inhale as you contract the overall space you are occupying. Until you can perform the movements, breathe naturally, then learn the breathing methods described. As you learn you will be able to put all the forms together in one series of movements. You may perform tai chai any time, anywhere, once or more every day. Note the different hand positions. Be very gentle to begin with, do not strain.

1a

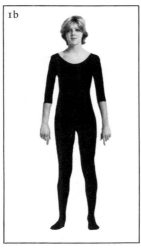

1b

1. *(left)* – Stand as shown, 1a. Let out the breath slowly; half clench fist, and maintain with minimum tension, the back of your hand facing forward, 1b; breathe in slowly and deliberately, raising hands at same time to nipple height, hold for short while, return to starting position, exhaling as you do.

2. *(below)* – Stand in neutral position; exhale. Breathe in slowly, raising arms upwards and outwards, 2a, and thigh horizontally, 2b; give gentle controlled kick, completing it as arms reach apogee, 2c; inhale fully without strain. Exhale slowly as arms return in smooth arc to starting position. Repeat with the other leg.

2a

2c

2b

TAI CHAI

3a

3b

3c

3d

3. *(above)* – Take up neutral position. Move arms gently and purposefully into position shown, while inhaling, 3a. Move weight on to the right foot, 3b, extending the left leg; execute the movement gently, bending the right knee as the balance point changes, 3c. Exhale. Inhaling, sweep hands down in arc, 3d, complete inhalation as you nearly touch your left foot; return to beginning of movement. Exhale to return to starting position.

4. *(right)* – Take up the neutral position; inhale. Exhale as you extend your left arm, simultaneously bending the left knee, sliding your right foot backward along the ground; you should have exhaled fully without strain at completion, as shown; inhale as you retract the left arm to the chest, at the same time transferring your weight to your right foot and moving back your left foot, your left foot barely touching the floor as it sweeps back to the neutral position; you should finish exhaling just as your hands reach the neutral position. Repeat with the left foot leading.

4

5. *(right)* – From the neutral position, take up position shown by gracefully turning left ankle quarter of a turn, barely touching the floor with the heel; extend right leg, keeping a sweeping move of arms, exhaling so that reaching position shown, you have exhaled completely; all your weight is now transferred to left foot; inhaling, sweep right leg to neutral position, allowing arms to take up neutral position; you will have turned quarter of a circle; repeat until you complete the circle. Now repeat using left leg.

6. *(above)* From the neutral position take up the position shown, inhaling gently as you do so, left arm bent and extended as depicted, 6a. Exhaling, transfer your weight to your right foot, at the same time sweeping with your left foot to take up position shown, 6b, the left arm more extended now, and the right having moved away from the chest centre; inhale gently and reverse the movements to take up the neutral position, 6c; repeat with right arm extension. As you improve you will bend the knees a little. When done in pairs more control is needed for unison.

TAI CHAI

7. *(right)* – Stand in starting position and curl your hands in a gentle claw, 7a. With positive but minimum tension inhale as you take up position of hands as shown, left leading, 7b; exhale as you direct left hand forward, at same time taking a step forward with left foot, letting most of the body weight come upon the left foot, 7c. Inhale as you retract left hand as shown, 7d, while simultaneously extending right hand, 7e; exhale as you reverse these movements, 7f; once they are reversed inhale and revert to starting position. Repeat leading with right foot.

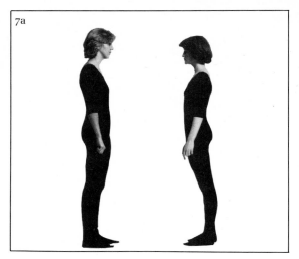

7a

7b

7c

7d

7e

7f

CALORIE CHART

Measuring calories exactly is an extremely expensive and time consuming operation – which is why you can look up six different charts and find that the calorie value of half a grapefruit can vary between 20 and 45 calories. Each type of food can vary according to the time of year, the place where it was grown, the soil it was grown in, how long it took to grow and the time which has elapsed since it was harvested. Variation in fat content, extremely difficult to measure, changes the calorie value of meat enormously; as does the amount of cooking. So use these calorie values as guide lines. The serious slimmer knows perfectly well that two thin well-cooked slices of streaky bacon have a far lower calorie value than two thicker lightly-cooked slices of back bacon. It is very easy to cheat while you are slimming, but remember that the only person who is being cheated is yourself.

Meat			Calories
bacon	grilled	1 oz (30 g)	115
beef	steak, grilled	1 oz (30 g)	55
		4½ oz (130 g)	250
	roast	1 oz (30 g)	65
		4 oz (115 g)	260
	minced	1 oz (30 g)	65
		4 oz (115 g)	260
	carbonnade	1 oz (30 g)	100
	corned	1 oz (30 g)	70
	hamburger	1 oz (30 g)	75
		4 oz (115 g)	300

Meat			Calories
chicken	roast	1 oz (30 g)	45
	portion	7 oz (200 g)	315
	curried	1 oz (30 g)	345
	poached	1 oz (30 g)	40
	giblets	1 oz (30 g)	100
duck	roast	1 oz (30 g)	90
	portion	7 oz (200 g)	630
gammon	baked	1 oz (30 g)	65
grouse	on bone, roast	12 oz (340 g)	290
guinea fowl	on bone, roast	12 oz (340 g)	370
ham	boiled	1 oz (30 g)	75
		3 oz (85 g)	225
kidney	grilled	1 oz (30 g)	40
lamb	chop, grilled	3 oz (85 g)	200
	roast	1 oz (30 g)	75
		3 oz (85 g)	225
liver	grilled	1 oz (30 g)	70
	pâté	1 oz (30 g)	100
pheasant	roast	1 oz (30 g)	60
		6 oz (170 g)	360
pork	chop, grilled	3 oz (85 g)	300
	roast	1 oz (30 g)	100
sausages	grilled beef	1 oz (30 g)	60
	grilled pork	1 oz (30 g)	90
tongue	boiled	1 oz (30 g)	85
turkey	roast	1 oz (30 g)	40
		4 oz (115 g)	160
veal	roast	1 oz (30 g)	65
		4 oz (115 g)	260

Fish			Calories
caviar		1 oz (30 g)	75
clams		1 oz (30 g)	20
cod	grilled	1 oz (30 g)	35
	on the bone	7 oz (200 g)	140
cod's roe		1 oz (30 g)	60
crab		1 oz (30 g)	30
fish-cakes		1 oz (30 g)	45
fish fingers		1 oz (30 g)	60
haddock	grilled	1 oz (30 g)	35
	poached	1 oz (30 g)	25
	smoked	1 oz (30 g)	30
halibut		1 oz (30 g)	40
		4 oz (115 g)	160
kedgeree		4 oz (115 g)	240
kipper		1 oz (30 g)	45
lobster		1 oz (30 g)	30
mackerel	grilled	1 oz (30 g)	45
	smoked	1 oz (30 g)	70
oysters	6	3 oz (85 g)	45
plaice		1 oz (30 g)	20
		4 oz (115 g)	80
prawns	shelled	1 oz (30 g)	30
red mullet		1 oz (30 g)	40
salmon	boiled	1 oz (30 g)	50
	smoked	1 oz (30 g)	45
	tinned	1 oz (30 g)	45
sardines	tinned in oil	1 oz (30 g)	75
scampi	boiled	1 oz (30 g)	30
	fried in breadcrumbs	1 oz (30 g)	90
sea bass		1 oz (30 g)	30
		4 oz (115 g)	120
shrimps		1 oz (30 g)	30
sole	poached	1 oz (30 g)	25
trout	grilled	1 oz (30 g)	30
	smoked	1 oz (30 g)	30
tuna	tinned	1 oz (30 g)	80

Dairy produce			Calories
butter		1 oz (30 g)	220
cheese	Brie	1 oz (30 g)	85
	Camembert	1 oz (30 g)	85
	cottage cheese	1 oz (30 g)	20
	Cheddar	1 oz (30 g)	110

Dairy produce			Calories
cheese	cream cheese	1 oz (30 g)	120
	Danish Blue	1 oz (30 g)	100
	Edam	1 oz (30 g)	85
	Gouda	1 oz (30 g)	85
	Parmesan	1 oz (30 g)	120
	Stilton	1 oz (30 g)	130
cream	single	tablespoon	45
	double	tablespoon	110
	clotted	tablespoon	140
eggs	small		75
	medium		80
	large		85
	yolk		65–70
	white		10–15
	boiled		75–85
	fried		130–150
	Scotch egg	5 oz (140 g)	350
lard/dripping		1 oz (30 g)	70
milk	whole milk	1 fl oz (30 ml)	20
	long life	1 fl oz (30 ml)	20
	goat's milk	1 fl oz (30 ml)	20
	human milk	1 fl oz (30 ml)	20
	buttermilk	1 fl oz (30 ml)	10
	skim	1 fl oz (30 ml)	10
	powdered	1 oz (30 g)	140
yogurt	natural	1 oz 30 g)	20
		5 oz (140 g)	100
	fruit	1 oz (30 g)	30
	nut	1 oz (30 g)	35
	low-fat	1 oz (30 g)	15

Vegetables			Calories
artichoke	globe, boiled	8 oz (225 g)	15
	heart, boiled	4 oz (115 g)	15
asparagus		3 stalks	10
aubergine	boiled	2 oz (55 g)	10
	fried	2 oz (55 g)	70
avocado		½ medium	100
bamboo shoots		2 oz (55 g)	15
beans	broad	2 oz (55 g)	30
	butter	2 oz (55 g)	50
	runner	2 oz (55 g)	10
beetroot		1 oz (30 g)	12
broccoli		2 oz (55 g)	10

Vegetables			*Calories*
brussels sprouts		2 oz (55 g)	10
cabbage	boiled	2 oz (55 g)	16
carrots	raw	1 medium	10
	boiled	2 oz (55 g)	20
cauliflower	raw	1 oz (30 g)	6
	boiled	2 oz (55 g)	15
celery	raw	1 stick	2
	boiled	2 oz (55 g)	5
chicory	raw	1 oz (30 g)	3
corn on the cob	boiled	5 oz (140 g)	170
courgette	raw	1 oz (30 g)	3
	boiled	2 oz (55 g)	6
cucumber	raw	1 oz (30 g)	3
endive	raw	1 oz (30 g)	3
garlic	raw	1 clove	1
leeks	boiled	2 oz (55 g)	15
lentils	boiled	1 oz (30 g)	30
lettuce	raw	1 oz (30 g)	3
marrow	boiled	2 oz (55 g)	4
mushrooms	raw	1 oz (30 g)	7
	boiled	2 oz (55 g)	6
	fried	2 oz (55 g)	100
onions	raw	1 oz (30 g)	8
	boiled	2 oz (55 g)	16
parsnips	boiled	2 oz (55 g)	35
peas	boiled	2 oz (55 g)	35
peppers	raw	1 oz (30 g)	4
potatoes	boiled	2 oz (55 g)	45
	new	2 oz (55 g)	42
	chips	2 oz (30 g)	180
	croquettes	2 oz (55 g)	100
radishes	raw	1 oz (30 g)	4
spinach	raw	1 oz (30 g)	10
	boiled	2 oz (55 g)	18
tomato	raw	1 oz (30 g)	4
turnips	boiled	2 oz (55 g)	10
water chestnuts	tinned	1 oz (30 g)	15
watercress	raw	1 oz (30 g)	10

Fruit and nuts			*Calories*
apple	raw	1 medium	50
	stewed, no sugar	1 oz (30 g)	10

Fruit and nuts			*Calories*
apricot		1	10
banana		medium	65
blackberries		1 oz (30 g)	8
blackcurrants		1 oz (30 g)	12
cherries		1 oz (30 g)	10
figs	stewed, no sugar	1 oz (30 g)	35
	dried	$\frac{3}{4}$ oz (20 g)	45
gooseberries		1 oz (30 g)	10
grapefruit		$\frac{1}{2}$	30
grapes		1 oz (30 g)	15
lemon		medium	15
loganberries		1 oz (30 g)	5
lychees		1 oz (30 g)	20
melon		4 oz (115 g)	16
orange		medium	50
peach		medium	40
peanuts	shelled	1 oz (30 g)	160
pear		medium	60
pineapple		1 oz (30 g)	15
plums		large	20
	stewed, no sugar	1 oz (30 g)	6
prunes	stewed, no sugar	1 oz (30 g)	20
raisins		1 oz (30 g)	80
raspberries		1 oz (30 g)	12
strawberries		1 oz (30 g)	10
tangerine		1	20
walnuts		1 oz (30 g)	150

Cereals			*Calories*
All Bran		1 oz (30 g)	75
bread	brown	1 oz (30 g)	65
	French	1 oz (30 g)	75
	granary	1 oz (30 g)	60
	white	1 oz (30 g)	75
	wholemeal	1 oz (30 g)	60
	wholewheat	1 oz (30 g)	60
cornflakes		1 oz (30 g)	110
cornflour		1 oz (30 g)	110
cream crackers		1 biscuit	30
crispbread		1 slice	20–30
crisps		1 oz (30 g)	165
flour	plain	1 oz (30 g)	100
	wholemeal	1 oz (30 g)	95
melba toast		1 slice	30

Cereals

			Calories
muesli		1 oz (30 g)	120
pasta	cooked	1 oz (30 g)	35
porridge	with water	4 oz (115 g)	50
	with milk	4 oz (115 g)	65
	with milk/sugar	4 oz (115 g)	120
rice	boiled	1 oz (30 g)	35
water biscuit		1 oz (30 g)	120
wheatgerm		1 oz (30 g)	100
yeast		1 oz (30 g)	100
yeast extract (Marmite, etc.)		1 oz (30 g)	35

Soups

		Calories
chicken	¼ pt (1.4 dl)	50
consommé	¼ pt (1.4 dl)	25
cucumber	¼ pt (1.4 dl)	50
fish	¼ pt (1.4 dl)	75
mushroom	¼ pt (1.4 dl)	50

Dressings, oils, sauces

		Calories
cheese sauce	1 oz (30 g)	55
custard	1 oz (30 g)	30
French dressing	1 oz (30 g)	125
horse-radish sauce	½ oz (15 g)	30
low-down dressing	1 oz (30 g)	30
mayonnaise	1 oz (30 g)	200
mustard	1 oz (30 g)	5
olive oil	1 fl oz (30 ml)	270
sunflower oil	1 fl oz (30 ml)	270
tomato sauce	1 oz (30 g)	30
vinegar	1 fl oz (30 ml)	1
Worcestershire sauce	1 oz (30 g)	50

Sweets and preserves

			Calories
apple pie		4 oz (115 g)	300
cheesecake	plain	3 oz (85 g)	300
crème caramel		4 oz (115 g)	150
fruit flan		4 oz (115 g)	250
honey		1 oz (30 g)	80
ice-cream		1 oz (30 g)	55
jam		1 oz (30 g)	80
lemon sorbet		5 oz (140 g)	190
marmalade		1 oz (30 g)	80
sugar	brown	1 oz (30 g)	110

Sweets and preserves

			Calories
sugar	white	1 oz (30 g)	110
	white	teaspoon	30
syrup		1 oz (30 g)	95

Alcoholic drinks

			Calories
beer		½ pt (2.8 dl)	90
Champagne		¼ pt (1.4 dl)	110
cider	dry	½ pt (2.8 dl)	100
	sweet	½ pt (2.8 dl)	120
cognac		1 fl oz (30 ml)	65
Dubonnet		1 fl oz (30 ml)	45
gin		1 fl oz (30 ml)	65
liqueurs	average	1 fl oz (30 ml)	110
Martini	dry	2½ fl oz (70 ml)	140
	sweet	2½ fl oz (70 ml)	150
port		1 fl oz (30 ml)	45
rum		1 fl oz (30 ml)	65
sherry	dry and medium	1 fl oz (30 ml)	35
	sweet	1 fl oz (30 ml)	40
whisky		1 fl oz (30 ml)	65
wine	red, dry	1 fl oz (30 ml)	20
	red, sweet	1 fl oz (30 ml)	25
	white, dry	1 fl oz (30 ml)	20
	white, sweet	1 fl oz (30 ml)	25

Non-alcoholic drinks

			Calories
apple juice	natural	¼ pt (1.4 ml)	50
bitter lemon		4 fl oz (1.1 dl)	40
carrot juice	natural	¼ pt (1.4 dl)	32
coffee	black	1 cup	4
	white	1 cup	20
	white with sugar	1 cup	50
Cola types		¼ pt (1.4 dl)	60
ginger ale		¼ pt (1.4 dl)	35
grapefruit juice		¼ pt (1.4 dl)	45
lemon juice		1 fl oz (30 ml)	2
orange juice	natural	¼ pt (1.4 dl)	50
pineapple juice		¼ pt (1.4 dl)	75
tea	with lemon	1 cup	2
	with milk	1 cup	20
	with milk/sugar	1 cup	50
tomato juice		1 fl oz (30 ml)	5
tonic water		¼ pt (1.4 dl)	30

HOW TO DETERMINE YOUR IDEAL WEIGHT

The human physique varies from person to person and rigid classifications are of little use except as conceptual references. This method, planned by Dr Anthony Harris, combines artistic ideals with anatomical research.

From a purely health view the ideal weights for mature women were established more than a decade ago by the mammoth surveys involving millions of people carried out in the United States. The charts resulting from these surveys were constructed on frame sizes chosen by rule of thumb with no objective criterion. It is little wonder that women trying to assess their ideal weight cannot decide what their frame size is. Sometimes height-weight charts are published without reference to frame size; women of average height (5 feet 5 inches, 1.65 cm) can vary by 30 lb (13.6 kg) without any of them being overweight. These charts give a precise method of determining frame size and figureweight.

Height is easily determined, but unless one is a skilled anatomist it is difficult to determine frame size. You can have broad hips and shoulders without being correspondingly deep in the pelvis or chest. When obese, total body measurements will not reveal the frame size, only the size of the fat and muscle upon the frame. And two frames may be identical in height, wrist, ankle and pelvic-width measurements yet be of different physique.

To overcome this the three main frame sizes (Venus types) are subdivided into categories according to bone size. It is unlikely that you will fit exactly into any of these Venus types, but if you

follow this line of thought you will see which range of weights you should fall into – the range of weights which allows you to maintain the proportions which belong to your type of physique. If you go much above or below this weight range, then you start to lose the healthy characteristics that you should naturally have. Look in the mirror and decide what kind of physical type you are. The flat tummy of the athletic physique may not be yours if you are a Renoir type. The curvaceous hips and bosom of the more muscled figure may not be yours if you have the delicate bone structure of Velasquez' Rokeby Venus. Assess yourself honestly and remember that if you are in no doubt that you are not Venus I or Venus II then you must be Venus III.

The upper part of your body may be preponderantly one frame-type and the lower part another; this is a common phenomenon and is known as dysplasia. If you suspect this assess for both and average the weights.

Frame Size

Cranach's painting *(opposite)* is an excellent example of a small to medium frame; Botticelli *(overleaf)* has depicted a modern athletic girl; Rubens' ladies *(p. 233)* are often overweight; in each of these paintings the artist's awareness of skeletal and muscular form is evident.

VENUS I

Small in width and depth; in side view usually distinctly slender. The form of the body may be rounded or angular; may or may not be cur-

VENUS II
The Birth of Venus by Botticelli (detail). *Uffizi, Florence.*

VENUS III
The Judgement of Paris by Rubens (detail). *Reproduced by courtesy of the Trustees, The National Gallery, London.*

vaceous in bust and hips. Do not be misled by a striking face with large, strong features, for although small frames are often associated with small faces and heads, this is not always so. We tend to think a round-faced person is at least stocky, but their bodies may in fact be the smallest type of Venus I. Many a Venus I appears to be a Venus II until seen sideways.

VENUS II
The most numerous and varied in form, from powerfully athletic to rounded and smooth, but there is always a distinct slimness of depth in rib cage and hips. Venus II may strike you as Venus III, until you see her sideways.

VENUS III
Less numerous than Venus I or II, rounded on every part of the body, with width and depth harmoniously round. Usually the shoulders are not as round as the hips. Athletic Venus II types have broader shoulders than Venus IIIs, but Venus III's shoulders will be more rounded in keeping with the general roundness of her body.

Bone category

HOW TO MEASURE

Wrist: use a tape measure; the circumference at the thinnest part is used, behind the wrist bone, not on it. Measure the hand you normally use, with fingers outstretched. Less than $5\frac{3}{4}$ inches (14.6 cm) is small, $5\frac{3}{4}$–$6\frac{1}{4}$ inches (14.6–15.9 cm) medium, more than $6\frac{1}{4}$ inches (15.9 cm) large.

Ankle: measure the thinnest part, above the ankle bone, not on it. Less than 8 inches (20.3 cm) is small, 8–$8\frac{3}{4}$ inches (20.3–22.2 cm) medium, more than $8\frac{3}{4}$ inches (22.2 cm) large.

Pelvic measurement: the measurement is made directly across the stomach on the top of the pelvic bone. Less than $8\frac{1}{4}$ inches (20.9 cm) is small, $8\frac{1}{4}$–10 inches (20.9–25.4 cm) medium, more than 10 inches (25.4 cm) large.

Find the words describing your measurements and use this list to find your bone category:

Category 1:   Three small.

Category 2:   Two small, one medium; or two medium, one small.

Category 3:   Three medium; or small, medium, large (in any order); or two small, one large.

Category 4:   Two medium, one large; or two large, one small; or two large, one medium.

Category 5:   Three large.

To establish your ideal weight

- Measure your height without shoes.
- Make sure you judge your frame size (Venus category) correctly.
- Take the measurements required for identification of your bone category.
- Now consult the chart opposite to find your ideal weight from the chart.

1926

Opposite: Ideal weight chart for women
© *Anthony Harris*

VENUS I — SMALL FRAMES

Height		1		2		3		4		5	
ft ins	m	lb	kg	lb	kg	lb	kg	lb	kg	lb	kg
5 0	1.52	96	43.5	98	44.5	100	45.4	103	46.7	105	47.6
5 1	1.55	99	44.9	101	45.8	103	46.7	107	48.5	109	49.4
5 2	1.57	102	46.3	104	47.2	106	48.0	110	49.9	112	50.8
5 3	1.60	105	47.6	107	48.5	109	49.4	113	51.3	115	52.2
5 4	1.63	108	49.0	110	49.9	112	50.8	117	53.1	119	54.0
5 5	1.65	112	50.8	114	51.7	116	52.6	121	54.9	123	55.8
5 6	1.68	116	52.6	118	53.5	120	54.4	125	56.7	127	57.6
5 7	1.70	120	54.4	122	55.3	124	56.2	128	58.1	131	59.4
5 8	1.73	124	56.2	126	57.2	128	58.0	132	59.8	136	61.7
5 9	1.75	128	58.0	130	59.0	132	59.8	136	61.7	140	63.5
5 10	1.78	132	59.8	134	60.8	136	61.7	140	63.5	144	65.3
5 11	1.80	136	61.7	138	62.6	140	63.5	144	65.3	148	67.1

VENUS II — MEDIUM FRAMES

Height		1		2		3		4		5	
ft ins	m	lb	kg	lb	kg	lb	kg	lb	kg	lb	kg
5 0	1.52	101	45.8	104	47.2	108	49.0	112	50.8	115	52.2
5 1	1.55	104	47.2	107	48.5	111	50.3	115	52.2	118	53.5
5 2	1.57	107	48.5	110	49.9	114	51.7	119	54.0	122	55.3
5 3	1.60	110	49.9	113	51.3	118	53.5	123	55.8	126	57.2
5 4	1.63	114	51.7	117	53.1	122	55.3	128	58.1	131	59.4
5 5	1.65	118	53.5	121	54.9	126	57.2	132	59.8	136	61.7
5 6	1.68	122	55.3	125	56.7	130	59.0	135	61.2	139	63.0
5 7	1.70	126	57.2	129	58.5	134	60.8	139	63.0	143	64.9
5 8	1.73	130	59.0	133	60.3	138	62.6	142	64.4	147	66.7
5 9	1.75	134	60.8	137	62.1	142	64.4	146	66.2	151	68.5
5 10	1.78	138	62.6	141	64.0	146	66.2	150	68.0	156	70.8
5 11	1.80	142	64.4	145	65.8	150	68.0	155	70.3	161	73.0

VENUS III — LARGE FRAMES

Height		1		2		3		4		5	
ft ins	m	lb	kg	lb	kg	lb	kg	lb	kg	lb	kg
5 0	1.52	109	49.4	113	51.3	118	53.5	123	55.8	127	57.6
5 1	1.55	112	50.8	116	52.6	121	54.9	126	57.2	130	59.0
5 2	1.57	115	52.2	119	54.0	124	56.2	129	58.5	134	60.8
5 3	1.60	119	54.0	123	55.8	127	57.6	133	60.3	138	62.6
5 4	1.63	123	55.8	127	57.6	131	59.4	137	62.1	142	64.4
5 5	1.65	127	57.6	131	59.4	135	61.2	141	64.0	146	66.2
5 6	1.68	131	59.4	135	61.2	139	63.0	145	65.8	150	68.0
5 7	1.70	135	61.2	139	63.0	144	65.3	149	67.6	155	70.3
5 8	1.73	139	63.0	144	65.3	149	67.6	154	69.9	160	72.6
5 9	1.75	144	65.3	149	67.6	154	69.9	159	72.1	165	74.8
5 10	1.78	149	67.6	154	69.9	159	72.1	164	74.4	170	77.1
5 11	1.80	154	69.9	159	72.1	164	74.4	169	76.7	176	79.8

These weights refer to women of twenty-five years of age in good health. The heights are without shoes, weights nude. For women from eighteen to twenty-four move down one category, since it is perfectly normal to continue to grow tissue up to twenty-five; thereafter growth tends to be overweight.

CHATELAIN

INDEX